ALL ACCORDING TO GOD'S PLAN

Religion in the South
John B. Boles, Series Editor

ALL ACCORDING TO
GOD'S PLAN

*Southern Baptist Missions
and Race, 1945–1970*

ALAN SCOT WILLIS

THE UNIVERSITY PRESS OF KENTUCKY

Publication of this volume was made possible in part
by a grant from the National Endowment for the Humanities.

Editorial and Sales Offices: The University Press of Kentucky
663 South Limestone Street, Lexington, Kentucky 40508-4008
www.kentuckypress.com

09 08 07 06 05   5 4 3 2 1

Library of Congress Cataloging-in-Publication Data
Willis, Alan Scot, 1968-
  All according to God's plan : Southern Baptist missions and
race, 1945-1970 / Alan Scot Willis.
     p. cm.
  Includes bibliographical references and index.
  ISBN 0-8131-2341-0 (hardcover : alk. paper)
  1. Southern Baptist Convention—Missions—History—20th century. 2.
Racism—Religious aspects—Southern Baptist Convention—History of
doctrines—20th century. I. Title.
  BV2520.W55 2004
  266'.6132'089—dc22
                              2004006223

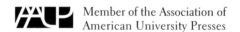   Member of the Association of
American University Presses

Dedicated with love to my soul mate
Sandy Burr

CONTENTS

PREFACE

Sitting at my desk surrounded by stacks of notes and photocopies—used, unused, or used and then excised—it seems reasonable to ask how I got here; how did I come to be writing about Southern Baptist missionaries and racism? Having grown up neither southern nor Baptist, I came to the topic as an outsider. I grew up in Denver, Colorado, where I had a fairly typical Catholic upbringing, although my father had been a Baptist while he was growing up. Furthermore, I grew up in a family who found racial prejudice unacceptable and certainly indefensible. Of course, I knew that racism existed in America, but I did not come into much contact with racists or their ideologies until I went to college. What I did know was that I loved history and had loved history since I was a young child. Indeed, the first book I ever read was a children's biography of Thomas Jefferson.

In college, becoming a history major was merely a continuation of prior interests, but several events awakened me to the persistence of racism. I remember many long talks about race in the hallways of Emory's dormitories, but two factors stand out in my awakening to continued racial problems in America: I attended a protest against a Klan rally (in retrospect, it seems I didn't believe that the Klan still had rallies, and that very fact awakened me to the persistence of racism), and I took a course from Dr. Patrick Allitt entitled "Race, Religion, and Gender in Modern America." At the conclusion of that course, I registered for an independent study with Dr. Allitt, and from that came my master's thesis on Georgia Baptists and desegregation. Now, fourteen years later, I teach a class similar to the one I first took with Allitt, which I've entitled "Protest Movements in Modern America," and that master's thesis has grown into a dissertation and, finally, a book.

As a college senior at Emory, I had set out to prove that white ministers in Atlanta had purposefully supported and promoted segregation and racism during the civil rights movement. I stumbled, instead, upon a then-divided Georgia Baptist Convention with ministers, leaders, and laity struggling to do what they believed was right in the eyes of God. I learned, among other things, that sources do not always fall in line with a preconceived agenda. I also learned that there was an almost inexhaustible source base for work on Southern Baptists.

As a graduate student at Syracuse, far from the South, I intended to pursue other avenues for a dissertation, but the Baptist missionaries kept captivating me. Particularly fascinating were Harris Mobley and Sam Oni, the missionary and the convert from Ghana who challenged segregation at Mercer University in Macon, Georgia, and provided the basis for the last chapter of my thesis as well as my first publication. Indeed, it was because I had stumbled onto the story of Mobley, Oni, and the desegregation of Mercer University that I finally decided to pursue Southern Baptists and racism from the missionaries' perspectives for my dissertation. It seemed, to me, the obvious choice. Yet other historians apparently had not entertained the same thought, for the topic remains, relatively speaking, untouched. In approaching this study, I focused primarily on articles published in missionary magazines. I wanted to understand what Southern Baptist missionaries were saying about race in public forums and how their religious beliefs shaped the way they viewed race relations. I soon discovered that a number of other Baptist leaders were also dedicated to the mission program, even though their official work was at seminaries or in other Baptist agencies. This discovery considerably broadened my evidence base but allowed me to maintain my focus on both missions and public discussion.

As an outsider, I am free from a personal stake in the reputation of the Southern Baptists. I have no need to either defend or attack them. However, as with any historian, I have my biases. Those biases lie with the ideas, not with the people. I am clearly more favorable toward people who express progressive views on race. I have tried to be fair to the Southern Baptist missionaries and progressive leadership and to present them on their own terms. I have tried to present their views in a systematic way, putting them in the context of the times and showing how they tried to counter much of that context. I cannot share their optimism, their individualism, or their self-certainty—and I am equally sure they would find my skepticism, liberal politics, and cultural relativism unacceptable—but I do admire their dedication to their cause and their willingness to speak publicly against the social norms of their times.

The formative ideas for "Our Preaching Has Caught Up with Us" appeared as an article entitled "'A White Man's Religion'?: Missionaries, Africa, and the Race Question," in *Proteus: A Journal of Ideas*, Spring 1998, Shippensburg, PA 17257-2299 © 1998 by Shippensburg University and are reprinted with permission. Also, certain parts of "Living Our Christianity" appeared as "A Baptist Dilemma: Christianity, Discrimination, and the Desegregation of Mercer University," in the *Georgia Historical Quarterly* 80 (Fall 1996). All photographs are courtesy of the Southern Baptist Historical Library and Archives in Nashville, Tennessee.

The danger of writing acknowledgments lies in the inevitable fact that some people who deserve recognition will be omitted. While working on this project—as a thesis, a dissertation, and a book manuscript—I have incurred more debts than I ever imagined possible or can possibly remember. So I should first thank those people whose names do not appear but whose help was invaluable.

Financial support came from the Roscoe Martin Fund at Syracuse University, the Department of History at Northern Michigan University, and the Lynn E. May Jr. Study Grant from the Southern Baptist Historical Library and Archives.

Edie Jeter at the International Mission Board, which was then the Foreign Mission Board, in Richmond, Virginia, assisted me in my work at the very time the archive was moving to a new building. Julie Belfield at the North American Mission Board, then the Home Mission Board, provided assistance with as well as insights into the research materials. Dana Martin at the American Baptist Historical Society offered his assistance and his patience when my schedule made my work there erratic. Bill Sumners at the Southern Baptist Historical Library and Archives helped make my time there productive. I must also thank John Boles for encouraging me to submit the manuscript to the University

Press of Kentucky. Without such encouragement I might have revised forever.

Friends and colleagues at Syracuse have made this project possible through their support and their insights. In particular, Marie Kelly's assistance in the early stages of the dissertation was invaluable. It's hard to imagine this project without her encouragement, friendship, and all the shared coffee. Bridget Carlin provided camaraderie and support. Kristin Anderson-Bricker, David Deacon, and Jim Eichesteadt all read parts of the dissertation and offered valuable advice. My gratitude goes out to Karen Bruner, who read the final draft of the dissertation in its entirety.

Several professors have provided invaluable guidance, encouragement, and insights. Three professors from Emory—Jim Roark, Dan Carter, and, in particular, Patrick Allitt—influenced my thinking about history and about religion and racism in American society. At Syracuse, Robert Gregory guided me in the study of modern Africa. Scott Strickland kindly read and discussed each chapter long before any were presentable. Of all the professors who have left their marks on my work as a historian, none has been so great an influence, or help, as my advisor, Elisabeth Lasch-Quinn. She encouraged me to pursue the dissertation I wanted to write, even when I thought a different topic would be more practical. She offered suggestions but always allowed me to find my own way through the issues. The dissertation would never have existed if not for her.

Colleagues and friends have been invaluable in turning the dissertation into a book. Most notably, Anthony Quiroz and T. Laine Scales made valuable suggestions for shaping a book out of the dissertation. Laura Kramer and Keith Kendall read revised versions and contributed significantly to the conversion of the dissertation into a book manuscript. Thanks also go to Chet DeFonso and Robbie Goodrich for helping me see that some day it would get done—and for springing for the beer.

Nannrel, my dog, stayed by me, literally, through multiple drafts. She gave up innumerable walks so that this book might get finished. But it is to my family that I owe the greatest debts. They exhibited great patience when I brought large stacks of books on family vacations. They allowed me peace and quiet to work during those rare times they even saw me. They made it possible, in so many ways, to keep going when it seemed as though the project would never end. My brother Mike, his wife Terry, my sister Mary, her husband Ricardo, my aunt Mary, and my parents all gave me the support needed to finish. Finally, with profound gratitude and love, I thank my wife, who patiently allowed me to work on the manuscript throughout our first year of marriage.

INTRODUCTION

This is a study of racism.

Racism, simply put, is the belief that one particular group of people is superior to some or all other groups of people. Clearly, the idea of racism involves the idea of race. Yet ethnic groups not typically considered "races" often suffer the effects of racism. So a more complex definition of racism is necessary. According to George M. Fredrickson, racism is "an ethnic group's assertion or maintenance of a privileged and protected status vis-à-vis members of any other group or groups who are thought, because of defective ancestry, to possess a set of socially relevant characteristics that disqualify them from full membership in a community or citizenship in a nation-state." This definition allows a consistent understanding of racism even though the definition of "race" has changed over the course of American history.[1]

This is also a study of religion.

Religion, even more simply put, is a belief in ultimate reality. This study deals with only one manifestation of religion: evangelical Christianity, in particular, the Southern Baptists. Central to this study is the Southern Baptists' belief that God's will can be known through a study of the Bible. Baptists believe that individual believers come to know God's will on their own. This in itself can be problematic. Introducing his own work, *The Historical Figure of Jesus*, E. P. Sanders notes that "people want to agree with Jesus, and this often means that they see him as agreeing with themselves."[2]

As a study of racism and religion, this work began with the intent of answering a fairly simple question: how do people's religious beliefs influence the way they think about race?

Simple questions rarely have simple answers. Instead, they spawn more complex questions. For example, what might happen if respected religious leaders called into question the prevailing beliefs about race in a society where those beliefs had been sanctified as Christian?

This was the world of the Southern Baptists after World War II. Southern Baptists were thoroughly enmeshed in southern society, a society segregated along racial lines. Few questioned the prevailing racial norms in their society. Indeed, as Melton McLaurin recalls from his North Carolina childhood: "All whites knew that blacks were, really, servants. It was their destiny to work at menial tasks, supervised, of course, by benevolent whites. All this was according to God's plan and was perfectly obvious to all but dimwitted Yankees and Communists." But it was not obvious to Southern Baptist missionaries either. Southern Baptist missionaries and mission leaders could not be dismissed as "dimwitted Yankees" or communists. They were solidly southern. They were virulently anticommunist. Their challenge to the southern race system came from the very heart of southern society: southern evangelical Christianity.[3]

In 1945, the Southern Baptist Convention was the second largest Protestant denomination in the United States. In the South, Baptist "culture" was pervasive. Presbyterians and Methodists typically had more in common with Southern Baptists than with northerners of their own denominations. The Southern Baptist Convention claimed the allegiance of more than half of the white population of all of the Deep South states, save Louisiana. In the upper South, the Convention attracted between 30 percent and 45 percent of the white population, as it did in the Southwestern states of New Mexico and Oklahoma. In 1942 it had affiliated churches in only nineteen states. With the establishment of a Southern Baptist church in Vermont on July 6, 1963, the Convention had entered all fifty states. Membership reached the ten million mark in 1964—up by more than two million since 1945—in 33,400 affiliated churches. Despite considerable growth outside the South, less than one church in thirty was outside that region throughout the postwar period. The Southern Baptist Convention remained throughout the postwar period dominantly southern, and it continued to dominate the South. One result was that, as Bill Leonard notes, "growing up Southern Baptist also meant you grew up Southern." That included believing in segregation and states' rights. But it also meant "you never sat next to a black person on a bus, in a restaurant, at school, or at a church."[4]

At the dawn of World War II, Baptist theologian Das Kelly Barnett wrote that a new prophetic theology that sought to involve Baptists in social issues was replacing the older, traditional, provincial, and dogmatic theology prevalent among Southern Baptists. The new theology was "dynamic in its appeal, social in its application, and dedicated in its purpose to the achievement of the intention of God in history"; it suggested that Christians should work to transform society and to make it more Christian. Prophets, according to Barnett, interpreted God's word for the present rather than foretelling the future: "The first task of prophetic and practical theology is the analysis of the conditions that have been indicated." Baptist leaders set themselves to the task of analyzing society. They often found, however, that their views were unwelcome. Historian Sam Hill writes, "The minister, called to be a prophet, is restrained by the social-psychological situation from violating the values in terms of which the congregation understands itself."[5]

The war experience provided a catalyst for this new theology, leading to the creation of the Peace Committee to work toward avowedly political goals and moving the Convention leadership to become increasingly involved in social and political issues. In 1947, the Committee on Race Relations—chaired by J. B. Weatherspoon (who had served on the faculty of the Southern Baptist Theological Seminary since 1929)—recommended that the Convention pursue an educational program on race and race relations through editorials, study programs, and classes at Southern Baptist colleges. The committee's report outlined the Convention's program for improving race relations in the South after the war.[6]

Southern Baptist missionaries and mission board leaders sought to involve the Convention in social issues. They were committed to the theology Barnett described; thus, they were progressives. Progressive Baptists filled the missionary and leadership positions at the three major mission organizations: the Home Mission Board, the Foreign Mission Board, and the Woman's Missionary Union. Furthermore, leaders of other Convention agencies, notably the Social Service Commission and the Christian Life Commission, shared this progressive view and commitment to missions. Many seminary professors and more prominent pastors also shared progressive views with the missionaries. Progressives were not theological liberals. Their goal was to involve the churches in southern society and to create a more Christian America without suffering, in the words of Professor H. Cornell Goerner, "the debilitating effects of theological liberalism." They maintained their dedication to individual conversion and redemption.[7] Progressive Southern Baptists expounded three major themes when discussing race: the biblical mandates of racial equality and unity, the international dimensions of the race question, and the personal responsibility of each Christian to work for better race relations.

Progressive Baptists believed that God had created all people in His own image. Throughout the postwar period the Baptist mission leaders called for Christians to recognize the unity of the human family. Divisions were man-made, unchristian, and, therefore, sins in the eyes of God. The idea of united humanity led Baptist mission leaders to see the race question as broader than black and white. God had intended unity for "all nations," and the Christian view of race demanded equal dignity for all people regardless of their ethnic background. Racial inequality contradicted such a view.[8]

The leadership, with its focus on mission work, saw the American racial situation in its international context. In various settings, racism manifested itself through colonialism, segregation, or the belief in "super-races" that had the right to dominate other peoples. Each led to conflict. Therefore, Baptists believed that world peace, demanded by God, required overcoming racism both in America and abroad. Baptists viewed the American and international race questions as inextricably intertwined.[9]

For Baptists, racism was primarily a moral question, and moral questions were individual questions. Solving the race problem was, therefore, a matter of individual moral change, and that mandated evangelism. Individual redemption remained the heart of evangelical religion, even as Baptist missionaries insisted the Gospels had a social message. The solution to the race problem lay in converting individuals—even, perhaps especially, those who may already be Christians—to the Christian view of race.[10]

The Baptist missionary leadership believed that ignorance bred misunderstanding and racism. Thus they believed that education was a key factor in overcoming racism. In addition, they believed that individuals could overcome their racism by making friends across cultural chasms. Friendships, like education, could break down the barriers that led to ignorance. This was especially true for youth. Baptists argued that racist beliefs were learned. If young people were taught acceptance and had positive interracial experiences, they would be less likely to become racist. It was, therefore, incumbent upon parents, and especially mothers, to teach their children the Christian view of race. Progressive Baptists and mission leaders intended to teach Baptist youth a view of race quite out of step with southern traditions.[11]

Critics might suggest that progressive Baptist missionaries and mission leaders actually did very little about the race problem in America. Baptist missionaries would argue that working for the conversion of individuals was the greatest work that could be done. They believed that the conversion of individuals to true Christianity was a prerequisite for the ending of racism as well as the only way the unity of humanity could be accomplished. Furthermore, as Goerner pointed out, "the ideal [of racial justice] must become real as *an ideal* before it can become effective in actuality." This study is primarily concerned with examining that ideal and how Southern Baptist missionaries and their progressive allies worked to make that ideal real so that it could become an actuality.[12]

Taken on their own terms, then, Southern Baptist missionaries and mission leaders articulated their views and acted in accord with their beliefs about religion, society, and God. Those beliefs had limitations, particularly the tendency to overlook, or at least understate, institutional discrimination. Furthermore, some individual Baptists, including Baptist ministers, defended segregation. This study demonstrates, however, that southerners, particularly Baptists, knew the progressive view of race and that continued racial discrimination was contrary to the views of a respected group of southerners who could not, in any way, be considered outside agitators. The outright, active rejection of those ideas necessitated a conscious effort that mere ignorance of them would not have required.[13]

Southern Baptist mission leaders publicly promoted their view of race through the popular literature of the Convention's three main mission organizations. In these public forums, Southern Baptist missionaries and mission board leaders persistently challenged the prevailing views of race and dominant practices of their region.

The evidence for *All According to God's Plan* comes from this popular literature. Much of it was intended for a general Southern Baptist audience, while some was aimed more specifically at women or youth. Yet it was all widely available to Southern Baptists and even to other southerners. *Home Missions* and *The Commission*, monthly magazines offered by the Home Mission Board and the Foreign Mission Board respectively, had the broadest audiences, in terms of age and sex, of the magazines examined. In 1954, the year the Supreme Court delivered its desegregation ruling in *Brown v. The Board of Education*, *Home Missions* went to 124,500 subscribers, and *The Commission* went to 80,000 subscribers. Other magazines, like *Ambassador Life* and the *Window*, were aimed specifically at youth, and the *Baptist Student* was intended for college students. *Ambassador Life* was the official publication of the Royal Ambassadors program, which enrolled nearly 130,000 boys aged nine and up. The *Window* went to young women between the ages of sixteen and twenty-five who were members of over 5,000 chapters of the Young Woman's Auxiliary. These publications, along with *Royal Service*, were produced by the Woman's Missionary Union, although *Ambassador Life* moved to the Baptist Brotherhood in the early 1960s, and many of the articles were intended to be educational program guides for various organizations' meetings. The leadership hoped members of those organizations would act upon their suggestions, or at least ponder them seriously. Indeed, "missionary education of young people is the central purpose in the life of Woman's Missionary Union; it is it's [sic] most fruitful service to the life of the denomination at large." Many of the articles in *Royal Service*, the Union's publication for adult women, focused on teaching Christian values to youth.[14]

The Baptists' popular literature significantly helped shape the Convention. Bill Leonard wrote that the denominational programs created a "surprising uniformity among a diverse and individualistic constituency." Leaders within the Convention realized that as well. Indeed, as Albert McClellan, director of publications for the Southern Baptist Convention, explained in 1954: "The wonderful uniformity of Southern Baptist life exists, not by law but because of the spreading of information. . . . No denomination anywhere has a greater array of modern, well written literature." These sources, whether or not all scholars would agree with McClellan's hyperbole, allow for the examination of ideas in a public forum, and they promoted, almost uniformly, the progressive view of race and society. Had Baptist leaders and missionaries discussed their progressive views in private but not expressed them publicly, their history would be one more, perhaps tragic, example of moderate southerners being silenced by the culture of segregation. Instead, progressive Baptists refused to be silent. They put their thoughts in print for anyone to read, debate, and even refute.[15]

Mission board leaders, seminary professors, and prominent pastors frequently wrote for mission magazines. They had often obtained graduate, even doctoral, degrees at universities and seminaries. Prominent among these were H. Cornell Goerner and T. B. Maston. Formally appointed missionaries also wrote. Some, like Joanna Maiden, became frequent correspondents with mission magazines. Yet the Baptists' belief that every believer is a missionary meant that any Baptist was invited to write to or submit an article for a mission magazine. These writings should not be dismissed. As historian Beth Barton Schweiger points out, "the most fiercely anti-intellectual among the pious took ideas deadly seriously, and even illiterate Protestants were people of the Book." Though only a rare few Southern Baptists were illiterate in the postwar years, Schweiger's point is clear: ideas are central to religion, and they are not restricted to the leadership. These ideas are an important part of religious, social, and intellectual history.[16]

Many Southern Baptists took the opportunity to express their views on missions and race by writing articles for or letters to the mission magazines. Some wrote frequently, some infrequently, and others only once. Little or nothing is known about many of them. Many women writers can be identified only as "Mrs." followed by their husband's name (I have used their given names when possible, but have identified their husband's name if that appeared in the byline of the source cited). Youth frequently wrote for their own magazines. The Baptists' insistence that young people were the key to Christian race relations in the future highlights the importance of these sources. Regardless of age or educational level, there was a remarkable consistency among the people who wrote for and corresponded with Baptist mission magazines. True, some correspondents wrote to disapprove of the positions taken by the Baptist leadership. Others, however, expressed their approval. Some even encouraged more progressive stands. In general, segregationists and racial conservatives voiced their opinions elsewhere, notably in state newspapers like the *Alabama Baptist*, where editor Leon Macon opposed integration. Resistance to integration and civil rights was plentiful among

Southern Baptists but not at the mission boards or the Woman's Missionary Union. As a result, the mission-oriented magazines display considerable consistency in their progressive views.[17]

The importance of women and youth to the progressive Southern Baptists' attempts to reshape the South's racial landscape can hardly be exaggerated. Yet the influence of Baptist literature for women and youth has been underestimated. One historian admits that the publications "may have had some impact on impressionable young readers" but argues that Southern Baptist men "could dismiss female or student concern about racial discrimination as either a reflection of the sensitivities of the gentler sex or as a product of the passing and unrealistic idealism of youth which would be tempered by the onset of adulthood and adult responsibilities." Baptist men may have done just that, and that may have contributed to the persistently progressive tone of publications for women and youth. Baptist literature for men, particularly the *Southern Baptist Brotherhood Quarterly*, gave less coverage to the race issue than did the other magazines studied, and *Ambassador Life* offered fewer stories on race after it moved from the Woman's Missionary Union to the Baptist Brotherhood in the early 1960s. Still, they did deal with race, and, when they did, they offered the progressive view. Furthermore, male Baptist leaders wrote for all the publications under consideration in this study, no matter the intended audience. Even if more conservative Baptists dismissed women's or young people's concerns, they could hardly help but notice that the denomination's mission leadership was solidly against the racial norms of the South.[18]

Religion is one of the most effective ways of transmitting a culture's values to the next generation, and Baptists believed that women, as mothers, had a special role in that transmission. Religion can legitimize the existing social structure, demonstrating to youth that it is "natural" and even "sacred" and, therefore, should not be changed. It can also, in the hands of progressives, undermine the system and demonstrate that it is contrary to the "sacred order" and therefore must be changed. By targeting women and youth, progressive Southern Baptists intended to show the next generation a different vision of race relations.[19]

Certainly, one measure of success is the degree to which later Southern Baptists' views on race reflect the progressive vision of the past. At the end of the twentieth century, conservative Baptists controlled virtually every major agency within the Convention, but "virtually no

Southern Baptists disagree with the U.S. Supreme Court's *Brown v. Board of Education* decision that ruled racial segregation unconstitutional." According to Andrew Manis, who examines Southern Baptist resistance to the civil rights movement, many conservative Baptists "will say that segregation was unchristian, something their forebears from the 1950s and 60s would have been loath to admit." The leaders acknowledge that "those who stood for segregation were wrong." Certainly, a number of factors are involved in that change, but conservatives' rejection of racism is based more on theology than law, much as the progressive rejection of racism was decades earlier. Religion, for Southern Baptists, no longer sanctifies segregation. For progressive Baptists and missionaries, it never did.[20]

Several factors frustrated progressive Baptists. Since the Southern Baptist Convention embodies the ideal of a voluntary association, its leaders are powerless to force their ideas on the congregations. Each church makes its own decisions. Indeed, Baptists believe that each Christian makes his or her own decisions regarding moral issues. The postwar progressive leaders could only cajole their coreligionists, hoping and praying that they would come to a Christian understanding of race relations. Thus, the gulf between the leadership and the congregations presented a problem. The leaders, often more educated and more aware of the world situation, addressed Baptists who viewed the world, and the church's role in that world, quite differently. Many Baptists believed that segregation was Christian and that the churches should defend the practice. Others simply believed that the churches should concern themselves solely with redemption and not with the workings of this world.[21]

The difference between the missionaries and the congregations is especially interesting considering the nature of Baptist mission appointments. Missionaries presented themselves to the boards after being called by God to serve in a particular field. The boards then approved or rejected the request. Yet missionaries generally shared the progressive views of race held by the mission board leaders, not the pervasive attitudes of the denominational and regional culture from which they rose. There were multiple reasons for this, but certainly one was their dedication to the Christian mission in the world. W. Seward Salisbury explained in 1964 that some Christians internalized their religious values, while others did not. This may seem obvious. Seward noted, however, that those who internalized their beliefs tended to view their role as serving their faith and humanity, while those whose religion was largely extrinsically oriented viewed religion as serving them. They used religion for its social connections but did not surrender to its demands, including the abandonment of prejudice. Clearly, Christians drawn to the mission fields surrendered to the call to serve their faith and found their religious values "interwoven into the fabric of . . . [their] personality." Baptist missionaries and their leaders, having internalized their faith, cried out against America's sins and pointed to the Christian path. They were prophetic rather than reflective.[22]

Missionaries and their ideas were particularly important for Southern Baptists. One church historian, William R. Estep Jr., considered that Foreign Mission Board leaders like M. Theron Rankin and Baker James Cauthen "enjoyed hero status among Southern Baptists." Historian Stephen Neill argues that the main trend in postwar missions was the growth of nondenominational societies. Most denominational efforts stagnated. Yet, Neill noted, "an exception is the work of the Southern Baptists, which in increase in range and numbers and in vigor of policy is second to no other in the world."[23]

With the renewed effort, race became an increasingly important topic. Progressive Baptists believed that racism had been at the heart of World War II and had to be overcome if a permanent peace was to be achieved. Further, the race situation in America affected Baptist evangelical efforts overseas. After the Supreme Court's decision in *Brown v. The Board of Education,* Baptist missionaries became increasingly concerned about the hypocrisy in an American South that continued to defend segregation while claiming to be Christian. That concern increased as the civil rights movement illuminated that hypocrisy for Americans and for people around the world. By the mid-1960s, Baptist educational institutions were increasingly integrated, though resistance to the progressive message continued. The Convention adopted stronger stances on race through the end of the sixties. In the 1970s, the Convention turned its attention to internal theological differences, focusing on biblical inerrancy and culminating in the seemingly irreparable rift between the "moderates" and "fundamentalists" of the late twentieth century. Still, even if it was eclipsed by other disputes, race never disappeared as an issue. Indeed, the conservative leadership at the end of the century echoed the progressives' view on this one issue.[24]

From 1945 to 1970 the Southern Baptist mission leadership was oriented toward social concerns and focused on the race question. The following study examines, in the first chapter, the biblical mandates for missions and racial equality upon which the Southern Baptist missionaries and mission leaders based their views. The two chapters that follow show how the Baptist leaders put the American race question in its international context, first broadly and then specifically regarding Africa. The fourth chapter examines the progressives' more general critique of postwar American culture by focusing on the dual "sins" of materialism and racism. The following two chapters focus on the Baptists' home mission efforts among minorities. The first deals mainly with Latinos and Native Americans, demonstrating that the Baptists viewed the race question in much the same way regardless of which ethnic groups were involved. The last chapter focuses on the leadership's views of race relating to blacks.

There was, of course, a range of ideas among progressive Baptists. Some were blatantly paternalistic while others were less so. A few managed to overcome paternalism almost entirely. Early in the postwar years some argued that racism and discrimination could be ended while segregation could be maintained. Others condemned segregation from the beginning. Their views were rarely worthy of the appellation "revolutionary." Yet all were progressive for two reasons: each believed that the Convention had a distinct and important role to play in solving America's race problem, and each argued for an end to racism. While their visions varied, all progressives called for a bettering of race relations from where they stood at that time.

The southern racial hegemony required the consent, often passive but sometimes active, of the preponderance of the white South. Southern Christians helped legitimate the system by endowing it with religious sanction. Accordingly, many southern Christians felt that God had mandated segregation and that integration went against God's plan. Progressive Baptists and missionaries, however, spoke through one of the South's most influential cultural institutions and announced, quite to the contrary, that God's plan was one of racial unity. Segregation and racism were the sins. Unwilling to be silenced, progressive Baptists, missionaries, and mission organization leaders questioned the grounds upon which the southern racial system rested. Animated by their belief that racism undermined their mission efforts, they demonstrated that segregation, white supremacy, and racial discrimination were unchristian. In doing so, Southern Baptist progressives presented a forceful argument against racism and contributed to real change in the South.[25]

1

"GO YE"

Missions and Race in
Progressive Baptist Theology

Southern Baptist leaders stressed the importance of using the Bible as a guide to the Christian life. On this point they were in full agreement with the congregations. The leadership also used the Bible to demonstrate the importance of missionary efforts. Again the congregations agreed. When the progressive leadership pointed to the biblical principles of human equality and unity to demonstrate that southern racial norms were unchristian, many Baptists disagreed. This led to an extended debate over the Bible's teachings regarding race and the Christian's role in society.[1]

Progressive Baptists faced several problems in bringing their denomination to a Christian view of race relations. The leadership believed that the role of Christianity was to point the way to a Christianized society. Many Baptists, however, believed that their society was already Christian. Baptists also believed in the free pulpit, meaning that Baptist pastors could speak from their own Christian consciences, whether or not they agreed with the Convention and mission leadership. Further, Baptists believed in the priesthood of all believers, which meant that each Baptist had to approach the Bible on his or her own, according to his or her own conscience.[2]

The radical individualism in the Southern Baptist Convention clearly allowed for a variety of beliefs regarding the relationship between Christianity and society. Those ideas generally fit into two of H. Richard Niebuhr's categories as outlined in his signal work, *Christ and Culture*. Missionaries and progressive leaders held what Niebuhr called the "conversionist answer to the problem of Christ and culture." In this view,

T.B. Maston, the prophetic voice of progressive Baptists. Photo courtesy of the Southern Baptist Historical Library and Archives, Nashville, Tennessee.

Christianity's role was to change society and make it more Christian. Outside the leadership, however, many Baptists tended to hold the "Christ of culture" view, which suggested the culture within which they lived was already Christian. Christ was simply absorbed into the culture, and the culture's institutions became "Christian." This conflation of Christianity and cultural norms created a civil religion that, as historian Andrew Manis points out, held the allegiance of a significant portion of the Baptist laity and sanctified segregation. Progressive Baptists generally shared Niebuhr's view that Christianity should transform culture, while recognizing that the "Christ of culture" was considerably easier to follow than the Christ who would transform culture.[3]

Race was the most important area of disagreement between the progressive leadership and the more conservative elements of the denomination. Thomas Bufford Maston, who had studied under Niebuhr as a graduate student at Yale, led the Southern Baptist leadership in its fight against biblical racism. Maston, born in Jefferson County, Tennessee, in 1897, grew up in a society where segregation was both legal and pervasive. He attended Carson-Newman College in Jefferson City, Tennessee, and Southwestern Baptist Theological Seminary in Fort Worth, Texas. After he earned a PhD in Christian Ethics, he returned to

Southwestern as a professor and taught there from 1923 until the end of his career. He remained a force in the denomination until his death in 1988. His arguments against the biblical sanctions for segregation were numerous, but he summed them up simply in 1959, writing that "there is no valid biblical or theological defense for the segregation pattern."[4]

In 1946, Maston wrote *"Of One": A Study of Christian Principles and Race Relations* for study by the Woman's Missionary Union. It was not his first pamphlet on race—he wrote that in 1927. *"Of One,"* however, became one of the most discussed books the Home Mission Board ever published. Thirteen years later he published two more books on the issue: *Segregation and Desegregation: A Christian Approach* and *The Bible and Race*. Maston intended *The Bible and Race* to replace *"Of One,"* and the Woman's Missionary Union dedicated three months to studying the new book. Additionally, Maston wrote numerous articles for denominational magazines, including a three-part series, "Southern Baptists and the Negro," which appeared in *Home Missions* in 1966 and was reprinted in the *Baptist Student*. Other Baptist leaders pointed to Maston's work when they discussed the biblical teachings regarding race. As a result, his words permeated the works of Baptist leaders throughout the postwar era. William M. Pinson Jr., executive director of the Baptist General Convention of Texas in the late 1990s, wrote that colleagues in Seminary believed that "if Southern Baptists have produced a prophet in this twentieth century, it is T. B. Maston."[5]

Baptists prided themselves on being a "people of the book." For Maston, this meant that "in the area of race, as in every other phase of life, the will of God is the final determinant of right and wrong for those who are in the family of God." Maston's views were widely shared. One Baptist who agreed, Mrs. R.H., wrote to *Royal Service* regarding the publication's position on race, saying that "to me there is one single guide which is a question, 'What would Jesus do?' I firmly believe that any sincere Christian would not have a bit of trouble answering that question. The hard thing is to abide by the certain answer."[6]

When Baptist leaders claimed biblical sanction for their mission efforts, the membership agreed. Claude T. Ammerman, pastor of First Baptist Church in Troy, Alabama, announced: "The Bible is a missionary book." Jesus had given the missionary movement its "commission" in Matthew 28:19–20: "Go ye therefore, and teach all nations, baptizing them in the name of the Father, and of the Son, and of the Holy Ghost;

Teaching them to observe all things whatsoever I have commanded you; and, lo, I am with you always, even unto the end of the world." Jesus, Ammerman said, intended the Gospel to be preached to the entire world without impediment. The Bible gave an account of the early mission efforts of the apostles and remained "the best handbook on missions, setting forth its motive, methods, and aims." Since Baptists were "Bible-loving and Bible-honoring people," Ammerman believed they must therefore be "a missionary people."[7]

Baptists, as "a missionary people," believed that missions were the responsibility of all Baptists. Mission boards could hire only a few full-time missionaries, but all Baptists were equally obligated to the mission effort. Mrs. Fred Neiger wrote in *Royal Service*, "We cannot read Acts 1:8 without realizing that every Christian is a missionary." In that passage, Jesus instructed his followers, "But ye shall receive power, after that the Holy Ghost is come upon you: and ye shall be witnesses unto me both in Jerusalem and in all Judea, and in Samaria and unto the uttermost part of the earth." Neiger reminded Baptists that each of them had both the obligation and opportunity to act as missionaries.[8]

Prominent theologian Paul Tillich argued that missions were the central feature of Protestant Christianity, and missions were certainly central to every level of the Southern Baptist Convention. Baptists often said, "Missions is one." Ungrammatical, perhaps, but they insisted that all missions, from the local community to foreign outposts, were intertwined. As Clifton E. Fite said, "State missions is a part of the world-wide, Christ-centered, church sponsored soul winning program outlined by Christ." The editor of the *Southern Baptist Brotherhood Quarterly*, Lawson H. Cooke, made a similar point: "'World missions' in the thinking of many of us has become synonymous with foreign missions. Unfortunately we do not seem to realize that Tennessee is as much a part of the world as is the darkest spot in Africa."[9]

Dedication to mission activity also provided a common ground of agreement that helped keep the Southern Baptist Convention together despite its enormous diversity. As J. B. Lawrence, executive secretary of the Home Mission Board, argued, "Our task, as Baptists, is to make Christ known to men everywhere. . . . This is the missionary impulse; and our denominational organizations and agencies are for the purpose of implementing and carrying this impulse out to the lost of every nation, kindred, tribe, and tongue in the world, at home and abroad." Rogers

M. Smith of the Foreign Mission Board explained that "in the Kingdom of God there are no frontiers." This idea underlay the board's efforts to evangelize the world. Smith further noted that mission work was "truly the primary purpose and privilege of every follower of Jesus Christ."[10]

The Baptists' worldwide mission efforts demanded that race relations at home become more Christian. Here, biblical dedication to racial equality and missions intertwined. Andy Blane, director of the Baptist Student Union at the University of Kentucky, argued that the time had come for winning the world to Christ. He worried because "some areas are revolting against our total culture because so much of it has been saturated with greed, exploitation, and color lines." Although Blane cited several problems, he essentially agreed with Foy Valentine of the Social Service Commission, who said that "the ultimate failure or success of the modern missionary movement may well depend on what today's Christians do with the race problem."[11]

Frank Stagg, professor of New Testament at the Southern Baptist Theological Seminary, agreed. He pointed out that by the mid-1960s, ten years after Blane wrote, roughly 85 percent of the people with whom Southern Baptist missionaries worked were not white. He noted, "Attitudes of superiority, patronization, discrimination, and prejudice pull the rug out from under the missionary endeavor." W. T. Moore, director of the North Tulsa Baptist Center for Negroes, feared that missionaries would be asked to leave certain countries because of race hostility in the United States. He noted that Jesus commanded Christians to "go into all the world" and that "all the world" included the United States. Racism, at home or abroad, directly impaired the biblical mandate to make disciples of all nations. For missions to be successful abroad, missionaries had to address the race situation at home.[12]

Congregational support for mission activity suggested that the conversionist view of Christianity could take root in the local churches, but Maston understood that southern Christians were more willing to apply the radical, transformative ideal of Christianity abroad than at home. He admitted that "it is comparatively easy to be radical when one does not have to face the real problem or results of his radicalism." American Christians were willing to support missionaries who took the transformative message of Christianity to the uttermost parts of the earth, but they did not want their own way of life challenged. Baptist mission leaders believed that the same message that applied in the far reaches of earth applied in the American South. Racism, however, prevented that message from being applied. Maston noted, "If we do not want our way of life challenged and our conscience disturbed, we had better not study seriously the ideals of original Christianity and their application to race relations."[13]

Radicalism was difficult for southerners to embrace, but James C. Barry of the Sunday School Board encouraged Baptists to think of radicalism in distinctly Christian terms. Christian radicalism was "religion rooted in Jesus Christ and having its source in his teachings," and "those who shy away from radicalism in the Christian life are left to be called by its opposite—'rootless, shallow, touching only the surface, affecting the non-essentials.'" Still, radicalism was easier dealt with when it was far from home.[14]

As Maston noted, Christians celebrated foreign missionaries, "particularly those who have opened new geographic frontiers." However, in keeping with their traditions, many of the same Christians "ostracize those who seek to open up frontiers for Christ in our midst." Lillian Smith, author of *Killers of the Dream*, wrote about a newly appointed missionary who in 1947 admitted to her that "I wanted to stay in the South and help rid it of lynching and segregation. That is what I really wanted to do. But there was Mother . . . you know how disgraced she would have felt if I stayed and helped here. She would have died if she had seen me eating with a Negro. . . . But she is proud of me now, going to Africa as a missionary." Even among dedicated Christians, then, pressures to conform were enormous.[15]

Mission leaders like Stagg and Moore believed that the "all nations" aspect of the Commission of Matthew 28 "suggests its geographic, national, and racial inclusiveness." They argued, like Maston, that Jesus intended his disciples to "go as readily to one racial, national, or class group as to another." That element was central to the missionary nature of the Christian movement. Maston argued that the Acts of the Apostles demonstrated that Jesus intended the Gospel to break through barriers of race and nation. He noted that Peter ate with Cornelius, one of the "uncircumcised," and declared in his housetop vision that "God has shown me that I should not call any man common or unclean." Maston wondered, "Has the church learned even yet that God does not look on the color of the skin or the class or culture one comes from? Have we learned yet that He shows no partiality, that He is not a respecter of persons?"[16]

All Baptists essentially agreed that God's will was revealed through the Bible, but many Southern Baptists had long believed that the Bible sanctioned segregation. When progressives instructed them differently, they wondered how the leadership could claim that biblical principles, supposedly inviolable, no longer supported segregation. The idea proved remarkably persistent. Nearly ten years after the Supreme Court declared segregated schooling unconstitutional, Ken E. Edwards wrote that he would "never understand" how Baptist leaders allowed a "Supreme Court unconstitutional ultimatum to suddenly change [their] opinion as to the Bible, Christianity, and God's intention in forcing the amalgamation of the races." Edwards's belief that the Baptist leadership began teaching the biblical principles of equality only in response to the *Brown* decision was erroneous, but he was not alone in believing that Baptist leaders had let the Court dictate their interpretation of the Bible.[17]

T. B. Maston recognized that the Bible was being used to "justify the customary patterns of race relations, just as it was used a few generations ago to defend slavery." The most frequently cited biblical passage in support of segregation was the "Curse of Ham," found in Genesis, chapter 9. In it, Noah cursed Canaan (one of Ham's sons) and his descendants, condemning them to be the "servants of servants." Maston understood the urge to use the Curse to justify segregation, noting that "the use of this Curse is a good illustration of man's longing for respectability, of his strong desire for divine approval of what he has done." Ralph A. Phelps Jr., president of Ouachita College in Arkansas, agreed, saying, "As long as people claim to believe the Word of God and to follow the will of God, then God must be pictured as favoring what they are doing." Both believed, in Maston's words, that the Curse of Ham was being used "to defend the prevailing racial pattern, a pattern which falls far short of the Christian ideal."[18]

T. J. Preston was among those Baptists who cited the Curse to justify segregation. He argued that the descendants of Ham had been "relegated" to Africa, adding that "all Bible readers know that the Lord, speaking through the prophets to the Jews, commanded they do not mix with other races about them." He wondered, "If the Lord had wanted us to all live together in a social way, why did He separate us in the beginning?"[19]

Humphrey K. Ezell agreed with Preston. Ezell began serving as a Baptist minister thirty years before *Brown* and found the idea of integration repulsive and unchristian. He believed, in particular, that the Curse of Ham was permanent. He suggested, contrary to most Christian thinkers, that the atonement for human sin achieved by Jesus' crucifixion did not release blacks from the curse because it only released people from the "shared depravity" of the sins of Adam and Noah. Whites, he claimed, did not share the depravity of the curse; therefore, the curse was not affected by the atonement. His argument was well outside mainstream Christian thought and suggests how far biblical segregationists would be willing to go to prove their point.[20]

On the other hand, progressive Baptist leaders denied the curse's relevance to the race situation in the American South. R. Lofton Hudson, pastor of Wornall Road Baptist Church in Kansas City, Missouri, and writer of a weekly column for Baptist state papers, claimed, "This idea that Ham's sons were Negroes is completely without foundation." Hudson explained that the idea was unheard of before Americans tried to use it to justify slavery. T. B. Maston said that a careful study of the passage would "reveal that it has no significance for the present racial discussion." He found no biblical evidence for believing that Canaan's descendants were Africans. Indeed, he said, it was "quite clear that the Curse of Canaan did not, does not, and never can properly be applied to the Negroes." Maston further argued that even if the Curse of Ham had had racial significance it would not have been perpetual, and certainly would not have outlasted the atonement. Furthermore, defending segregation as Christian, as part of the will of God, did "irreparable harm" to "the Christian ethic and the Christian cause." He concluded, "Let us not claim the authority of God for that which is so contrary to his nature and to his revealed will."[21]

Ultimately, the greatest fear in the South concerning integration and "social equality" was the "amalgamation of the races." The possibility of interracial marriage terrified southern whites who believed in the "purity" of the white race. Again, segregationists pointed to the Bible to sustain their belief that God never intended for people of differing ethnic heritage to marry. Progressive leaders wrote little about interracial marriage, but when they did, they denied that there was a biblical injunction against intermarriage. Progressive leaders looked to Maston to write about this difficult subject, for they believed, as Foy Valentine did himself, that Maston was "the best man in the country to do it." At the heart of Maston's argument was his belief that "if people were not so prejudiced, and hence could think straight, they would realize how unfounded are most of the fears regarding intermarriage."[22]

In the late 1940s, while many Baptist mission leaders themselves were still wary of calling for social equality, Maston argued, "Must we not admit that Peter's vision persuaded him that spiritual equality involved social equality? If God accepts men and women of various races into His family, on what basis can we justify our unwillingness to associate with them?" Christians, Maston claimed, had to recognize that God made all persons in His image, as explained in Genesis 1:27, and that God was no respecter of persons. Furthermore, Christ had died for all people, and salvation was available on an equal basis. If that were so, as one Presbyterian woman realized during an integrated Sunday School class with Mexican Presbyterians, there should be no signs barring blacks and Mexicans from businesses and public places. If Christians took to heart the biblical teachings about race, those signs would have to disappear.[23]

In light of this, Maston admitted, "It may be extremely disturbing to us as Southern white Christians, but let us sincerely search for the fullest implications of the spiritual truths we find in the Gospel." "If God is no respecter of persons, should not the ultimate goal in our individual lives and in the social groups to which we belong be the elimination of all distinctions and discriminations based on color or class[?]" Maston knew that would be "a long, long step" for white Christians, but he also knew that it was "a step plainly revealed by an examination of Peter's vision on the housetop."[24]

The fear of integration and interracial marriage was tied to stereotyped views of black sexuality. James J. Kilpatrick, author of *The Southern Case for School Segregation*, cited higher rates of illegitimacy among blacks as proof of their sexual promiscuity. He believed that if blacks were allowed to go to white schools they would organize interracial sex clubs. Segregationists also pointed to the marriage of Walter Stoval and Charlayne Hunter, the first black woman to attend the University of Georgia, as proof that integrated schools led to intermarriage.[25]

Sam Bowers, a Baptist Sunday School teacher, served as Imperial Wizard of the Ku Klux Klan in Mississippi. He assumed blacks were sexual degenerates and believed that that degeneracy violated "God's first law of nature" and ran counter to the "white man's instinct for racial purity." After his conversion experience, Bowers studied the Bible and determined that "no one less than Jesus Christ himself was calling him to the priestly task of preserving the purity of his blood and soil." He saw himself as preserving the true Christian life—the segregated life—against the communist-inspired, atheistic dictates of the Supreme Court. He went far beyond most conservative Baptists by advocating armed resistance to integration, though many would have agreed with him that integration would lead directly to intermarriage.[26]

Progressive Baptists rejected both the idea that interracial marriage was unchristian and the idea that desegregation would lead directly to interracial marriage. Maston did not believe that interracial marriages were "wise" and occasionally discouraged them in private, in part because of the social pressures against them. He believed, however, that people who sought "divine approval" for their opposition to interracial marriage had misinterpreted scripture. He told Baptists that God had ordered "his chosen people" not to intermarry for religious reasons that had nothing to do with race. God had given the command because spouses of other religious groups "would turn away your sons from following me, to serve other gods," which was irrelevant in a society where the vast majority of blacks were Christians. Still, the prohibition was "widely used in the contemporary controversy, even being used by some to justify the whole segregation pattern."[27]

When progressives rejected arguments against interracial marriage some Baptists in the pews objected. In the early 1960s, after *Royal Service* ran a story about a Japanese woman who married an American, letter writers objected to the implied message that interracial marriage was acceptable. Hanako Noden had brought her American husband to Christianity, but after she was widowed, few friends were willing to visit her. While the situation was consistent with the common view that "the woman is the leader in making her home and family conscious of the true beauty of Christian living," the story sent a clear message that Christianity transcended racial barriers. An unsigned letter in response, which *Royal Service* decided to print despite its anonymity, read: "We try to teach our youth about inter-racial marriage. God had a purpose in making people different races and to live in different parts of the world and it is a sin to change the laws of God." The editors were disappointed that anyone could "drip so much hatred from her pen."[28]

The fear of interracial marriage arose, in part, from the belief that "mixed blood" offspring were somehow deficient, an idea espoused by polemicists like Herman Talmadge, a Southern Baptist and governor of Georgia in the early 1950s. Yet the idea of "mixed blood" ran counter to biblical principles. As Katharine Parker Freeman of the Woman's Missionary Union noted, "Race is no problem to God. . . . In the mind of God there is only one race, the human race." The belief that there was only one race was rooted in the Acts of the Apostles passage from which T. B. Maston took the title for *"Of One": A Study of Christian Principles and Race Relations.* Paul had declared that "God hath made of one blood all the nations of man." Maston announced, "What a long way we would go in solving our problems concerning race . . . if we simply accepted men and women as members of the human family rather than as members of a particular race, class, or caste!"[29]

Baptist leaders also invoked science to support their view of a single human race. Hugh Brimm noted that a gathering of anthropologists in Paris announced that the "so-called racial differences in mankind" were a result of hereditary and environmental factors and that "no basis can be found . . . for holding that mental superiority or inferiority and race are in any way related."[30]

When Maston replaced *"Of One"* with *The Bible and Race,* he maintained the theme of "one blood." He noted that segregationists pointed to the second half of the passage, which indicated that God had set "bounds of their habitation." Progressive Baptists offered a different interpretation. Maston instructed Baptists that Paul pointed to the predetermined bounds of habitation from the perspective of the "oneness of God and the unity of mankind." Accordingly, Paul meant his reference to boundaries and limitations to prevent the Athenians, or anyone else, from developing a Messiah complex. Biblically, there was only one race, one "family" with God as the Father. If anyone had overstepped their bounds of habitation and developed something of a Messiah complex, it was whites.[31]

Maston believed that "those who through faith have come into the spiritual family of God are brothers and sisters in Christ." Maston explained the familial relationship, saying, "They all can and do pray that universal, unifying prayer, 'Our Father.' Regardless of class or color, every child of God is a brother and should be 'a brother beloved.'"[32]

Like most progressive Baptists, Leonard A. Duce, assistant dean at Baylor University, believed that communist, or other non-Christian, answers to racial problems were unacceptable. Just as no one could be "right with God and wrong with his fellow man," Duce noted that "wherever human efforts to build true social relationships have ignored the basic need of being right with God, only conflict and war have resulted."[33]

The idea of Christian "brotherhood" raised certain questions. Most important among them was "am I my brother's keeper?" Ralph A. Phelps noted that the question was "first asked by jealousy-crazed killer Cain." The question was repeated over the centuries by people who wished "to wash their hands of any responsibility for their fellow man." In particular, Phelps noted, "It was and is being asked by many communities in the United States as they seek ways to perpetuate a caste system designed to keep minority races impoverished in ignorance and squalor." Phelps noted that people continued to deny their brotherly responsibility and concluded, "Christianity has come to a day when it must start giving God's answer, not Cain's, to the question of social responsibility."[34]

Progressives viewed social responsibility as central to the teachings of Jesus. When Jesus was asked for the great commandment, he said it was the supreme love for God and immediately added a second commandment: "You shall love your neighbor as yourself." Maston argued that the two commandments stood or fell together. Doris DeVault, head of the Young Woman's Auxiliary at the Woman's Missionary Union, added, "If we love our neighbors as ourselves, we will seek for them the same opportunities and privileges we desire, regardless of class, creed, race, or nation."[35]

Just as the lawyer asked in the Gospel of Luke, some southern Christians wondered, "Who is my neighbor?" Progressive Baptist missionaries offered an answer consistent with their missionary outlook: they expanded the notion of "neighbor" to include all people. In the *Baptist Student*, Mary-Ellen Garrett, a long-time missionary in Africa, noted that Jesus responded to the lawyer with the parable of the good Samaritan. Garrett believed that Southern Baptists were so familiar with the story that they overlooked the depth of its meaning. The story of the good Samaritan was one of the most widely known biblical passages. Few southerners, however, realized how much animosity existed between the Jews and the Samaritans. Garrett explained that the Jews referred to the Samaritans as "dogs" and that "it must have been difficult for the Samaritan to stop. Real courage was involved. . . . Here we see one with *the courage to cross race barriers.*" The test of being a neighbor was the "ability to look with compassion" on other people. The Samaritan, the "dog," had proven to be the real neighbor.[36]

Also drawing on the story of the good Samaritan, Vivian Hackney wrote, "Anyone who needs my assistance is my neighbor, and God has commanded me to hold that one in as high esteem as I hold myself. Can I throw rocks at my neighbor? or shove him into the gutter? or kick him?" Certainly many Baptists agreed with Hackney, and most likely never actively engaged in racial violence. But Hackney challenged them further. She demanded, "Can I stand by, silent, while others mistreat my neighbor?" She believed that "to fit myself to live effectively in God's changing world, I must believe—and act out that belief—that my Heavenly Father loves everyone." Her challenge was poignant. While the Southern Baptist Convention, like other major denominations, had voiced support for the *Brown* decision and passed resolutions regarding race throughout the 1950s and 1960s, many local congregations remained silent. Silence abandoned the Christian mission in the world and bred an environment where violence was "inevitable." Silence was an unacceptable alternative for Christians. For T. B. Maston, it was a simple matter that "the church cannot perform God's prophetic function in a community unless the prophetic voice is in the pulpit and the prophetic spirit is in the pew." Silence on the race issue meant a church failed to be prophetic.[37]

Writing in the mid-1950s, prominent Christian thinker Reinhold Niebuhr argued that silence meant "the communities seem totally at the mercy of the intimidation of this revived Ku Klux Klan [the White Citizens' Council]." Niebuhr admitted, "Perhaps it is too much to expect even good men to have the stuff of martyrdom in them." A decade later, Baptist pastor Chevis Horne of Martinsville, Virginia, saw the silence of the churches as a clear abandonment of the transformative mission of the churches, noting that some churches responded to the racial crisis with aloofness and passivity. He argued, "This kind of church is at the mercy of powerful social, economic, and political forces in the society. Rather than shaping its culture it is shaped by the culture." Baptist ministers found themselves silenced despite their adherence to a free pulpit.[38]

Ministers should have been free to express their opinions on race and any other issue because of the Baptists' dedication to the free pulpit. The idea of the free pulpit indicated that a Baptist pastor had the right to preach whatever his own examination of the scriptures led him to believe. Pulpits, however, were rarely "free" during the race crisis.[39]

Walker L. Knight, editor of *Home Missions* in the later 1960s, noted that the pulpit was hardly free if the pastor was constrained by the congregation in what he could say. Congregational restraints caused many pastors to avoid the race issue, and not just in Baptist churches. Methodist ministers, too, felt the pressure, though their pulpits were more protected since they were appointed by the conference bishop. For Baptists, the church alone determined who it would have as pastor. As a result, Knight believed that "what is missing in many pulpits is a clear expression of the ideal of the New Testament, that race *is* irrelevant and only redemption is important." Pastors feared financial loss and tensions in the church, which prevented them from speaking on the race issues and, thus, prevented the pulpit from being truly free. Such silence reinforced the view that southern culture, with segregation, was indeed Christian.[40]

One Georgia pastor was lucky enough to have his congregation uphold the principle of a free pulpit. Brooks Ramsey of First Baptist in Albany had "given himself freely to efforts toward 'channels of communication' between Negro leadership and city officials." When three blacks attempted to attend his church, however, ushers prevented them from joining the service. Ramsey disagreed with the ushers' actions, saying, "This is Christ's church and I can't build any walls around it Christ did not build, and Christ did not build any racial walls." The church, despite such differences, voted to retain Ramsey as pastor, noting "the right of our pastor to exercise a free pulpit according to his own sincere Christian conviction even if, at times, such conviction differs from that of some members of the church." Ramsey challenged another congregation years later, publicly supporting the sanitation workers during the strike in Memphis in 1968. That year, Ramsey invited an African minister to preach on Race Relations Sunday, causing some members of the congregation to attempt to remove him. The attempt failed, but others were not so lucky. When the board of deacons at University Baptist Church in Chapel Hill, North Carolina, could no longer tolerate W. Wesley Shrader's integrationist views, it asked for, and accepted, his resignation.[41]

Silence prevented the church from effectively playing its role in society. Walker L. Knight wrote that silent pulpits "are captives of the culture of present society." Worse yet, "to be silent is to imply that the Bible says nothing, or if it does that the minister does not believe it." Knight believed that race was the most pressing issue facing the churches but also the one about which most pastors were silent: "We lose our integrity by our silence, and the church loses its integrity because it does not practice what the Scriptures teach: that Christ died for all men. We might well ponder what [H.] Richard Niebuhr said: 'there is no conflict between theory and practice, between thought and action. The central conflict always is between the theory we profess and the theory upon which we act.'" [42]

Recognizing the persistent silence of southern Christians, Baptist leaders called on individuals to examine their consciences and to determine if they were prejudiced. According to Maston, many Christians had not faced their prejudice, thinking it was confined to hate for blacks, which they did not feel. Further, they had not realized that prejudice was unchristian. Maston wrote, "Many conscientious white Christians have never realized that fundamental Christian truths, theoretically accepted as valid, are applicable to the race situation of the South. One of the main hopes for progress in the future is that more and more of us will be able to say with Peter, 'Now I really understand that God shows no partiality.'" Maston wondered if Baptists were "willing to ask the Spirit of God to show us our sins in the area of race relations?" Even Peter had resisted. Frank Stagg told Southern Baptists that, of the twelve apostles, only Philip was "color blind" from the start. He argued that the other eleven apostles and "millions since have struggled to free themselves of prejudice, which cannot be Christian." It took a vision atop Cornelius's house to make Peter believe "in the depths of his soul" that God showed no partiality. Maston believed that if Southern Baptists let the Spirit work in their souls, then "the majority of us will become conscious that we have sinned, that we have fallen short of God's expectations for us." [43]

Recognizing prejudices was only the first step in overcoming them. Katharine Parker Freeman warned that "prejudice is so sinister in its working that even after acknowledging the facts, we may still be warped in our opinions, the underlying cause being that we want to think like other people." She recognized that prejudices persisted even in people who admitted they were prejudiced because the culture so distorted people's thinking and because of people's innate desire to "belong." She understood that "it is much more comfortable to conform!" [44]

Overcoming prejudice was necessary for inviting the spirit of Christ into one's life. Maston pointed out that the "one test of how much of the spirit of Jesus we have is how free we are from color consciousness, from racial prejudice." White Christians had to be able to pray "Our Father" with members of all races. If they could not, Maston wrote, they had "failed to catch the spirit of our Father and their Father." *Agape*—Christian love based on service—manifested the spirit of "our Father and their Father."[45]

Some Christians argued that agape was "too idealistic" for an "evil world." Maston agreed that Christian love was idealistic, but he believed that "there is no full achievement of Christian ends without the use of Christian methods; and certainly love and the love ethic have an important place in any Christian approach to human problems." According to Maston, anything that creates barriers to fellowship between people and God and among people is sin. Those barriers "keep us from fulfilling God's purpose for us in human relations." Racism was clearly a barrier between peoples.[46]

Like many progressives, Maston believed race relations to be primarily a moral issue and that "the moral forces should take the lead in its solution." Specifically, "it is the church's business to be in the vanguard of the moral forces of society." Since the South was predominantly Baptist, "we must conclude that the racial problems of the South are primarily Baptist problems, there is no way for us to escape our responsibility." Throughout the postwar years, Maston called on churches to lead the way in solving the race problem, writing that "from the days of the New Testament until today, the Gospel of Christ has been the good news that has not only brought salvation to men everywhere from the penalty and power of sin, but it has brought vision, hope, and courage to the disheartened, the underprivileged, the down-trodden, the enslaved of the world."[47]

The Baptist leaders insisted that biblical teachings needed to direct all aspects of the lives of Christians and the churches. While they agreed with their constituents that the fundamental mission of the church was "to preach and to teach the principles of original Christianity in their purity," they disagreed with those Christians who argued that the churches should not become involved in political or social questions. Furthermore, progressive Baptists often defined political questions as moral questions. In this way, they had become involved in such causes as the prohibition movement while claiming to be apolitical. Many

Baptists, however, believed that becoming involved in social issues strayed from religious purity. T. J. Preston was among those who worried about the churches taking social and political stands. Preston told Baptists that desegregation was a purely political question and, therefore, the Southern Baptist Convention and its state affiliates had no right even to discuss the matter. Such Christians separated their social, professional, and religious lives.[48]

Many Christians, however, severed their Christianity from the rest of their lives even inside Christian institutions. John H. Marion Jr., director of Christian relations for the Presbyterian Church, US, writing about Christian colleges, said, "Though biblical facts are normally taught with a loving and devout fidelity, they are usually carefully segregated from all dark and practical realities—at least so far as their application to our present social order is concerned." The *Baptist Student* offered Marion's opinions to Baptist college students in 1948, encouraging them to ponder the relationship between Christianity and the social order.[49]

Conservative Baptists claimed that Jesus had not participated in a social revolution. Christianity, in the words of an unnamed "prominent layman," was "man's relation to God; his relation to his fellow man is not a part of Christianity." T. B. Maston and two of his former students at Southwestern Baptist Theological Seminary, Ralph Phelps and Foy Valentine, disagreed with that view. Maston noted that the church must "apply the ideals [of Christianity] to life and seek to lead the people to practice the Christian principles in every area of life." He said, "It is a mistake to interpret the kingdom in social terms alone," but added that "no conception of the kingdom is adequate that does not include the social." Phelps added that such a position was "neither scripturally nor rationally sound." While he was secretary of the Texas Christian Life Commission, Valentine wrote that the world was plagued by social inequities and that it was "imperative that modern Christians in general, and Southern Baptists in particular, face up to their responsibilities in the realm of applied Christianity."[50] Valentine, who had lived on the interracial Koinonia Farm in southwest Georgia, went further, noting that Jesus "came preaching the gospel to the poor, giving sight to the blind, healing the sick, associating with social outcasts, and planting the seeds for the greatest social revolution of history." Christians, thus, were obligated to be a part of that social revolution.[51]

Josef Nordenhaug, editor of Foreign Mission Board's *The Commis-*

sion in 1949, wrote that many people looked for a "convenient religion." They did not want the tension that came with the Christian endeavor to transform the world. They wanted, instead, a "religion from which they can take a vacation when it suits them." Many Americans had found just such a religion, but Nordenhaug noted that such "bargain-counter" religions, whatever they might be, were not Christian: "A Christian is permanently and inextricably bound to Christ in all seasons." The depths of the southern race problem, widely recognized by Baptist leaders, required a true and deep Christianity to challenge it.[52]

Billy Graham, Baptist and renowned evangelist, appraised the upsurge of religion in America during the 1950s. Like Nordenhaug, Graham determined that it was hollow; it had not been accompanied by higher standards of morality or more Christian attitudes on social issues, specifically regarding race. Paul M. Stevens, director of the Baptist Radio and Television Commission, quoted Graham as saying, "If every church member were committed to Christ, I doubt if we would be having the racial violence . . . the high divorce rate, the terrible slum areas of our cities." Many new, and some old, Christians apparently avoided the serious soul-searching of conversion. John C. Bennett of Union Theological Seminary hoped that Graham held the key to a true revival: "His great influence should do much to disturb complacent Christians and to release the truth of the Gospel that has been hidden from churches themselves in many places."[53]

True Christianity was demanding. The Christian, according to Ralph Phelps, must live as a Christian and be willing to be "terribly inconvenienced for the sake of his religion; he must take up his cross daily and follow Jesus." In *Royal Service*, Jacqueline Durham cited Romans, arguing that the Christian ethic was not confined to the church. It was to be practiced in daily living: "It cannot stop with the people around us, but must help determine the quality of society."[54]

Maston recognized that in the 1950s and 1960s it was difficult for many people to apply Christian teachings regarding race. He understood that many people lived in areas of severe racial tension where there was considerable pressure to conform to social traditions. Yet he also argued that race prejudices could be overcome through the power of God. For proof, he again pointed to Acts 10:28, where Peter came to the full realization of the meaning of his rooftop vision. In an article for the

Window, Maston encouraged young Baptist women to "ask our heavenly Father to give us the wisdom to know what we should do and the faith and courage to do it and to do it in the right spirit."[55]

Mission leaders realized the enormity of their demands. They fully understood the difficulty involved in rejecting long-established customs. Yet they insisted it was necessary. Billie Pate, promotion associate for Young Woman's Auxiliary, wrote, "The principles of a missionary organization sometimes run counter to popular opinion. YWA is based on the concept of the expansion of the gospel of Christ into all the world, but no less into all of life. When these principles are exerted in community situations that oppose them, conflict is temporarily created. So we welcome you to tension and conflict." Theron D. Price, professor of Christian history at the Southern Baptist Theological Seminary, argued that the church was "the organ for the accomplishment of God's saving purpose for the whole world." That mission meant "the church serves as a challenge over against the society in which it lives. It aims at more than teaching people to feel pious while living by the same standards which are in the 'world.'" Price, like Pate, believed that the church "points beyond its own border to the saving of all men." He went further. Each church, he said, "must be an instrument in God's hand to bring the light to those who walk in darkness."[56]

Foy Valentine noted that many potential solutions to the race problem had been offered over the years, but only one was viable: "God has given man the only adequate solution to it in Christ Jesus who loved us all and gave himself for us that we might know in him true peace and brotherhood." Valentine believed that it "was in such a dark area as that of race relations that Christ's call to be Christian, to be light of the world, takes on its clearest meaning."[57]

The disjunction between the leadership and the congregations reflected, in part, the membership's persistent, if somewhat unfounded, fear that stressing social issues, such as racism, would lead Baptists away from their traditional religion to the Social Gospel. Many Southern Baptists rejected the Social Gospel as being unbiblical. Even those who promoted the social message of Christianity frequently avoided calling it the Social Gospel for fear that the membership would view them as theologically liberal. The leadership in the postwar years developed the social message of the Gospel without forgoing their emphasis on individual conversion and redemption. By doing so, they maintained what they considered a safe distance from the theological liberalism of the Social Gospel.[58]

Race relations provided churches an opportunity to apply fundamental Christian principles to life and to act as Christians. Maston believed that "by faithfully proclaiming the Christian conception of race relations the churches can take the lead in what is primarily a moral problem and may be able to recapture to some degree the prestige and the moral leadership they have, to a considerable extent, lost." Maston maintained the emphasis on individualism. He argued that solutions to social problems required both enlightened minds and willing hearts. He continued, "It is the church's business to furnish the willing hearts, those with souls that seek sincerely for divine truth and apply that truth to the problems of life."[59]

Some Baptists disagreed with the characterization of race relations as primarily a moral issue. The First Baptist Church of Farmerville, Louisiana, announced: "We do not believe that the segregation-integration issue is a moral or immoral matter. . . . To us it is not a matter of Christianity or non-Christianity, and no such issue was newly created by the Court Decision of 1954." Similarly, William L. Bush of Shreveport, Louisiana, wrote to Porter Routh that segregation was "a political and social problem which Jesus Christ himself cannot solve." Progressive Baptists uniformly disagreed, believing that it was a moral issue and that only Christianity could solve the problem.[60]

Churches had an important contribution to make to the changing of society around them. Ross Coggins argued that any time a minority suffered "humiliation or exclusion because of an indefensible social structure, the church must bear prophetic witness to the fact that social structures which oppress stand under the judgment of God." Coggins pointed to the church's responsibility to change the society around it and overthrow institutionalized racism.[61]

Christians had not proven fast learners, especially when it came time to apply Christianity to the problems of everyday life. Maston cited Galatians 3:28, where Paul said that there was neither bond nor free, "for ye all are one man in Christ Jesus." He admitted that "it took Christians a long time to learn that brothers should not be slaves," but he also argued that "there are men and women caught in the mighty grip of our class and racial caste system who are in real, if not legal, slavery." As long as such a situation persisted, "the task of Christian brotherhood is not complete."[62]

Maston urged Southern Baptists toward the Christian ideal by asking them to "consider briefly what it would mean if churches took seriously the fact that they are 'Churches of God,' that they are 'the body of Christ.'" He believed churches had to recognize that they were not fraternal orders or civic clubs. He argued that racial distinctions, however real they may be in society, should not apply to churches. Churches existed to "make men and the community of men conscious of the presence of the living God." Furthermore, Christians had to behave as Christians. Maston wrote, "The members are so to live among men that they will point them to God." Maston argued that the courts could break down legal barriers between races and classes, but that the "deep-seated walls of prejudice can be broken down only by the inner presence of the resurrected Christ. He alone can really make Jew and Gentile, Negro and White, one."[63]

By practicing segregation, churches explicitly failed to foster God's kingdom on earth. Maston knew that many white Christian churches did not welcome blacks for worship services or membership. He asked, "How can we justify the exclusion of the Negro from many and possibly most of our churches?" He wondered how Baptists could explain the exclusion to themselves, or to black Christians. Further, "how can we explain it to the Lord, who is the head of the church?" He believed, instead, that "as a fellowship of or in the Spirit the church should demonstrate in its own fellowship the kind of world we would have if society itself were redeemed." The church was the only organization that could demonstrate "God's ideal or goal for human society" on earth.[64]

Segregation in churches violated the basic nature of the church. Maston argued that God alone had the right to determine the membership of the churches. He admitted that there were churches, including some outside the South, which were "thoroughly committed to the continuance of segregation in society and also within the church." Some leaders contended that segregation was in harmony with the will of God. Maston retorted, "We believe that such an attitude, which is the epitome of racial pride, cuts the very heart out of the Christian gospel and the Christian ethic. It imperils the soul of the church itself." He saw that most Southern Baptists, if they were not outright defenders of segregation, gave it their "silent assent." The Baptist laity also recognized the problem. Mrs. RBH wrote a letter to the editors of *Royal Service* citing several biblical passages, including Peter's housetop vision in Acts. She lamented that prejudice was "a cause of trouble in my own church. May God help us to wake up before it is too late."[65]

The churches, as human institutions, came under pressure from their members and from the wider society to conform to community practices. Maston reminded Baptists, "One function the church is supposed to perform for its members and for the community is to maintain a constant tension toward the Christian ideal for the individual and for the world." Church members in the South often failed to maintain that tension. Maston argued that many Christians in the South revealed that they were "babes in Christ" during the racial crisis. He added, "Many of them have revealed that they are more Southerners than Christians." They refused to see the relevance of Christian truths to the racial situation. In doing so, they damaged the cause of Christianity throughout the world. Maston reminded Baptists, "Christ is not concerned exclusively with any one segment of life. He has authority in every realm, and He wants that authority to be realized and recognized."[66]

One Georgia pastor believed that much of the difficulty in moving the churches to more progressive views of race came from nominal members. After a group of five blacks attended services at his church, "fears were fanned by two or three members' insistence that 'if you give them an inch, they will take a mile.'" A deacon had shaken hands with one of the Negroes and had "received more criticism because of this act of common decency than any other person who has taken a stand in favor of seating Negroes." More important was the fact that most of the people who opposed seating the blacks "were not really involved in the life of the church. Some were regular Sunday morning attenders, but in most cases they did not even attend that often." None were good stewards with money and only two were, by the pastor's standards, "good" church members. Despite the pastor's announcement that "a vote to exclude anybody from our sanctuary was a vote against 1,800 Southern Baptist Missionaries" the church voted 150 to 95 against seating blacks.[67]

In the South, as Maston and other progressive leaders noted, some Christians bowed to social pressure to follow southern customs instead of Christian truths. Maston pointed to the Gospel of Mark where Jesus told the Pharisees and the scribes "you leave the commandment of God, and hold fast the traditions of men." Jesus then charged them even more directly with misinterpreting God's will, saying, "You have a fine way of rejecting the commandment of God, in order to keep your tradition!" To Maston and other Baptist leaders, defending segregation was a prime example of holding fast to the traditions of men. Indeed, historian Bill Leonard notes, "Perhaps no major Protestant denomination retained so much of its nineteenth-century identity as long as the Southern Baptist Convention." He argues that Southern Baptist denominational unity was "based less on rigid doctrinal synthesis than on denominational and regional identity."[68]

Maston believed that the resistance to change was deeply rooted in southern culture, creating problems for effecting a "Christian transformation" in society. He suggested that Baptists were "basically against change of any kind—theological as well as social," adding, "They frequently identify cultural conformity with theological 'orthodoxy.'" According to Charles Wellbron, pastor of the Seventh and James Baptist Church in Waco, Texas, the relationship between culture and Christianity provided Christians with their most difficult problem: "one of the fundamental problems that a Christian faces in his spiritual life is the one of distinguishing adequately between moral principles and social customs. It is also one of the most difficult things to do." In a society that claimed its customs were "Christian," the distinctions could be difficult, especially for young Christians. As a result, many Baptists identified the traditions of the South with Christianity itself and resisted seeing that they were incompatible.[69]

One Baptist minister was so disgusted with some Christians' continuing adherence to tradition instead of God's commandment that he told a friend and fellow pastor, "I am a Southern Baptist theologically, I'm not sure that I am one sociologically." Many "cultural Christians" believed, in the words of Daniel R. Grant of Vanderbilt University, "you aren't supposed to talk about righteousness during the week—only on Sunday unless possibly at the Wednesday night prayer meeting." People divorced righteousness from politics and business and social life. Grant, however, insisted that righteousness had to infuse all of a Christian's activities: political, social, and economic.[70]

For Southern Baptists, the difference between Christ and culture was blurred in the very name of the Convention. Charles Chaney of Palatine, Illinois, wrote that Baptists often emphasized the "Southern" even as the Convention spread throughout the United States. After the

1968 annual convention in Houston passed a progressive, if weakened, resolution on race, Chaney wrote, "In the heat of debate I heard informed Southern Baptists asseverate that they were *Southern* Baptists, had always been *Southern* Baptists and always would be *Southern* Baptists (emphasis theirs)." Chaney continued:

> are we willing to change? Where is our first allegiance? Is our supreme loyalty with Christ or with culture? This is the question that must be faced. It cannot be Christ and culture, at least not if we want to really evangelize all of America. The prior question, I suppose, is still, "Do we really want messengers from all over the United States and from all races in the United States at a meeting of the Southern Baptist Convention?" That is the consequence of evangelizing *all* of America. Faced with that probability the evangelistic zeal of some may decline suddenly. But assuming that our purpose is to win all men in America to Christ, then Christ and Southern Culture is not an option.
> It should be obvious that if we must choose between Christ and culture, that we will choose Christ. But culture has an insidious way of getting inside even the way we think about Christ.[71]

Such a conflation of religion and culture led Frank Stagg to fear that pastors were not challenging their congregations. Instead, he wrote, "the church in America today is threatened by the culture with which it has almost identified itself." After noting the flight of Southern Baptists to the suburbs, he wrote, "Churches are in danger of being captured by the suburbs in which they seem to prosper. They often reflect the character of the suburb, making little impact on the suburb's character." He concluded "only the severest self-criticism with a willingness to accept correctives can save the church from irrelevancy and impotence in the years ahead."[72]

Sam Hill Jr. believed churches had to point the way to a better, more Christian society. Hill had graduated from the Southern Baptist Theological Seminary and earned a PhD from Duke. He told Baptists: "those who say that religion and politics are two topics which they never discuss together have not yet caught the social implications of Christian commitment." He explained, "The Christian strategy is never withdrawal or retreat—but involvement in the affairs of this world of persons." Hill was particularly concerned about the divisions within the Convention and wrote, in the *Christian Century*, "It is unlikely that any major religious group in America faces as critical an immediate future as does the Southern Baptist Convention." Hill pointed directly to the relationship between Christianity and culture, explaining that "although Southern Baptists outside the south are sect-type, radical in their isolation from or opposition to the prevailing culture, in the south they are church-type, accepted by and involved in the culture of the region." Race was clearly central to the growing rift within the Convention, and it was the one aspect of southern society that was changing the most in the 1950s and 1960s. Hill warned, "So integrally related are the Southern Baptist people to the regional culture that the new south's arrival threatens the equilibrium of the institution . . . and the relevance of its ministry."[73]

Hill believed the growing rift between the denominational leadership and the congregations was due, at least in part, to the rising levels of education among the younger clergy and leadership. The leaders of various denominations were increasingly college educated. Many had earned graduate degrees. Yet, Hill believed, there was a persistent anti-intellectualism in southern Christianity, suggested by the common phrase, "I'd rather be a fool on fire than a scholar on ice." He believed, however, that anti-intellectualism was not founded on biblical principles and that scholarship and fervor were not incompatible. Finally, he noted that "it is imperative that the Christian student gain the facility to rise above nationalism and any other form of provincialism in interpreting world happenings, and that requires keeping abreast of social and political trends and events."[74]

Still, in the postwar world rising levels of education were not restricted to the ministry. If anything, they were more widespread than ever before. William Self, pastor of Wieuca Road Baptist Church in Atlanta, noted that church leaders had long supported education and that in the postwar era it was available to more people than ever before. Certainly more and more people were going to college. This was not, as Hill feared, creating an unbridgeable chasm in the churches. Instead, Self argued, it meant that the "underbrush" of "immature and unexamined theological positions, inadequate moral framework, provincialism, and folk religion" was being cut away. In its stead, "healthy and relevant attitudes can grow." Self reflected the Baptist leadership's faith that future generations could build a more Christian society. He clearly believed that the churches were gaining a new "theological maturity and social awareness." He believed that the religious revival of the postwar period had finally grown to maturity by the mid-1960s and noted that "a religious pep rally substituted for the worship of a holy God is its own indictment and will not long endure in the emerging church."[75]

As the churches struggled with cultural changes, many found themselves somewhere between the irrelevancy Hill feared and the maturity Self predicted. Southern Christians often proved to be "babes in Christ," unable or unwilling to follow the will of God in the face of cultural pressures. Ronnie Stutes, a student at the University of Southwestern Louisiana, wrote, "I am concerned because cultural factors often override Christian influence. I see people who claim to be Christians calling other men innately inferior and often manifesting hate toward them." Some had a conversion experience, but lived their lives as if that were both the beginning and the end of their Christian obligations, never doing anything to live up to the name "Christian." Others had truly come to believe that southern institutions were Christian. Either way, they sought justification and reassurance from the churches. The Southern Baptist leadership refused them both.[76]

Race threatened to rip the Southern Baptist Convention apart. The fissures between the leaders and the congregations, rooted in differing interpretations regarding the relationship between Christianity and culture, ran deep. The divisions grew as the progressive leadership, with the benefits of seminary education, tried to move the Convention toward a "gospel that is social," a move many Baptists in the pews rejected as theologically liberal. Part of the clearing of the underbrush that William Self believed was occurring was actually an exodus of conservative Baptists. Historian David Edwin Harrell demonstrates that the most important independent church movement after World War II was the departure of white, racially conservative congregations that could no longer remain within a Convention they believed was dominated by racial progressives. Still, the Baptist free-church tradition, which prevented the Convention from maintaining any doctrinal discipline among the churches, also prevented the race issue from destroying the Convention altogether. Baptist independence allowed the coexistence of competing ideas regarding the relationship of Christianity and culture, especially where it concerned the race question.[77]

Baptist missionaries firmly believed that the power to transform society was rooted in Christianity's power to transform the individual. Since Christianity transformed individuals, the larger culture had to be transformed one individual at a time. But the "excessive emphasis on individualism and personal piety" weakened the social application of Christianity. A Christian transformation of southern culture, such as the leadership hoped for, would be slow in coming, if it were to come at all.[78]

2

ALL NATIONS IN GOD'S PLAN

Peace, Race, and Missions in the Postwar World

World War II dramatically altered international relations. In search of a mechanism for preventing future wars, leading members of the world community met in San Francisco in 1945 to charter the United Nations. Baptist leaders approved and sent a delegation to the meeting. Although the United Nations' meeting was secular, they believed it reflected their belief in the unity of humanity and the inclusion of all nations in God's plan. They believed that a lasting peace was only possible in a Christianized world; thus they focused on missionary efforts, both at home and abroad, to promote world peace. Further, they believed that overcoming racism was essential to the successful evangelization of the world and for peace. While many Baptists saw overcoming racism as necessary for a world conversion to Christianity that would make a lasting peace possible, others made the connection between racism and peace more directly. Myrtle Robinson (Mrs. C. D.) Creasman, the Woman's Missionary Union's vice president for Tennessee, wrote, "As long as there are racial prejudices, racial injustice, racial hatreds, and unrighteous racial ambition, there can be no permanent peace."[1]

Progressive Baptists saw World War II as a watershed event in world race relations. W. R. White, writing for *Home Missions*, noted that people had traveled extensively and "their contacts with other races and nationalities have given them a better understanding and a more inclusive appreciation." He argued, "The tremendous racial conscious-ness that has been aroused in this war must be faced." He was certainly not alone in that view. According to E. C. Routh, editor of *The Commission*, "the war has widened the acquaintance of every tribe and

41

tongue. African men, for example, have gone to the ends of the earth to return with new aspirations, new ambitions, the desire to learn more about the Americas, Europe, the Orient, the islands of the sea." Routh was optimistic about the changes taking place in Africa. He said that "Allied forces gained first hand acquaintance with every political division of Africa and reported amazing possibilities in that continent, many of which hitherto had been largely unknown." The increased contact between people of differing backgrounds highlighted the international dimension of racial prejudice and the need for a Christian solution to racism.[2]

Baptists believed that colonialism, and its inseparable racism, had been among the chief causes of the war. Colonialism would have to cease, albeit gradually, before true peace could be established. W. O. Carver, emeritus professor of missions from the Southern Baptist Theological Seminary in Louisville, Kentucky, argued, "Not for even one generation longer can all the power and force and ingenuity of the white races maintain a position of preferred tenants of God's earth which he has peopled with twice as many colored as white men." French and British efforts to shore up the old colonial system in Asia and Africa worked against peace. Simply put, "the clash of color" had to be resolved or "not all the skill of diplomacy and manipulation of natural resources [could] preserve a peace that would have at its heart arrogance and exploitation."[3]

This attack on colonialism was all the more important in the emerging cold war. Colonial powers were allies against communism. Historians Mary L. Dudziak and Penny Von Eschen both argue that the cold war narrowed the scope of legitimate protest. Criticism of colonialism itself, much less its racial implications, could not be accommodated. Historian Eric Foner notes that the "vision of racial inequality in the United States as part of a global system rather than as a maladjustment between American ideals and behavior did not long survive the advent of the cold war." Yet progressive Baptists not only critiqued colonialism; they also tied it directly to segregation in the United States. They persisted in tying American racism to its global context while also noting that it was a failure of America to live up to its ideals.[4]

Progressive Baptists saw that the racist attitudes behind both colonialism and segregation in America were much the same. Creasman noted that once people believed in their racial superiority, they would try to dominate "lesser" peoples. Notably, in the late nineteenth century "the white nations of Europe, considering themselves superior to black people, felt they had the right to take possession of Africa and to use black labor for their own enrichment." By the same token, whites in America thought they had "a right to claim all of the blessing of democracy for themselves while denying it to the Indians, Mexicans, Negroes, orientals and other minority groups in America's population." Baylor professor Charles D. Johnson dealt more specifically with segregation in contemporary America when he wrote, in 1946, "To maintain a system of government that denies educational opportunity to millions of people is to perpetuate social crime on an international scale." Johnson's comments appeared in his *Southern Baptist Brotherhood Quarterly* article on the United Nations, in which he also noted that, despite the Thirteenth, Fourteenth, and Fifteenth Amendments to the Constitution, "several states, north and south, have discriminatory laws."[5]

Other mission leaders agreed with Creasman and Johnson that the international race question was much the same as the domestic race question. The core issue was the same: white oppression of nonwhites. Theodore F. Adams, a member of the Foreign Mission Board and pastor of First Baptist Church in Richmond, Virginia, told the Woman's Missionary Union, "We need to recognize that the racial issue is world-wide. That our own problems of race relations at home are but a part of a larger problem that all the world must face." In America it was done through segregation; in Africa and Asia the mechanism was colonialism. Hermione Dannelly Jackson of the Woman's Missionary Union prompted young women to ponder the point, noting that "we belong to and are promoting the Kingdom of God on earth. We cannot insist on liberty, justice, and equality only within the arbitrary boundary lines of our own country. Our concern is for all men everywhere."[6]

At the close of the war, Carver feared that the United States might become "the patron of empires, the guardian angel of imperialism, and prosperous leader of a new era of materialism." He considered it "tragic" that Winston Churchill and Jan Smuts, two leaders previously lionized by Southern Baptists, were working to preserve imperialism and entrench colonialism. Churchill resisted the end of the British Empire, and Smuts sought to bring South-West Africa under South African control. Churchill particularly needed to be on friendly terms with South Africa and Rhodesia because of England's currency problems and the "dollar gap," which could be aided by holding on to those areas—either as dominions or colonies—that were wealthy in minerals, especially gold.[7]

While the Baptists were critical of imperialism and attempts to preserve it, George W. Sadler, the Foreign Mission Board secretary for Africa, Europe, and the Middle East, argued that Americans should not gloat over the troubles of the empires. Instead, they should be "awed by the new responsibility that has come to us as a result of the bankruptcy of Britain." The Baptists' new evangelical efforts in the British colonies focused on health care and education, but some Baptists, wary of the Social Gospel, argued that ministering to the worldly needs of people was not true evangelism. Sadler disagreed: "it is God's love in action. It is God's grace expressing itself through Christ-centered teachers and Christ dominated doctors and nurses."[8]

The need for "worldly" as well as spiritual help around the world fit well with the Marshall Plan, which distributed enormous amounts of aid to war-torn countries. Other parts of the world not covered by the plan desperately needed aid as well. President Truman, a Baptist, speaking in Columbus, Ohio, said, "There is a supreme opportunity for the church to continue to fulfill its mission on earth. No other agency can do it. Unless it is done, we are headed for the disaster we would deserve." That mission involved fighting the "forces of selfishness and greed and intolerance," both at home and in international relations. Truman urged Americans "to prove your faith and your belief in the teachings of God by doing your share to save the starving millions in Europe and Asia and Africa." Most Southern Baptists agreed but still believed that spiritual needs were preeminent. Porter Routh, the secretary of the Southern Baptist Convention's Executive Committee, wrote, "To be sure, . . . [man] has needs in the realm of the economic, the social, and the political, but these needs must be met in the name of Jesus Christ before they can bring him into the road of peace."[9]

Realizing that racial prejudices exacerbated world tensions, J. B. Lawrence of the Home Mission Board argued "unless the racial problem is solved, we cannot have world peace." Writers for *Home Missions* agreed. One feared that "in Africa, in India, the Near and Far East, racial conflicts may any day provoke an incident that will touch off the next world war, and the end." Only one solution was available: "love of Christ in the hearts of men." Lawrence warned Southern Baptists that racism and discrimination would "greatly hinder and retard our efforts to evangelize the world."[10]

H. Cornell Goerner, professor of missions at the Southern Baptist Theological Seminary, announced that Jesus and the prophets "understood the comprehensiveness of God's loving purpose. No one was left out. All nations were included in his plan of redemption." Christianity, spread to all nations, could provide the only solid basis for a lasting peace. Like other Baptist mission leaders, Goerner believed that racial problems in the United States made the evangelization of the world more difficult. In 1947, he wrote a short book, *America Must Be Christian*, arguing that America's behavior in the years immediately after World War II would determine the future of the world. Goerner warned, "America must be Christian not only in name but in national behavior, or our civilization will perish and our own nation with it." He explained that "race prejudices hamstring American missionaries everywhere. We cannot go much farther in persuading others to become Christian until we are willing to go deeper in applying Christian principles in our own land." Baptists were not alone in pointing out the damage done to the mission cause by racism at home. Southern Presbyterian missionaries also noted that segregation and discrimination in the United States adversely affected their efforts. Yet the expanse of the Baptists' mission effort, and its centrality to the Convention, gave that argument particular force. [11]

Shortly before leaving the Southern Baptist Theological Seminary to take over duties as the secretary for Africa, Europe, and the Near East at the Foreign Mission Board, Goerner again wrote on the relationship between racism and missions: "missions is the process whereby the saving gospel of the Lord Jesus Christ is progressively shared with men of all races and nations, looking toward the time when every knee shall bow and every tongue confess that Christ is Lord." By definition, missions involved crossing barriers of class, language, and race. Goerner reminded Baptists that "all over the world members of the so-called 'colored peoples' are acutely aware that in past centuries they have often been ruled, exploited, and dominated by so-called 'white' . . . people." In the later 1950s, while African nations, led by Ghana, were obtaining political independence from Europe, Goerner wrote that as members of the "colored races" became independent, they resented any suggestion that they were inferior, and might "take personal offense at a supposed slight or insult to any other 'colored' race." Africans, Goerner wrote, were divided on several issues, but they were "powerfully united in their common resistance to any vestige of the old idea of 'white supremacy.'"[12]

Missionaries were caught in the middle of a tense racial situation that emerged with the end of colonialism. Southern Baptist missionaries, with their white skin, were often associated with colonizers. That was a difficult enough challenge, but modern communications had made the world "one great whispering-gallery." While all news traveled fast, Goerner believed that news of racial problems in the United States "spread with unusual speed." He feared that such news items could "quickly destroy good will and understanding which the missionary has laboriously built up over the years and may create embarrassments and problems which greatly hinder his work."[13]

Following Goerner, Daniel R. White wrote that "Jesus did not share the narrow prejudiced view of the people of his day." White, the Southern Baptists' fraternal representative in Spain, believed that Christians of the twentieth century needed to reject narrow, prejudiced views of the day. He reminded Baptists that whites were a minority of the world's population, that Marxism was spreading, and that news of racial problems in the United States turned many Africans and Asians away from Christianity. In the month White's article appeared in *The Commission*, the bombing of a black church in Birmingham had demonstrated the lengths to which some white southerners were willing to go to maintain segregation.[14]

Victor Glass, secretary of the Department of Work with National Baptists at the Home Mission Board, was more optimistic than Goerner or White. Writing in 1966, after both the Civil Rights and Voting Rights acts had passed, Glass believed that there was "more goodwill in race relations than at any time in American life." He reflected the Baptists' insistence on individualism, explaining, "This is so now because goodwill is on a different basis. It is between persons rather than races." Nevertheless, problems remained. And, Glass told Baptists, "World opinion is on the Negro's side." He mentioned that over forty newspapers around the world carried front-page photographs from the Freedom Rides of the early 1960s. That could also be good. Glass wrote, "No longer can we say 'out of sight, out of mind.'" Furthermore, more African and

Asian nations were taking their seats in the United Nations. Glass admitted, "We need to be reminded again that this is a 'colored' world."[15]

The international situation influenced the race struggle in the United States. Glass wrote, "Negroes have tasted the heady elixir of freedom and they like it. They have seen their African brothers treated well in the councils of the United Nations. They have quit asking for freedom; they are demanding it, and getting it. They know it is theirs by birth, and no one has the right to grant it to them as a favor, or withhold it as a threat." The solution to the racial problem in missions was manifold but the essence simple. Glass explained that the foremost imperative for missions in a racially tense world was to "undergird our mission philosophy with theology instead of trying to explain it in terms of culture, anthropology, or a way of life." To do so, Glass believed, would release the mission effort from both cultural imperialism and racism by showing that it was truly intended for all peoples.[16]

Baptists believed that each individual Baptist had a responsibility to work for world peace through the evangelization of the world. They believed that each individual's actions impacted the wider world, though in less obvious ways than institutions like the United Nations. To demonstrate that idea, Congressman O. K. Armstrong of Missouri and his wife Marjorie Moore Armstrong, a frequent writer for Baptist mission magazines, held a birthday party for the United Nations. They invited a Brazilian and Hungarian family over for birthday cake. Marjorie Armstrong wrote that it was "simple, but it dramatized for my boys two things. The UN is still a living organism after seven years, but peace after all is a personal matter of practicing good neighborliness." Her efforts reflected the ideas offered by E. W. Thornton, professor of history and government at Oklahoma Baptist University. He wrote, "Although we deal in global concepts when studying the problems of peace, we may begin right at home to *practice* it. International understanding, so essential to world peace, is after all a very personal matter." Thornton stressed the importance of good relations between students and their international classmates: "our own hospitality or indifference may well be a determining influence upon their outlook when in later years they become leaders in their home lands."[17]

The United Nations was limited in what it could do for world peace largely because it was a secular institution. Peace had to enter the hearts and lives of people around the world, and Baptist leaders believed that only Christianity was suitable for that task. Christianity was "the one force in history that is grounded in the ideal [of unity] and produced by the power that makes for unity and brotherhood." Only with Christianity could the spirit of international cooperation dominate diplomacy. Laws and treaties were needed, but Baptists believed that laws could not change the hearts and minds of individuals. In their report on world peace, Baptists argued, "Invaluable as they may be, international agreements embodied in political organizations, the establishment of brotherhood among men awaits the regeneration of individuals and the real Christianization of leaders."[18]

Even people associated with the United Nations realized the limitations of international agreements. Several years after the founding of the United Nations, one Baptist student, A. E. Lacy Jr., wrote that the United Nations was dependent upon the willingness of its members to follow the principles set out in the charter. Without a conversion to Christianity, that might not happen. He reported that a member of the United Nations spoke at Georgetown College in Kentucky. Lacy, unfortunately, did not name the speaker, but quoted him or her as saying, "When we first adopted the Universal Declaration of Human Rights, I was very optimistic. I thought all we had to do was to have all the nations sign the covenant, and the pressure of public opinion would cause racial discrimination to cease. I soon found out that a 'piece of paper' wasn't enough."[19] A "piece of paper" could not solve racial tensions without the regeneration of the individuals, and that was the obligation of missions. Reflecting on that obligation, J. W. Marshall, the Foreign Mission Board's secretary for missionary personnel, argued that "Christ commissioned us to preach the gospel to all nations. He offered no other remedy for war." Other Baptists agreed. William Flemming of Fort Worth, Texas, had written, "The fighting part of the war seems to be over but nothing short of the spirit of Christ can bring about the peace for which we fought."[20]

The Southern Baptists' belief that peace was a personal obligation for individuals meant that peace could be accomplished only by worldwide conversion to Christianity. H. Cornell Goerner noted the supreme importance of Christianity in the search for peace: "the Bible is perfectly plain in its teaching that peace is conditioned upon surrender to the will of God." Goerner reminded Baptist youth that the prophet

Baker James Cauthen and Mrs. Cauthen with Nigerian officials. Photo courtesy of the Southern Baptist Historical Library and Archives, Nashville, Tennessee.

Jeremiah rebuked the Israelites who were crying "peace, peace" when there was no peace and told them, "Today it is vain to talk about peace, to hope and pray for peace, unless we are willing to have a peace based upon good will and righteousness, beginning in our own hearts and lives."[21]

Some politicians agreed with the Baptist missionaries about the necessity of a worldwide religious revival. Baptist missionary Rosalee Mills Appleby cited politicians who looked to religion to help secure peace. She quoted the venerable British statesman David Lloyd George as saying, "The only thing that will save the world from utter destruction and the nations from a world war vastly more terrible than history has yet recorded, is a universal revival of the Christian religion." Baptist mission leaders believed that Baptists were "united in the conviction that Christ is the answer—the one and only answer to the precarious world in which we find ourselves."[22]

Baptists believed that world economic upheaval, colonialism, racial animosity, militarism, and an escalating war of ideologies between East and West all combined with the scarcity of true Christians to present serious obstacles to peace. In the face of such challenges, Southern

Baptists embarked upon an ambitious mission effort. M. Theron Rankin, the executive secretary of the Foreign Mission Board, had been right when he predicted that "our people are eager to do far more in the future than they have ever done before, and they are looking hopefully to the Foreign Mission Board to give them the lead in doing this." Southern Baptists' response to the boards' efforts were tangible, as an ever-increasing number of missionaries reported for service. Rankin died of leukemia in the early 1950s but not before the board entered twenty new countries and initiated what William R. Estep considers to be the period of greatest expansion in the board's history.[23]

Despite limited material resources, Baptists believed that the spiritual resources available to missionaries were truly limitless. Believing that well-planned world evangelization was the only way to ensure peace, J. W. Marshall thought that "Southern Baptists [would] give with abandon to support a plan for preventing another war." In the mid-1950s, Rankin's successor at the Foreign Mission Board, Baker James Cauthen, circulated a letter to the missionaries declaring, "We rejoice over the increased interest in and support of the world mission program of Southern Baptists." He cited the efforts of mission boards, the Woman's Missionary Union, pastors, and the Sunday School board, as well as "other influences" for that increasing support. Encouragement for their efforts had even come from the highest level of political power. President Harry Truman, himself a Baptist, told a select group at the White House that "foreign missionaries have done more for world peace than any other group."[24]

Racism, colonialism, missions, and the cold war all came together in a particular way in southern Africa. D. F. Malan, whose United Party won the 1948 elections in South Africa, ousting Jan Smuts, began formalizing the apartheid system that dominated that nation for the following four decades. George W. Sadler argued that the attitudes of the new South African administration "repelled" many Africans, who would then turn to the East and communism instead of Christianity. He saw South Africa's repression of its black residents as not merely tragic but also unchristian. As the situation worsened, Baptists began to predict civil war. By 1953, Hendrick Verwoerd, Malan's successor, had instituted much of the apartheid system. That year, Mrs. Edgar L. Bates, North American chair of the Baptist World Alliance Women's Committee, noted, "Nowhere else in the world is there such a sore spot, nor are there such tensions between black and white." She pointed out that thousands of Africans were being settled in townships near Johannesburg. Among the problems with the townships, Bates noted that there was only one Baptist church, and it seated only three hundred people.[25]

Australia, too, earned the disdain of progressive Baptists. Mrs. J. Walsh Watts wrote that "though immigrants are now pouring into Australia, there is no welcome for any but the white races." Religious organizations attacked the racist immigration policies of the Australian government. Baptists declared that Australia's "refusal to subscribe to the principle of equality for all peoples and religions serves as a constant and dangerous irritant in Pacific and world affairs." The mission leaders were concerned about immigrants in the United States as well. Yet at no time did Baptist mission leaders attack the racist immigration policies in effect in the United States until the Johnson-Reed Act (popularly known as the Nation of Origins Act) was finally replaced in 1965. That act had effectively set immigration limits based on ethnicity. Even the leadership seemed to have been more able to attack racism when it was not likely to have a direct impact on their lives.[26]

Katharine Parker Freeman took Americans to task for condemning other nations. She explained that Americans "abhor racial discrimination which other people have" and cited South Africa specifically. She believed that segregation in the United States was not as extreme, but asked, "Can it be denied that many of our customs are aimed at making Negroes and others feel inferior?" She reminded Baptists that "every time an injustice is done to a Negro here, the story appears almost immediately in India, and Africa, and Russia; it flashes around the world, and each time the prestige of our country or section is lowered." Freeman, like other progressive Baptists, believed that the solution lay in Christianity and that Christians had to actually practice their beliefs. Some people, she noted, thought that being a church member gave them "the privileges of a Christian" but overlooked the obligations of being one.[27]

Myrtle Robinson Creasman agreed that the problem was international. As early as 1945, she explained that "the whole world expects America to prove her democracy by her treatment of minority groups." Both in race relations and in international relations, "right attitudes must express themselves in right actions. The nations must be just in their treatment of each other. Only principles of universal justice applied to international relations can bring universal peace." She noted that the "Christian citizen is a world citizen." Being Christian citizens, they would hold right attitudes, which would cause people to behave in a just manner. Creasman believed that "the ultimate outcome of international and interracial justice will be world peace." The Christian citizen was a world citizen because Christianity was a world religion.[28]

Southern Baptist mission efforts focused first on the individual, hoping to turn the hearts and minds of individuals to God. Baptists believed that peace was an individual responsibility. Though Baptists recognized that most people worked in "small places in the Kingdom," they argued that they were not isolated. Earl Hester Trutza, who, with her husband Peter, founded the Southern Baptist Training Schools in Bucharest and Budapest, explained: "we touch many lives daily. Every human contact has some effect, so what each of us does is very important. Our attitudes and our actions contribute toward peace or war." Others agreed. Jameson Jones directed Baptist young women to be peacemakers, "the people who make peace, the people who live in peace—the people of vision, of understanding, of loving kindness."[29]

With race, as with peace, individual Baptists worked in "small places," and they understood the limitations that that placed on their efforts. Hugh Brimm of the Social Service Commission admitted that "you and I . . . cannot, within a week, overcome the effects of racial discrimination; we probably cannot hope to change the warped thinking of the race-baiters and the hate mongers in public office." Yet there was much that Christians could do as individuals. They could show respect to people of other races, learn to accept people for who they were, avoid concepts of status, and get to know people from other ethnic groups.[30]

People discovered the importance of individual regeneration in a variety of ways. Tennessee Senator Estes Kefauver, a Baptist and one of the few southerners who refused to sign the Southern Manifesto, related the story of his young daughter's discovery of the principle. He noted she had been rather rambunctious one day. To keep her busy he cut up a map from the newspaper and set her to the task of reconstructing the map. She completed the task considerably more quickly than he had expected. When questioned as to how she had learned the world's geography so well, she responded that the reverse side had a picture of a man and she knew that if she "got the man right, the world would be right." Kefauver related the story to remind Baptists that the world was made up of individuals and that as individuals were regenerated, the world, too, would be regenerated.[31]

There were successes. A Community Mission society in Raleigh, North Carolina, studied *Blind Spots*, a Southern Baptist publication on race relations. The society's leader, Katharine Parker (Mrs. L. E. M.) Freeman, noted that reading a book was not always enough, but that it was important. She said, "The only tangible result of which I am aware from our study is a turn-about [in] attitude on the part of a man whose wife was interested enough to borrow our books on race and get him to read them." Freeman argued, "That one result was priceless."[32]

The Southern Baptists' emphasis on individual redemption was, at times, a hindrance to its progressive leaders. Baptists in the pews often rejected the social message of the leadership in favor of focusing on individual redemption. The leadership attempted to show that both were important. W. O. Carver noted that Baptists faced the problem of "bringing religion down out of the clouds onto the earth; out of the too exclusive stress on the future with too little concern for the present." For missionaries, the two were inseparable. E. C. Routh, editor of the Foreign Mission Board's monthly publication, *The Commission*, reminded Baptists that while the primary emphasis of missions was the "saving of souls," the Gospel, "with all of the implications of its teachings, is vitally concerned with the spiritual, mental, and physical welfare of all men."[33]

One possible reason why Christianity had failed to achieve interracial and international unity was the inability, or, perhaps, unwillingness, of Christians to see the relevance of the Bible to race questions. Ed Arendall, pastor of First Baptist Church in Atmore, Alabama, cited Romans 10:12–13, in which Paul announced, "For there is no difference between the Jew and the Greek: for the same Lord over all is rich unto all that call upon him." Arendall lamented that "many people are willing to grant this kinship of races in the past, but balk when faced with races today." Leila Lequire, a missionary in New Mexico, used the same text to argue, "Nor is there any difference between the Indian and the white man except for the color of the skin and the lack of opportunities which have held the Indians back."[34]

Christian teaching entered the realm of the here and now as Baptists tried to put their beliefs into action. Christian teachings were often more difficult to live by than they appeared at first glance. Writing for the Woman's Missionary Union's publication, *Royal Service*, Mrs. J. M.

Dawson of Waco, Texas, argued that it was "especially incumbent on women" to spread the Gospel and work for peace. Her plan was simple: "what can each of us do? The answer is so simple as to seem almost commonplace. *Just be Christian.*" She added, "Yet who does not admit this is the most difficult achievement." Likewise, Miss Thelma Brown wrote about a discussion of racism in her small prayer group in Tennessee. The discussion focused on ways of building interracial goodwill in the spirit of Christ. Brown wrote, "We finally decided, however, that the whole interracial problem could be solved by applying to every single individual the principle of the Golden Rule." There were, however, far-reaching implications. Brown explained that to follow the Golden Rule "is to put yourself in the other person's place and to see and think and feel as he does. To do that means more than wishing or even praying that we do unto others as we would that they should do to us. It means knowing their historical, cultural, economic, and social background. It means that we should understand why and how our neighbor is similar or different from ourselves and what he needs. In other words, we cannot measure all of the various racial groups in America or other parts of the world by our highly favored yardstick."[35]

Some women acted on the mandate "just be Christian" by trying to establish a more united world. Itsuko Saito, a Baptist missionary and native of Hawaii, attended the Cleveland gathering of Baptist women from around the world. She noted the friendships between people recently divided by war and claimed "all barriers were gone. They were sisters in Christ." Spreading Christian sisterhood was a vital step in the pursuit of peace. Saito continued: "as Baptist women organize by continents, a worldwide fellowship can be more easily accomplished. Dare we attempt anything so tremendous when nations cannot unite on political and economic questions? The answer was a unanimous 'yes' as this matter was presented to the women. With the help of God, we can demonstrate that Christ can weld the nations of the world in love and peace where hate and war now exist. Baptist women are challenged to lead in uniting on a worldwide basis to carry the banner of the cross into places of darkness."[36]

Baptist gatherings created an atmosphere that fostered cross-cultural personal contact. In 1947, barely more than a year after Winston Churchill had declared that an iron curtain had fallen across Europe, dividing it between the free world and the communist world, the Baptist World Alliance sponsored a youth conference in Copenhagen, Denmark. T. G. Dunning, the Alliance's Youth Committee chairman, noted the diversity of the people who met in "one united fellowship." People from communist countries mingled with people from democratic countries, civilians mingled with soldiers, and "Negroes sat among the white people in various parts of the church." Yet "far more significant than its diversity was the essential unity of the gathering." That unity reflected the fact that God had created a united world.[37]

When Baptist youth from around the world gathered in Toronto a decade later, commentators noted the ease with which they interacted. In Toronto, people of all races had "sat down together and, without frustrating inhibitions, discussed freely and frankly the major problems of the world." The world was an even more precarious place than when Baptist youth had met in Copenhagen. By 1958, the Soviet Union had launched *Sputnik* and had nuclear capabilities. On the other hand, colonialism was clearly coming to an end in Africa, the last bastion of imperialism; Ghana led the way in 1957. Frank K. Means, who had taken over as editor of *The Commission*, said the prevailing harmony in Toronto was possible because "these young people recognized that in Christ there is no East or West, no North or South, red or yellow or white or brown or black." He noted optimistically that "unless they forget the principles enunciated and the climate and fellowship which prevailed in Toronto, they will make significant contributions toward Christian progress tomorrow." Both Dunning and Means reflected the faith progressive Baptists put in personal contacts across racial lines and in future generations to overcome the racism of the past.[38]

Person-to-person contact with people of wide-ranging backgrounds was available to many Americans who did not even realize it. One way was through friendships with international students. The *Baptist Student* announced that "an unprecedented educational migration is now taking place." The United States, after the war, had become the "educational center of the world." One result was that "a foreign mission field has moved here and is now on the threshold of our educational centers." Further, "one world mindedness, or cultural, international, and global unity, can now be created by our institutions of higher learning." The institutions could not, however, foster that global unity unless individual students acted. Bill Cody, the associate editor of the *Baptist Student,* encouraged students to invite foreign students to their homes to experience the "warmth and wholesomeness of a real Christian home."[39]

By becoming friends with international students, American students would see the basic unity of humanity. According to Jane Ray Bean, "sharing breaks down barriers of difference. In sharing, students discover how much they are basically alike." Ultimately, "continents are bridged, differences are lessened, and the world grows smaller through the cultivation of friendships."[40]

In California, Baptists organized a more formal system of welcoming international students. Beginning in 1951, the Baptist International Center served students in Berkeley. Dwight Wilhelm wrote, "Hundreds of students from many countries have passed through the halls. Many have come to know Christ while there and have gone back to their homes to tell others of the Saviour they have found." The center was a living experiment in international relations. Wilhelm continued, "They are of many races—some are rich, others poor; some hold positions of importance in their country, many are unknown. But at the International Center all are equal no matter what their race, color, or rank, for God 'hath made of one blood all nations of men for to dwell on the face of the earth.'"[41]

The unity of humanity was the one true road to peace. In the midst of the confusion and conflict of the postwar world, W. O. Carver believed, "the one encouraging factor is that there is an actual and growing belief in the essential oneness of the human race and of the conviction that deliverance from our strife and conflict and all our wars lies along the line of cultivating and developing an actual unity among the peoples of the earth." George W. Sadler added that the world faced a simple choice: "world community or world suicide." He explained: "It was impossible in Abraham Lincoln's day to have a world that was half slave and half free. It is impossible now to have a safe world in which half of the people hate or are suspicious of the other half."[42]

Even though Baptists understood the tendency of nonwhites to identify with other nonwhites, they saw it as an artificial division that God had not intended. All people of all races shared in God's plan for humanity. Unity within a particular race but not with other races countermanded God's fundamental plans and denied reconciliation. Theodore F. Adams argued that Baptists had to recognize that "'God made all nations of one blood to dwell on the face of the earth' and that we must learn to live together, white and black, red and yellow." W. O. Carver noted that "Christianity proposes that we realize that God made for unity all men to dwell on the face of the earth . . . that in Christ all are members of 'one new humanity.'" J. B. Lawrence agreed: "All nations, kindred, tribes and tongues in every land stand on the same footing in the redemptive program of Christ."[43]

When Baptist missionaries looked at the world, they saw divisions, not brotherhood. People were not living in harmony and unity. They were not living as true Christians. Mrs. Taul B. White, writing the program materials for use in Women's Missionary Societies, said, "What are the things dividing people today? From the individual to the world, we face barbed wire entanglements: national, racial, social, economic, and political. They are made up of different nations, different languages, different colors of skin, different degrees of wealth, different religions. You ask how Jesus solved these problems. We are startled that for Jesus there was no problem. The barriers were not there for his mind and heart."[44]

The barriers, then, were human constructions. Loyd Corder, secretary for Direct Missions at the Home Mission Board, pointed out that natural barriers, "the barriers of time and space are being conquered." By the mid-1950s, communications technology reduced those barriers in ways never before possible. Yet, Corder warned, other barriers existed. He pointed to "social customs, economic circumstance, religion, language, and race" as barriers that "stand between so many of our people and the saving Gospel of Christ." [45]

Of all the threats to Christianity and world peace, Baptist leaders viewed communism as the most serious. Communism exploited racial and economic tensions, created discontent, and, perhaps most important, denied the relevance of Christianity and the very existence of God. Racial tensions in America were easy for communists to exploit because the natural barriers of time and space were being conquered. Rapid communications meant that whatever happened in America had worldwide implications. As the civil rights movement in the United States got underway, Dr. and Mrs. William R. Norman noted that the Nigerian press was quick to publicize race problems in the United States. Whenever Americans asked them if such incidents hurt the mission effort overseas, they responded, "They certainly do."[46]

Communism offered false hopes. H. Cornell Goerner reminded

Baptists that communists promised that they would eliminate all racial distinction and give freedom to those who still, even after two world wars, labored under the yolk of colonialism. Goerner understood that "a new Africa is in the making," and it was up to Christians to offer the way of Christ and peace rather than the way of communism—the way of "bloody revolution, bitterness, and hatred"—for overcoming the legacy of racism and colonialism.[47]

Baptist commentator Charles A. Wells noted that many Americans believed peace depended largely on what the Soviets did or did not do. He proposed, however, that "Communism would never have got started [sic] in the world if men had not built walls of selfishness around their wealth." Greed was only one issue. Wells continued, "Racial prejudices and race hatred in this country have made it much easier for the Communists to propagandize against America in the world . . . we can't keep building walls around ourselves and have an open road to peace. We need fewer walls and more roads."[48]

Baptists, and other religious leaders, believed that communism functioned as a religion, a false one to be sure, but a religion nonetheless. That made it far more dangerous than had it been merely an economic or political system. The most famous Baptist evangelist of the postwar period, Billy Graham, was in Los Angeles in 1948 when he heard that the Soviet Union had successfully tested an atomic device. He told the Los Angelenos, "Communism is a religion that is inspired, directed, and motivated by the Devil himself." The chairman of the Committee of the World Council of Churches, John C. Bennett, agreed with Graham that communism presented itself as a religion. In his work *Christianity and Communism,* he warned against identifying Christianity with capitalism but noted that communism operated as both an economic system and a religion.[49]

According to W. R. White, the Soviets were "taking advantage of the mass awakening and the racial consciousness of the world." Like other mission-oriented Baptists, White saw a clear relationship between the domestic situation and the world situation. Unless things changed, he said, "Communism will continue to exploit our problems in the South and will continue its penetration." White called for a vigorous mission program as a response to the communist threat. His sentiments were echoed by J. B. Lawrence, who told readers of *Home Missions* that "the answer to Communism and all the isms that infest and infect civilization today is the gospel of the Lord Jesus Christ."[50]

T. B. Maston agreed that Christianity was the answer to communism, but he noted that some good changes were taking place because of communism's challenge to American democracy. One of those changes was the Supreme Court's decision declaring school segregation by race unconstitutional. Writing about the Supreme Court's *Brown v. The Board of Education* decision, Maston said, "Communism helped to create the atmosphere that was favorable for the Court's decision, but in a way different from what is sometimes charged. It has challenged and is challenging the United States on every hand. Our failure to apply consistently our democratic principles and Christian teachings to racial minorities at home and to the great racial majority around the world is one of the weakest spots in our American way of life. Communism has called attention to and sought to capitalize on this weakness or failure. The Communists have used it rather effectively to challenge our nation for the leadership of the peoples of the world."[51]

Missionaries in the field agreed with Convention leaders in the United States. In opposition to the gospel of love, Clyde Dotson argued, "Communism is sowing the seeds of hatred in many hearts." Dotson worked in Southern Rhodesia. where racial tensions were worse than even in the American South. There, in the shadow of South African apartheid, the "breach between white and black" was growing ever wider. Dotson announced, "It is only the power of the gospel of our Lord Jesus Christ that can help people under such circumstances."[52]

Outside the mission organizations, Baptists expressed the same deep concern about communism that pervaded the South. Miss Annie Mae Smith of Marlin, Texas, was so concerned about the activities of communists around the world that she wrote Baker James Cauthen about its threat to Christianity. Cauthen responded, telling Smith, "It is obvious that Communism presents a major threat to the values we hold dear in the world today. Its ideology is basically opposed to the idea of God and is contrary to the things Christians hold dear." Cauthen reminded Smith that there were many Christians who worked for Christ in the face of persecution in countries dominated by communists. He also recommended that she consult H. Cornell Goerner's books on missions, in which Goerner stressed the necessity of helping Christians behind the iron curtain. Cauthen wrote, "That is exactly the reverse of anything that the Communists would desire to see done, but it lies at the very heart of our responsibility in the world today."[53]

The cold war and communist threat framed the world in which Baptists promoted their vision of a unified humanity. In such a world, continued support for military preparedness was easy for politicians to promote. Baptists certainly rejected any attempts at isolationism, but they also rejected what they believed to be an increasing militarism. Truman's "get tough" policy, they believed, backfired by making Stalin tighten his grip on Eastern Europe.[54]

In September of 1945, Baptist mission leaders pointed out that the war had brought increasing religious toleration in the Soviet Union, including the official recognition of the Russian Orthodox Church. Russian Baptists were the largest group of evangelicals in the Soviet Union and were in a "more favorable light" than before the war. E. C. Routh, editor of *The Commission*, suggested "we need to be patient with the Soviet Union. Marshall Stalin is suspicious of other powers. When we review the relationships of the past, he may have some justification for his suspicions." Further, "as individuals and as a nation we need to be Christian in our dealings with the Russian people." As the lines of the cold war hardened in the later 1940s and 1950s, Baptists continued to stress the need to understand the Russian people and to work with Baptists behind the Iron Curtain.[55]

Baptists were concerned that "fear and death [had] replaced faith and life in the world's conversations." The change was related, at least in part, to the atomic bomb. Baptists like Harold G. Sanders, pastor of First Baptist in Tallahassee, Florida, lamented that "scientists rather than preachers have become the prophets of doom." Indeed, they had. A small group of scientists inside the strategic community developed plans for the use of atomic and nuclear weapons should conflict break out between the United States and the Soviet Union. Baptists, however, believed that the idea of peace through power was an acceptance of the inevitability of war and that planning for war was a step in bringing war. They argued, instead, for a change in attitudes. Jenny Lind Gatlin, associate editor of the *Baptist Student*, stated what was perhaps obvious: "militarists believe in war." She believed that "the American people should turn to training for peace." Only peace achieved through Christian love would create a world where war was not a fact.[56]

Many Baptists believed that the military was gaining too much power in American society. In both 1951 and 1952 the Social Service Commission reported to the Southern Baptist annual convention that the military was making unprecedented inroads into the power structure. Specifically, the Commission noted, "Never before in American history has the military establishment had so much money to spend, so many officers and ex-officers in important civilian government posts, so much influence in the formation of foreign policy, or such an ambitious publicity department as it does today." Baptists recognized, with the rest of the nation, that "in these days of war and rumors of war" a strong defense was necessary, but increasing the power of the military was not the answer. Some politicians shared their anxiety about the increasing power of the military. Indeed, President Eisenhower expressed concern about the increasing power of the military-industrial complex. Baptist leaders pointed out, in *Home Missions*, that "we need something that will establish a calm center in our heart of hearts . . . we must reaffirm our faith in what life can be." The answer to a rising militaristic mentality was, again, the evangelization of the United States and the world. Evangelization could change the worldwide conditions, which were fertile ground for the growth of despotism.[57]

The solutions to the problems posed by mounting world tensions were intensely individual, yet the government had a role to play. Dedicated Christians in government service stressed nonmilitary solutions to the world crises. *Home Missions* reported that Senator John Foster Dulles told the First Presbyterian Church of Watertown, New York, that the nation's reliance on material and military strength was "dangerous." While Congress was attempting to fight communism with military and economic aid, Dulles, who shortly thereafter became President Eisenhower's secretary of state, argued, "It is perfectly clear that these plans will not succeed if they merely put material things into the hands of men who do not have a spiritual faith and do not feel a sense of human brotherhood and social responsibility." Dulles, however, practiced a policy of peace through power and engaged in what historians have called "brinkmanship," a policy at odds with the Southern Baptists' antimilitarist views.[58]

Just as preparation for war made war more likely, preparation for peace would make peace more likely. Baptists emphasized that peace was a way of living and thinking contradictory to militarism. Thus they opposed efforts in Congress to pass a universal military training bill, which would have required all American men to undergo military training. Even in the midst of the Korean conflict, Baptists opposed universal military training. Marjorie Moore Armstrong, whose husband would have to vote on the proposed legislation, took her children out of their afternoon classes to attend the debate on the bill. She noted that the proponents of universal military training hoped to wear their opponents down but that "a strong group—a majority we hope and pray!—still believe militarism is obsolete, an armaments race leads to war, and that U. M. T. is a form of slavery for America's young people." Baptists believed that, should universal military training become law, "then the American people can soon expect the 'next step according to plan' in the militarization of our beloved nation." That next step was the conscription of women. For Baptists, however, the most compelling reason to defeat the program of military training and to end the arms race was the fact that preparation for war led to war.[59]

By 1955, the active fighting on the Korean peninsula had come to an end and the United States was, again, at peace. Universal military training, however, remained an issue. The Christian Life Commission reported that year that "America does not need and our people do not want any military plan that will fasten upon us a permanent system of military conscription in a time of peace." Joe W. Burton, editor of the Southern Baptist publication *Home Life*, wrote, "Our own security, Americans now believe, is to make ourselves so strong that no nation will risk an encounter in any field of battle. And yet, we know that the hope of maintaining such an armed truce is groundless, for when two nations commit themselves to preparation for war, the day of battle must surely come."[60]

In the mid-1950s, political turmoil erupted close to home. Fidel Castro began his efforts to overthrow the regime of Fulgencio Batista in Cuba with an ill-fated attack in July of 1953. After having been pardoned in 1955, Castro returned to Cuba to stage a successful revolution that culminated in his taking control of the Cuban government in January 1959. The relief that the Foreign Mission Board had expressed when a communist insurgency in Guatemala had been squashed was dashed completely. Militarism became an even greater threat as the triangular relations between the United States, Cuba, and the Soviet Union threatened to explode. Yet Baptists focused on the effects of the revolution on their mission work and on the situation facing Cuban Baptists and refugees. They realized that Spanish-speaking Americans and immigrants faced discrimination just as much as other minorities.[61]

The changes in Cuba did not destroy the Baptist work there, which had begun in the late nineteenth century at the urging of the Florida Baptist Convention and had been overseen by the Home Mission Board since 1886. Aaron F. Webber wrote to *Royal Service* in January of 1960, saying, "This is a day of revolutionary optimism in which to witness for Christ in Cuba." Webber questioned the American policy of supporting Latin American leaders merely because they were anticommunist. He claimed, "The United States loses ground in Latin America every time its influence is used to shore up the fortunes of a dictator. The ease with which our Government appears to accept the fallacy that a dictator is a defense against Communism, and that 'the enemy of our enemy is our friend,' has cost us real friends in Latin countries." Webber argued that the United States owed the new Cuban regime at least as much patience as it showed those dictators. If that were done, he argued, communism would not take over on the island. Despite the fact that the United States had been the first country to recognize Castro's regime in Cuba, the Eisenhower administration failed to show much patience. In the spring of 1960, before Castro turned decidedly toward communism, Eisenhower reduced sugar imports from the island by half, and Nikita Khrushchev announced that the Soviet Union would purchase the difference.[62]

In the early 1960s, the Home Mission Board continued to operate missions in Cuba. In 1961 the board placed "implicit confidence" in its Cuban missionaries "to decide according to their own appraisal of the situation whether from the standpoint of personal safety and/or the well being of the mission work it is wise for them to return to the United States." Six missionaries opted to remain in Cuba. They reported considerable success in gaining converts. In fact, Courts Redford reported to the Home Mission Board that they had "the largest number of conversions that they have ever had." Through 1961, missionaries in Cuba instituted several new projects, and two of the island's churches became self-supporting.[63]

Mission work was essential in the fight against communism. Mildred Dodson (Mrs. William) McMurry, of the Woman's Missionary Union, wrote that confronting communism in Latin America required a public space where "citizens, teachers, and students from all corners of the hemisphere can gather and get to know each other in an environment free of prejudice of class, creed, color, and culture."[64]

The churches had the opportunity to be the gathering place McMurry suggested, but Walker L. Knight, editor of *Home Missions*, knew that some churches were not up to the challenge. By September of 1962, it was clear that Castro's Cuba would be communist. Knight wrote that the refugees arriving in Florida "presented Southern Baptists and other Christian groups with a unique home mission opportunity" but noted that one church's efforts to help with refugees were stymied because the racial issue involved disturbed some of its members. One member with more progressive views wrote to Knight, saying, "How quickly men drop the veneer of Christianity when confronted with a problem which threatens their established social values."[65]

By 1964, the Cuban missions situation had deteriorated even more, but Baptist leaders revealed a persistent, even naive, optimism. Courts Redford, executive secretary of the Home Mission Board, reported that "work in Cuba continues to go along with limited interference from the government." Redford's "limited interference" included the closing of several churches and the imprisonment of Baptist workers. He noted, however, that the seminary and the clinic in Havana remained open and that "our Baptist leaders in Cuba have maintained a very high spirit in their service and a wonderful faith in the power of God."[66]

The tide of Cuban refugees rose throughout the 1960s. Miami's Spanish-speaking population nearly doubled between 1960 and 1968. According to Ione Gray and Dallas M. Lee, "within a short time nearly thirty Spanish-language congregations were under way, most of them Spanish departments in Miami's existing Baptist churches." Gray and Lee quoted, but did not name, one pastor who worried that the churches might actually get left behind in the process of integration. He told them, "We're integrating schools and housing and jobs . . . I would hate for the church to be the only phase of the Cuban's life where he is segregated." Reflecting the Baptist leadership's view that prejudice grew from ignorance, the pastor said, "I have a natural fear of any kind of segregated society. Right now we might segregate with the highest of motives, but I'm afraid of what this might lead to. Segregation fosters ignorance of each other and ignorance fosters fear." Hubert O. Hurt, Florida's director of Language Missions, told Gray and Lee that the pastor's views represented "a healthy approach." He stressed the importance of offering to the Cubans Spanish language services and programs where they could go if they desired. Hurt said, "The important thing, however, is that the

Spanish-speaking be free to do as they see fit. If they wish to integrate, they certainly should be able to do so in our churches."[67]

One Cuban refugee, Arley Rodriguez, arrived in the United States to become part of Reverend Russell Pogue's family. Pogue pastored First Baptist Church in Petersberg, Texas, and Arley quickly joined all the church groups appropriate for a seventeen-year-old girl. By 1962, Rodriguez had entered Wayland Baptist College, in Plainview, Texas. Martha Ann Clay, one of Rodriguez's friends at Wayland, wrote that "adjusting to life in the United States after living in Communist Cuba has not been too difficult," perhaps because Rodriguez had not lived in a communist Cuba particularly long. Still, Clay's comments show the Baptists' fear of how quickly communism could infiltrate and change a society and individuals within that society.[68]

The Home Mission Board continued to operate in Cuba despite difficulties. In 1963, the Cuban government expelled missionaries Lucille Kerrigan and Ruby Miller, and in 1965 Herbert Caudill and his son-in-law, David Fite, were arrested. Fite was convicted of "illegal currency transactions." Under such circumstances, the board transferred power of attorney to the Western Cuba Baptist Convention in 1967, explaining that it could no longer maintain or administer property in Cuba because of the political situation in that country. The board also decided to allow Cuban nationals who had come to the United States to work for the organization without fulfilling citizenship or residency requirements. When, in 1969, Caudill, Fite, and their families were allowed to leave Cuba, it marked the first time in eighty-three years that there were no Southern Baptist missionaries on the island.[69]

Throughout the postwar years, Southern Baptist mission leaders saw evangelization as a key component of world peace. World peace necessitated improved race relations. For progressive Baptists, racism in America and racism around the world were intimately related. Racism in America could damage the Baptist mission effort around the world. Racism abroad led to international hostility and could lead to war. As Africa gained its political independence, Baptist missionaries focused considerable energies on evangelizing Africa. Furthermore, the race question was acute in Africa and directly related to the race question in the American South. Missionaries understood that race was "the most dangerous area of our vulnerability."[70]

3

"Our Preaching Has Caught Up with Us"

African Missions and the Race Question

At the end of World War II few Europeans believed that their African colonies would soon become independent. They saw the demands of the Pan Africanists who met in Manchester, England, in October of 1945 as, at best, hopes for the distant future. Africa, however, was changing rapidly. By the mid-1950s, it was clear that independence would come soon. Ghana led the way in 1957. In 1960 Nigeria followed, and by 1965 the majority of the continent had gained self-rule. Some Africans remained under colonial rule, especially in southern Africa, but after 1970 the system was clearly anachronistic.[1]

For the Southern Baptist missionary leadership, Africa represented the clearest example of the racist implications of imperialism. It also represented the clearest connection between the international and domestic race situations. Indeed, Southern Baptist missionaries in Africa and leaders concerned about Africa made poignant attacks on racism at home and around the world. Like Baptist mission board leaders in the United States, missionaries were adamantly anticommunist. Unlike African converts, they could not be accused of failing to understand the situation in the South. So long as Southern Baptists took seriously the evangelization of Africa, racial discrimination in the United States was hypocritical. Baptist missionaries, board leaders, and mission converts told Southern Baptists exactly that. The Southern Baptists' missionaries in Africa preached a color-blind Gospel, promising all people that they were equal in the eyes of God. One of those missionaries, Harris Mobley, examined the situation while home on furlough from Ghana and concluded that "our preaching has caught up with us." It was time, the missionaries insisted, that Southern Baptists catch up with their preaching.[2]

The Foreign Mission Board presented its postwar program, "Advance," to Southern Baptists in the June 1945 issue of *The Commission*. The board intended to rehabilitate missions that had suffered or closed because of the war and to expand its mission work beyond prewar levels by advancing into unevangelized regions. Most important, the board hoped to encourage self-supporting, indigenous Baptist churches and church leadership. Missionaries looked forward to the day they would work together with these churches in "God's total enterprise of world redemption." Nowhere was the work of Advance more enthusiastically undertaken than in Africa. Nowhere did racism in the United States damage the effort more than in Africa.[3]

Africa offered both peril and promise. While mission efforts there would be difficult, L. Howard Jenkins, president of the Foreign Mission Board, told Southern Baptists that "In Africa, the possibilities seem unlimited. The doors are wide open." When Jenkins wrote, Baptists had only forty-five missionaries to Africa, all in Nigeria. Jenkins prodded Baptists, saying, "We must send many more to Africa." By 1965, their efforts had increased tenfold, with 447 Southern Baptist missionaries working in eighty-three cities and towns across ten African nations.[4]

As a part of the overall postwar program, Southern Baptist missionaries sought to educate Americans about Africa. I. N. Patterson, a missionary who served as head of the Nigerian Baptist Convention in the 1940s, told Baptist youth that "an African student in an American university recently complained about the ignorance of America concerning awakened Africa." The student said Americans still thought in terms of nineteenth-century explorers, missionaries, and adventurers like David Livingstone and Henry Morton Stanley It was time, he said, that Americans stopped talking about the "dark continent."[5]

Mission leaders believed that Americans wanted to learn more about the world. They also believed that educating Americans about Africa would help Americans overcome racism. Marjorie Moore Armstrong announced that "the United States has rediscovered Africa." More media were covering events in Africa than at any time since Stanley went searching for Livingstone. While Armstrong admitted that the increased concern for Africa was prompted by worries of communist intrusion, she was proud that "long before Soviet Communism was heard of, the

Christian world mission took Africa into account." Still, Armstrong understood that even Christian Americans held provincial views. She asked readers of the *Window*, "Have you ever heard the statement: 'the average American is disqualified for world citizenship because of his almost inherent dislike of the unlike'[?]" Armstrong reminded readers that Christian love embraced everyone, regardless of how "unlike" they might be. She also reminded readers that whites were a minority in the world.[6]

Editors of the *Window* announced that "a girl wants to know the score . . . she wants to be intelligent about what goes on in the world—in her hometown and in remotest Africa." The study of mission activity would provide that information. Carroll Hubbard, a Royal Ambassador from Louisville, Kentucky, wrote "Mission Study Makes a Difference" for *Ambassador Life*. Hubbard claimed that "many studies educate, inspire, and broaden one's horizons, but no study gives the vision that mission study gives. . . . Mission study is a magic bridge. The study of books on world missions brings us face to face with all the needs of the world. Barriers are broken down and understanding sympathy is aroused, a nearness, a kinship of feelings results. Royal Ambassadors help to provide this magic bridge. Let us travel it to help wipe out racial prejudice and make one world become a reality."[7]

Mission education and publications did make a difference, at least for Ralph Rummage of Tulsa, Oklahoma. Rummage told Baptist boys that the two factors leading to his decision to become a missionary in Rhodesia were a missionary's message and an article in the Foreign Mission Board's publication, *The Commission*.[8]

As part of their mission education efforts, writers for both *Ambassador Life* and the *Window* told their readers that African youth were quite similar to themselves. They encouraged their readers to build bridges with youth around the world, especially through the "Pen Pal" programs. Both organizations provided addresses to readers who wanted to begin a correspondence. Myra Nell Noyes of Brunswick, Georgia, began corresponding with Abiola Adewole of Nigeria as a member of the auxiliary and continued for several years. When Adewole got married, Noyes sent her a white Bible, the traditional wedding gift given to members of the auxiliary.[9]

Pen pal correspondence provided a direct link across the ocean, but mission leaders realized that not every youth in America would engage in such an exchange, so magazines for youth continued to promote understanding through their articles. J. I. Bishop, director of the Royal Ambassador program, wrote that "Nigeria is filled with boys who, if transplanted to the United States of America, would be just like hundreds of Royal Ambassadors here. . . . Under the skin, they are *just like you.*"[10]

Some young Baptists were able to gain more direct cross-cultural experiences. One student from Memphis State University, Patsy Parker, traveled to Ghana for the dedication of a Baptist hospital. Several Africans asked Parker why young women in America would want to build a hospital thousands of miles away. Parker answered, "In our mission organizations we have studied the needs and opportunities in Ghana for proclaiming the name of Jesus." Mission education in America built a hospital in Ghana that would minister to both the spirit and the body.[11]

Mission education was aimed at the American ignorance about Africa. That ignorance combined with racial tensions in the United States to undermine America's prestige on the continent. Africans and missionaries attacked racism as unacceptable in a world with independent nations throughout Asia and Africa. Racism in America could turn Africa's leaders against the West and against Christianity, which they often saw as the "white man's religion." Jean Favell, a Southern Baptist missionary in Ghana, claimed that Muslims stressed Christianity's association with the West. She wrote, "We hear more and more the Muslims claiming that Christianity is the white man's religion and that Islam is the only religion fit for the African." Baptists noted that Muslims at Al Azhar University in Cairo claimed that "Christianity maintains the subservience of the Africans and plays into the hands of those who [would] like to dominate and exploit indefinitely." According to evangelist Billy Graham, for every convert to Christianity, seven Africans joined Islam. Islam was also more successful than communism in gaining followers. Communism was only prominent in southern Africa, while Islam had considerable influence in at least seventeen African countries.[12]

Baptist missionaries believed that if they could sever Christianity from the oppressive and racist legacy of Western imperialism, Africans would be more receptive to its message. Severing the connection between Christianity and Western exploitation, however, could prove difficult. M. Theron Rankin, executive secretary of the Foreign Mission Board, warned Baptists that communists examined the West, looking for faults they could use to associate Christianity with imperialism. He concluded that "whereas we were once looked to as the champions of the oppressed, we are now classified with the oppressors." According to Professor W. O. Carver of the Southern Baptist Theological Seminary, imperialism persisted after World War II only because "the might and the money of America . . . [were] used to restore and perpetuate the British, Dutch, French, and even Belgian empires in Africa and the Orient." Additionally, America's prestige was born of a military victory that rested on the use of two atomic bombs. Marjorie Moore Armstrong argued that in the postwar world people were afraid of America more than they respected it.[13]

The legacy of imperialism haunted Southern Baptist missionaries simply because they were white. Armstrong reported that a missionary had once told her in confidence that "it takes so long to live down the reputation of the white man in West Africa. My white skin identifies me with the slave trader, the whiskey dealer, and the bearer of venereal disease." The situation persisted even though the majority of missionaries sympathized with African desires for independence and equality.[14]

Despite the missionaries' efforts to overcome barriers of skin color, race was a factor in foreign missions. H. Cornell Goerner considered it "a truism; a self-evident, inescapable fact." In 1949, Goerner told Royal Ambassadors who might want to be foreign missionaries that "if you discover in your heart prejudices and contempt for persons of a different color or meager opportunity, then you had better stay home." They should stay home, at least, until God had helped them overcome their prejudices.[15]

Race prejudice damaged foreign missions in multiple ways. Missionary W. E. Wyatt wrote from Nigeria to tell Baptists about the "real price we are paying to keep our Baptist schools, churches, and other institutions segregated." Wyatt wrote late in the summer of 1963, while the highly publicized events in Birmingham, Alabama, were fresh in the minds of both Americans and Africans. He admitted that integration might cost dollars, but said "segregation is costing human souls." Wyatt admitted that "it seems unfair that this generation has to face and solve . . . all the evils and problems imposed upon it by unthinking and prejudiced forebears." But that did not change the facts. While Wyatt did not have the answer to America's problems, he told Baptists, "I believe God does." Whatever the answer would be, Sydney Pearce, who served in Kenya, hoped it would come soon. She asked,

H. Cornell Goerner (seated) of the Foreign Mission Board and James T. Ayronide of the Nigerian Baptist Convention. Photo courtesy of the Southern Baptist Historical Library and Archives, Nashville, Tennessee.

"When will Southern Baptists become outraged enough over the oppression taking place in [the United States] that they will correct this thing which has now become an actual hindrance to the work of the Lord around the world[?]"[16]

Wyatt and Pearce were not alone. By late 1963, between the events in Birmingham and the March on Washington, many Americans had come to agree that racial discrimination created problems for America's foreign policy, but Baptist leaders were more concerned with missions. Leaders at the Woman's Missionary Union believed that educating young people about race would lead to better, more Christian race relations in the future. In 1962, Mildred Dodson (Mrs. William) McMurry wrote, "We should have as our goal the elimination of prejudice *for the sake of the Gospel we profess to follow.*" William M. Dyal Jr. told Baptist young women to avoid "aloofness." Dyal, an assistant in the department of missionary personnel at the Foreign Mission Board, noted that "aloofness to race has produced immense hostility in our world. . . . The vocabulary of Christian witness to the world has no room for the word 'prejudice.'" Betty Bock, director of the auxiliary, suggested that members of the auxiliary "discuss as a group your attitudes and feelings towards Negroes." They should ask, and honestly answer, "What attitudes do I have toward persons of different races? Which are Christian? Which are unchristian?"[17]

America was showing the world its least Christian attitudes. As head of the Foreign Mission Board, Baker James Cauthen oversaw its entire operation. He told Baptists gathered at the Ridgecrest Assembly in June of 1963, in the midst of the crisis in Birmingham, that "we are aware of the deeply troubled racial situation in our beloved land." He further emphasized: "We cannot escape the fact that the witness we are bearing for Christ in many parts of the world is gravely affected by these racial problems." For Cauthen, it was more than a matter of a lost soul here or there, tragic as he believed that was. He warned Baptists that racial tension might force the board to close some of its mission stations.[18]

The rise of nationalism in Africa increasingly affected Southern Baptist foreign missions in the 1950s and 1960s. M. Theron Rankin recognized that Africans could accuse Baptist churches themselves of imperialism. He announced, "We must steadfastly pursue the objective of promoting indigenous Baptist churches which are directly responsible only to God." In the postwar world "a missionary must win and hold the respect of his associates and be able to work with or under national leadership."[19] As regional secretary for Africa, George Sadler emphasized that continent's importance in the postwar world. He noted that "the part of the globe that was known for many years as the 'Dark Continent' is speedily claiming its rightful place in the scheme of things that . . . we have the courage to call 'one world.'" Missions, Sadler believed, would play a vital role in shaping postwar Africa: "God and the British government are counting on us to make available the agencies of peace and spiritual power."[20]

W. O. Carver argued that "more and more Africans are being educated in the modern manner and are not content with being subordinate to the whites. The prestige of the white man and trust in him are waning." African leadership would be paramount in the churches as it would be in politics. That, however, did not release the Baptists from their responsibility to evangelize Africa. "The future of Africa is our concern," Sadler told the Foreign Mission Board. He later reiterated his belief that "we have grave misgivings about the future of an un-Christian Africa," which could succumb to communism or Islam. Missionaries had been in the lead of educational efforts in Africa. Missionaries recognized that the rising expectations of African leaders were, at least in part, a product of those efforts. Whites, missionaries and laity alike, had now to reap what the missionaries and mission schools had sown.[21]

Like Carver, Rankin believed the situation facing foreign missionaries was becoming increasingly difficult. Among the reasons was America's wealth. He noted, "We are looked upon as people who live in luxury, who demand ease of living and special privilege wherever we go, whose religion is what we call, 'the American way of life.'" As a result, Africans no longer welcomed missionaries simply because they were Americans. Rankin lamented, "Today as an American [the missionary] must overcome prejudice, antagonism, and in many cases even hatred." This was one reason that missionaries hoped to shift church and convention leadership to African Christians.[22] Barbara Epperson, a missionary serving in Nigeria, noted that "by 1950 the term 'Africanization' had become a part of every Africa-conscious vocabulary," and the Nigerian Baptist Mission set up a committee to oversee the process. Epperson pointed out that between 1950 and 1955 "national personnel have been proving their ability in medical, educational, and evangelical work."[23]

Africanization proceeded most quickly in Nigeria. The Southern Baptist mission in Nigeria, founded in 1850, was the Convention's second oldest, younger only than the mission in China. At the close of World War II, the Nigerian mission remained the only Southern Baptist mission in Africa. By 1950, the Nigerian mission's centennial, Baptists had expanded their work in Nigeria, but they entered only one other African region, the Gold Coast. Over the next fifteen years, while Baptist work spread throughout sub-Saharan Africa, Nigeria remained the Southern Baptists' cornerstone. When Baptists spoke about Africa, they did so with their experiences in Nigeria foremost in their minds.[24]

As missionaries hoped, Nigerian Baptists increasingly took leadership in their religious life in the postwar era. James T. Ayorinde served as the pastor of Nigeria's largest Baptist church from 1948 until 1962. He became the first Nigerian president of the Nigerian Baptist Convention in 1950, taking the gavel at the centennial celebration. Ayorinde had been born in a Muslim home to illiterate parents. He not only learned to read and became an English teacher, but Ayorinde attended American universities, earning his master's degree at Oberlin and his doctorate in theology from Virginia Union.[25]

When Ayorinde took the gavel, there were 202 Baptist churches in Nigeria with roughly 24,000 active members, quite an increase from the six Baptist churches at the turn of the century. According to H. Cornell Goerner, nearly all of those churches, scattered throughout a nation roughly the size of Texas, had Nigerian pastors. In 1950 some 320,000 children were attending mission schools. Indeed, only some 30,000 children in Nigeria attended non-mission schools, though there were roughly 3.5 million school-aged children in Nigeria. Mission schools provided the education for the bulk of the rising professional class and intelligentsia. The overall Christian presence in Nigeria was significant and growing. Between 1953 and 1963, the estimated percentage of the population considered Christian rose from 22 percent to 34.5 percent. In 1970, it was roughly 44.9 percent. These numbers, however, included some who belonged to syncretic sects and identified themselves as Christian on government census forms but were not claimed by mainstream churches. Furthermore, Nigeria's enormous population meant that there were more Christians there than in several nations where the percentage of Christians was higher, such as Burundi, Congo, and Equatorial Guinea, which reported, in 1970, roughly 74 percent, 92 percent, and 81 percent, respectively.[26]

Also in 1950, the Nigerian Baptist Theological Seminary began granting degrees. The seminary in Ogbomosho had existed for several years, but only its recent affiliation with the Southern Baptist Theological Seminary in Louisville, Kentucky, gave it the legal basis under British colonial law to grant degrees in theology. As a result, Nigerian Baptists seeking theology degrees would no longer have to leave the country to obtain them. Goerner told Baptists that "it is difficult for one who has not been in Nigeria to understand the full meaning of this new era in theological education for Nigerian Baptists, for such indeed it is. It will help to dignify the ministry and provide an added incentive for study." Goerner believed that the true strength of Southern Baptist efforts in Nigeria and throughout Africa lay in the local evangelicals, not in the foreign missionaries sent from Richmond.[27]

The need for ministers was enormous in Nigeria. Jane (Mrs. Pat)

Hill, a missionary in Ogbomosho, told Baptists there were scarcely enough pastors to fill the pulpits in Nigeria. She noted that in 1953 there were 266 Baptist churches in Nigeria, and only 239 pastors to serve them. Moreover, there were 211 unorganized churches waiting for pastors. If both Goerner and Hill were right in their counting of Baptist churches in Nigeria, 64 churches had been organized in just three years, and, as soon as enough pastors could be found, another 211 were waiting to organize. With such a demand for pastors, the seminary at Ogbomosho was all the more important, even if it would be overwhelmed.[28]

The Nigerian Convention established both home and foreign mission boards, which missionary John E. Mills claimed would greatly aid the evangelization of Africa. He argued that "the Nigerian Christian who invites his brother to share *his* religion is a far more effective witness than the *foreign* missionary can be." Nigerian Baptists quickly began work in neighboring Gold Coast, where Reverend I. A. Adejunmobi had led Baptist churches in a series of revival meetings even before the Nigerian Convention officially created a foreign mission board. Such enthusiasm prompted Frank K. Means, as editor of *The Commission*, to declare, "The Africans themselves are eager to have a part in winning their continent for Christ."[29]

Nigerians also took the reins of Baptist schools. E. Milford Howell, writing from Wari, Nigeria, told readers that Africans headed more and more schools, including two teacher training centers. In 1947, Samuel A. Lawoyin, a Nigerian Baptist, left his position as headmaster of the Baptist boys' school at Abeokuta to study theology in Virginia. The headmaster's position then went to another Nigerian, E. L. Akisanya, the first alumnus of the school to take the position. Howell reminded Baptists that there was "still much to be done," but the future was bright. He concluded, "With this trend of African Christians taking places of responsibility, a new day is ahead."[30]

Mission schools were the cornerstone of Baptist work in Nigeria and made Africanization possible. In his article "All Things to All Men," John E. Mills argued that Baptist schools had a unique opportunity for evangelism. He believed that the widespread recognition of education's importance would continue to give mission schools a unique position in western Africa, where no system of public education existed. Education also provided a way of circumnavigating the "iron curtain of

Mohammedanism" that had fallen over northern Nigeria. That "iron curtain" helped explain why Sierra Leone and Liberia, despite generations of African Christian presence and considerable missionary efforts, had only a small minority of Christians. In Sierra Leone, the situation facing Christian missionaries remained discouraging. In 1970 only 8.2 percent of the population was Christian. In Liberia, with a historical tie to black Americans, the numbers were more promising at 31 percent.[31]

Mills claimed, "Perhaps more Mohammedans have been won through our schools than in any other way." Elizabeth Ferguson, a missionary teacher serving in Nigeria, wrote that, for many of the Muslim boys at her school, "their public profession [of Christianity] will mean being disowned by their parents." Still, Africans actively sought education and often aligned themselves with whoever provided that education. According to Cal Guy, "the African of tomorrow will be Mohammedan, Communist, or Christian depending on who teaches him to read."[32]

Mission schools dominated education in Nigeria. In 1951, the Baptists enrolled thirty-one thousand students in their schools, accounting for nearly 10 percent of all Nigerians attending school. Samuel A. Lawoyin, a Nigerian Baptist studying at Virginia Union University who later headed the Nigerian Baptist Convention, explained that World War II had awakened both nationalism and the desire for education. Imperialists would not offer education to the Africans, he said, because their paramount interest was to exploit the continent's resources with "very little or no regard for the people." The remaining educational choice, Lawoyin believed, was between the communists and the Christian missions. He did not mention Islamic education, which clearly was a choice. Baptist leaders in America and Africa hoped and prayed that neither communists nor Muslims would gain control of the continent during the turmoil of unprecedented changes brought by independence. Christian schools, they believed, would play a key role in keeping both communists and Muslims at bay.[33]

Mission education challenged African cultures in a number of ways, including providing education for girls. M. Theron Rankin pointed to the Baptists' school for girls in Agbor, Nigeria, as evidence. There "scores of young women are being prepared to assume the responsibility of home makers and spiritual leaders." Stella Austin, a missionary in Agbor, noted that the women's school was also producing a social revolution. She wrote, "As in all places where Christ is unknown and his name not honored, it has been true in Nigeria that women have had very little to do with community or national affairs. Now that Christianity is making an imprint, young women are being educated and are beginning to take their places of service." Agbor's first honor graduate, Jolade Ojeleye, gave her valedictory address in December of 1955. Noting that graduates had come from ten distinct tribes, Ojeleye claimed they had come together with no racial disputes and reasoned that "God has planned it so."[34]

Educating women in Nigeria was especially important, missionaries believed, because of the prominence of Islam in the region. According to Ruth Swann, who wrote for the *Window*, Muslim women knew only "a position of submission." She told Baptist young women that Muslim women accepted their fate of "being considered less than human." Mary H. Saunders, a missionary in Igede, Nigeria, agreed. She noted that "the women know little but hard work." Far worse than that, however, "many tell me they want to go to church and accept Jesus, but they have been bought by and married to Mohammedan men. The men seem to think they are to make all the decisions concerning their wives and children, and they will not allow their wives to accept Jesus." Baptists, both missionaries from America and Africans, rejected the idea of men having control over their wives' religious beliefs. Paul Ebhomlelien, a Nigerian Baptist, hoped that Christianity would spread more quickly in his district. He also hoped that "women will be given their right places in the community" once Christianity replaced idolatry in his region.[35]

Mission schools offered courses on Christian homemaking and home economics, suggesting that Baptist mission education involved Westernization. Missions in Africa could never completely avoid cultural imperialism. Indeed, the very basis of missions, the belief that people need to be converted to the one true faith, suggests a belief in religious superiority. That could often lead to a belief in cultural superiority, even if unintentional and not racially based. This presented Baptist missionaries with a difficult challenge as they tried to overcome their prejudices and still convince Africans that Christianity, which Africans often saw as Western and white, was the one true religion.[36]

Baptist leaders believed that Christianity afforded women a freedom that other religions denied them. Although their views on gender often remained traditional in the American sense, they were often radically different from the ones they encountered in Asia and Africa. But Baptists also provided examples of women's achievements that were atypical even in America. Most conspicuous were women doctors. Dr. Margaret Sampson, the first Southern Baptist woman appointed as a medical missionary to Nigeria, served at the clinic at Shaki. In Africa, "women doctors work[ed] against prejudices in Africa as in America." However, once the Nigerians discovered that the Western medicine dispensed by women doctors like Sampson worked, they became bolder in seeking their assistance. Over the next few decades, Baptists would send several women doctors to Nigeria, including Joanna C. Maiden, an outspoken critic of the American racial situation.[37]

Africa was a rapidly changing continent. George Sadler recognized that all of Africa was "in a state of ferment." He also noted that it had in recent years "become a continent of such tremendous concern that publications like *Life* magazine and [the] *Saturday Review* devote[d] entire issues to discussion of conditions there." Sadler pointed to the Gold Coast, which would become Ghana, the first British colony in Africa to gain independence. He claimed that "in their struggle for political freedom, the people are also striving for spiritual freedom from sin and idolatry." He was optimistic. Certainly many African leaders, like Kwame Nkrumah of Ghana, had been educated in mission schools. But Sadler was too optimistic about the Baptists' opportunities in Africa. Many Africans intended to maintain the cultures that the colonial powers—and missionaries—had attempted to change. In Kenya, for example, such efforts took the form of the Land Freedom Army, popularly known as Mau Mau, which Westerners saw as a revival of the paganism and idolatry Sadler thought Africans were eager to abandon. In Zaire, Joseph-Désiré Mobutu seized power in 1965 and in 1972 banned religious broadcasting, church youth groups, and religious publications.[38]

Nevertheless, the latter 1950s were a period of general optimism in Africa. The Gold Coast won its struggle for political freedom and, on March 6, 1957, became the first colony in tropical Africa to claim its independence, changing its name to Ghana. Kwame Nkrumah, who had attended college in the United States, led the nation to independence. Missionary Mrs. Howard Smith told Baptists that Nkrumah was "keenly aware" of the special position Ghana held for becoming independent first. Nkrumah told his parliament, "If we show ourselves disunited, inefficient or corrupt we shall have gravely harmed all those millions in Africa who . . . looked to Ghana to prove that African people can build a state based on democracy . . . and racial equality."[39]

Ghana paled in size and strategic importance—both in world politics and Baptist missions—to Nigeria. As Nigeria prepared for independence, which would come in 1960, the Baptist mission passed a resolution concerning racism and its effects on their efforts. In 1957, Southern Baptist missionaries serving in Nigeria announced that they had "become increasingly aware of the degree to which relationships between the Negro and white races in America determine the effectiveness of carrying out our mission task in Africa."[40]

Southern Baptist missionaries were echoing the views of Nigerian Baptists, who had pointed to the American racial system in 1955. That year the Nigerian convention passed a resolution stating that "Nigerians are acutely aware of the problems of race relations in America, they identify themselves with the American Negro, and they consider racism in any form unjust." The messengers reminded Southern Baptists that racism damaged their mission efforts and called on them to seek a Christian solution to America's racial problems. They also requested that the Foreign Mission Board circulate their resolution throughout the American South. Dr. E. A. Dahunsi had addressed the Convention concerning his experiences as a teaching fellow and instructor at the Southern Baptist Seminary in Louisville, Kentucky. He recalled several instances of discrimination he and his wife encountered in the United States, explaining that the most hurtful "came from Southern Baptists through whose missionaries we had come to know Jesus Christ and whose support enabled us to be in the United States." Still, Dahunsi believed many Baptists were seeking a Christian solution to the problem and said that these people had shown him considerable courtesy.[41]

When Nigeria gained independence on October 1, 1960, Missionary L. Raymond Brothers wrote that "the Southern Baptist mission program has greatly helped prepare the people for independence." Both Brothers and H. Cornell Goerner believed that Nigerians recognized the contribution of the mission. Goerner reported that S. L. Akintola, the premier of the western region, graduated from a Baptist school and then taught in one in Lagos. Akintola was also editor of *Nigerian Baptist*, and he had worked to bring modern hospitals to the country. Perhaps more important, Muslim leaders in the northern region expressed their gratitude for the Christian mission work in medicine and education.[42]

The situation in both Ghana and Nigeria changed after independence. Political riots spread even to those areas that Southern Baptists believed were most calm. One missionary, Ralph L. West, wrote to Goerner in 1961 that "there has been a great change in Nigerians since independence. The white man is generally downgraded. In pictures the white person is quite often unidentified or cut out of the picture altogether." Jean Favell, serving in Ghana, stressed the importance of training national leaders, adding that "all of us sense the growing hatred toward the white man." Like Favell, West recommended closer ties with Africans and stressed, "There must be less white affairs and *more* mixed parties and visitations." While West feared that these were uncertain days in Nigeria, he stressed that they were "days of great opportunity, if wisely used."[43]

One missionary, Harris Mobley, who served in Ghana, criticized his fellow missionaries in Africa for exacerbating the racial divides in Africa. While home on furlough, he addressed students at his alma mater, Mercer University in Macon, Georgia. It was April 1963, and Mercer was involved in a debate over integration sparked by the application of Sam Jerri Oni, a convert from Ghana and Mobley's personal friend. Indeed, Mobley and Oni intended his application to Mercer to challenge segregation at that institution. While many missionaries pointed to racism in America, Mobley attacked his fellow missionaries and called for a "new missionary." His comments made their way into the local paper, causing an uproar at the Foreign Mission Board. Mobley argued that his comments were never as severe as the *Mercer Cluster* reported, and his original manuscript differed considerably from the press reports. Nevertheless, Mobley did argue that not all missionaries successfully shed their paternalistic attitudes toward people of other races.[44]

Mobley reminded Mercer students that missionaries had to work among the people. He said, "Let us be Christian in our world mission today. Let us cease peddling pious piffle and plunge into the needs of our brother." He went on: "but in Africa I am afraid involvement is the least applicable word to describe the missionary's relationship to the African. Unlike the good Samaritan, we have simply refused to dismount and get involved in the wounds of the African." Mobley claimed that missionaries often lived apart from the African community, in almost colonial fashion. There were exceptions, of course, but not enough of them. Mobley demanded, "Hear me well. I am not dealing in missionary methods. What I am saying is that our methods have reflected our theology, and the image has emerged unchristian. Let the missionary have his house full of servants, his 'boy-master relationship.' Let him mimic the colonial past. Let him have his big American car, horn blowing, dust flying, Africans running off the road covered in dust or mud, but let him also know that he is thereby destroying the Christian Gospel."[45]

The African religious leadership was "fed up with playing second fiddle to the missionaries." Mobley worried that "our paternalism, cultural ignorance and disrespect have all but finished us." Some missionaries came with such little creativity, sensitivity, or respect for African culture that no matter how sincere they were, Mobley believed they could make a better contribution to world salvation by staying home.[46]

The Foreign Mission Board and Harris Mobley were at odds over more than the article. Mobley hoped to extend his furlough to pursue graduate work, a request that "surprised" Goerner. Nevertheless, the speech was at the heart of their difficulties. Goerner told Mobley that while he agreed that the manuscript was milder than the newspaper made it appear, it still contained "sweeping generalizations, some serious exaggerations, and a number of statements which although they contained some truth would need to be very carefully examined." The board assured Mobley that he was free to speak about the race issue as he wished but that much of the paper gave a "very unfortunate impression." Nevertheless, Goerner and the board hoped that Mobley would return to Ghana on schedule. Instead, he retired from missionary service in 1964 to pursue a doctorate in anthropology.[47]

Mobley's comments and the increasingly confrontational race situation in America coincided with increasing political turbulence in Africa. H. Cornell Goerner reported that the vice premier of the western region of Nigeria had sent a message to the American ambassador stating that the racial situation in the United States had become "unbearable" and that there would be a definite public reaction to that situation in Nigeria. Medical missionary Joanna Maiden related an exemplary incident to Southern Baptists shortly after the integration of the University of Georgia, which involved a riot. Maiden noted that a young ward assistant asked her if Georgia was an important place in the United States.

While she did not provide readers of *The Commission* with her answer, she wrote, "Perhaps a native Georgian could have answered him more gracefully than I did, but I am asked similar things about Virginia, my home state, and I can't answer without embarrassment." News did travel, and Nigerians did pay attention to the American situation. They also confronted missionaries about the racial situation, and African young people were deeply affected by the racism in the United States. Maiden's brief note exemplified what the leadership had been telling Southern Baptists for fifteen years.[48]

Another missionary told Mildred Dodson (Mrs. William) McMurry, "We teach and preach the Christian doctrine of the equality of men under God . . . the Africans take it from there." Indeed, some churches were quick to point out how much they had contributed to the emergence of a new Africa. Most pointed to education as well as doctrine, noting that Christianity had brought mission schools and literacy. Africans at the time, and historians since, have acknowledged the role of missionaries and Christianity in African society. As historian Noel King noted, however, Africans wished the churches would "purge themselves of foreignness," meaning foreign, or white, domination of the church leadership. Baptists were acting to accomplish this, but they were not moving quickly enough for everyone.[49]

As Southern Baptists pursued Africanization, the distinction between the American-operated missions and the locally controlled convention blurred. This was particularly evident in 1961, when African leaders participated in the All-Africa Conference for the first time. However blurred they may have been, distinctions were, according to Goerner, dangerous because "there is always the danger that 'difference' will be equated with 'discrimination.' The very word 'discrimination' has come to be associated in an unfavorable way with the word 'racial.'" He emphasized that the difference between the convention and the mission "must not suggest a sense of superiority of color" or be allowed to interfere with fellowship between the two. The differences remained only in the fact that the Foreign Mission Board in Richmond, Virginia, organized and operated the missions, while Africans led the conventions. Their ultimate goal was the same: world redemption.[50]

During the 1960s, however, the situation in Nigeria deteriorated dramatically. I. N. Patterson was optimistic as late as 1966, but the country was on the verge of collapse. Patterson told Baptists that the task of building a nation was incomplete. He added, "Increasingly it is becoming apparent that if the 250 tribes that make up Nigeria are to become truly one, this can only be done in Christ." Instead of becoming one in Christ, however, Nigeria sank into years of brutal violence and war. After the coup of January 15, 1966, the military officers leading the rebellion murdered several prominent leaders of the government, including the Baptist premier of the western region, S. L. Akintola. Goerner told the Foreign Mission Board, confidentially, that the revolution was popular among some people who believed it would bring an end to corruption. The new leaders also "decreed that in the future no reference would be made to a person's tribal origin or region of birth . . . in an effort to break the tribalism and regionalism which has been so prevalent." The effort failed, and the violence plaguing Nigeria contained an ugly ethnic tinge. As one missionary reported, "Hausa mobs in cities throughout the North mercilessly hunted down and killed every Ibo tribesman they could find." That reinforced the missionaries' belief that Christianity was the only force in the world powerful enough to end racism.[51]

As the violence wore on, the eastern region of Nigeria attempted to become an independent nation, spawning the Biafra War. Mission work faced severe difficulties. Joanna Maiden had been in the United States when the war broke out and was unable to return to Nigeria. More problematic, of course, was the situation facing the missionaries remaining in Nigeria. Of particular concern was the Baptist hospital at Eku, where Maiden had served. Rebel forces took over the compound in September 1967. Those missionaries who could fled to Ogbomosho, where they waited out the war, hoping to return to their posts when peace was achieved. Maiden, however, never returned to Nigeria.[52]

As missionaries in West Africa became more engrossed in the problems of an independent Africa, Southern Baptist expansion into East Africa also forced missionaries to face the hypocrisy of a segregated convention evangelizing Africans. In Tanganyika, later Tanzania after its merger with the island of Zanzibar, Africans were quick to point to that hypocrisy. Tanganyika, like Nigeria and Ghana, had a long-established Muslim community. Missionary James W. Carty noted that a Tanganyikan farmer, Jebulin Makala, told him, "The Muslims practice racial brotherhood more than do the Christians." Muslims hardly needed to remind Africans that they shared their darker skin tone.[53]

Tanganyika's government also pointed to the contradictions. Maxine

Law wrote that news of Mississippi's racial problems made the headlines for three days in late 1962. She noted that "the editor of the Swahili paper for Dar [es Salaam] told one of our missionaries that the government was going to stop admitting missionaries who came from churches in America where segregation is practiced." While Law was unsure if the government would act officially, there was a clear threat to the Southern Baptist missionaries who were associated, in the very name of their denomination, with the segregated South.[54]

To counter the Muslim claim, Baptists had to cross several "frontiers" in Africa. The most important frontier was in their attitude. Roslin D. Harrell wrote that "the missionary must try to avoid the attitude of paternalism." Missionaries themselves disagreed about how best to identify with the Africans, and the "theory that it is impossible for the Western mind to know the African mind is widely propounded these days." Indeed, Harrell admitted that "few, if any [missionaries], could truthfully claim complete identification with the African mind, personality, and culture." Yet the attempt had to be made. As a result, Velma Darbo Brown argued, "The missionary in Africa must learn to walk a mental and emotional tightrope."[55]

If missionaries in Africa fell off the tightrope it would be an open invitation to the communists. Christian mission forces clearly saw that communism was a threat to their work. Communists were able to both provide education and exploit the traditional ties between Christianity and Western imperialism. The Foreign Mission Board informed Baptists that Soviet leader Nikita Khrushchev called for the expulsion of missionaries from Africa. Khrushchev said, "Missionaries are the agents of formerly imperialistic nations which are using them in an attempt to reconquer their lost colonies."[56]

Communists took advantage of the association between Christianity and colonialism, but Baptists believed that communist leaders were really concerned about the possibility of mission successes. Hermione Dannelly Jackson, writing for the *Window*, recognized that communists wanted an end to Christian missions, but she offered different reasons from those put forth by Khrushchev. She argued, "Communists recognize the mission movement as a bond of good will between the people they seek to control and the United States." Some African leaders also disagreed with Khrushchev. Kwame Nkrumah invited religious leaders to a special dinner in 1963 to commend them for their work in medicine and education. According to Helen Bond, a Southern Baptist missionary who attended the dinner, Nkrumah "voiced hope that more schools and medical stations will be opened by religious bodies." She noted that the encouragement was welcome, given the uncertainty felt by many missionaries in Africa.[57]

Many African leaders rejected both Western imperialism and Soviet intrusions. They looked instead to African unity. H. Cornell Goerner and Mrs. Howard Smith both recognized the rising tide of Pan-Africanism. Smith wrote that Nkrumah hoped to create a "United States of Africa" and had called the All-Africa People's Conference, which two hundred delegates attended. African Baptist leaders in Ghana tended to agree with Nkrumah. In his presidential address, J. A. Imosun told the Ghana Baptist Conference that "as Africans we have a duty to the continent." He reminded Ghana's Baptists that "the liberation and development of the peoples of Africa are not the exclusive obligations of the politicians." He urged Baptists to lead African nationalism toward constructive, not destructive, ends. Imosun ended by saying, "Unity is the seed of possibilities. Let us plan it."[58]

Goerner noted that African students in Lagos, Nigeria, shared Nkrumah's belief that no part of Africa could be truly free until all of Africa was free. The students claimed that "all Africans are brothers with a common history of oppression and a common destiny of freedom." They directed their attack at the United States as well as the colonial powers. Even though the United States had not directly colonized any part of Africa, Nigerian students argued "that there is so much talk in the United States about winning Africa for the free world. Has it ever occurred to you that perhaps we don't want to be won, perhaps we don't regard your freedom as being particularly desirable[?]"[59]

Clearly, Africans saw the racial system in the United States as offering blacks something less than freedom. Missionaries feared that vision would mean Africans would not want to be "won" for Christianity, which they associated with colonial rule and Western culture. Thus, racism in the United States hurt both the political effort to "win" Africa for the West and the Baptist effort to "win" Africa for Christianity. That problem was perhaps most acute in southern Africa, where whites continued to dominate politics and economics with starkly racist policies.[60]

Southern Africa posed unique problems for missionaries, just as it did for politicians. Southern Baptists began their mission there in 1951.

At that time Clyde Dotson had noted that a school located in southern Rhodesia would be able to attract students from throughout the region, including Angola. He lamented that there were, as of 1951, no evangelical schools in all of Southern Rhodesia. Additionally, Dotson believed that "Communism is sowing seeds of hatred in many hearts and the racial policy of the Union of South Africa has widened the breach between white and black."[61]

Political problems worsened in southern Africa throughout the 1950s and 1960s, despite the creation of the Central African Federation that combined the British colonies of Nyasaland, Northern Rhodesia, and Southern Rhodesia. Meanwhile, white Southern Rhodesia was experiencing a population boom. In 1941, only about 69,000 whites lived in that country, but by the mid-1950s the number was nearer 160,000. Goerner reminded Baptists that "the African people, who constitute a large majority of the population, live in a segregated society in which a European minority is in control of the process of government." African leaders were demanding a greater voice in the government, while the whites took "vigorous measures to prevent the situation from getting out of hand." According to Goerner, the board's missionaries were caught in a difficult position between the Africans with whom they worked and the white government. He said, "Our missionaries are working with the African population almost exclusively, and naturally their sympathies tend to favor the Africans. They must at the same time observe the law and be conscious of the local customs. There is always the possibility that they might suffer in any African uprising merely because of the color of their skin, even though they might not share the discriminatory views of most of the European element in the population."[62]

Despite news of racial violence in America, evangelist Billy Graham believed that many Africans maintained a positive attitude toward America. He admitted that racial turmoil in America had "an adverse effect" but believed most Africans had faith that the government, under John F. Kennedy, would work for racial harmony and progress. Kennedy generally sympathized with the independence movements in Africa, though at times political considerations prevented his being able to support those efforts. This was particularly true of southern Africa, where American relations with both Portugal and South Africa complicated the matter considerably. For Kennedy, clearly, the strategic considerations were more important.[63]

For the missionaries, strategic concerns were less important. James N. Westmoreland wrote from Southern Rhodesia that missionaries were "saddened to learn that some churches refused membership to Negroes." Westmoreland believed that "if Christians at home could know what such things are doing to harm the cause of Christ around the world, I am sure they would re-examine their actions." By 1963 missionaries had been telling Christians in America about the impact of their racism on evangelism for nearly two decades, and yet problems persisted. Mission efforts went forward even if Christians in America were slow to change. Missionaries remained certain that world redemption was the only path away from world disaster.[64]

In Southern Rhodesia, Africanization was more urgent than elsewhere. Missionaries had to live in the European areas and could visit the African townships only by permission of the government. Even during relatively quiet times, missionaries could not hold meetings after six o'clock in the evening. Whenever violence erupted it was impossible for the missionaries to visit the churches or the homes of church members. Goerner believed that "the importance of developing capable African leadership for the churches, recognized everywhere, is strongly emphasized here, where missionaries labor under definite handicaps and limitation."[65]

The law was only one handicap to missionary efforts in Southern Rhodesia. Whites had dominated the economy, the politics, and the culture for generations, despite being outnumbered ten to one by Africans. As missionary W. David Lockard suggested, the Africans had seen little love in their years of experience with white "civilization." Naturally, some Africans argued that everything associated with whites, including Christianity, was inherently oppressive. Clyde Dotson noted that the Africans became increasingly blunt in their rejection of Christianity on racial grounds. Dotson reported that an African had approached him and declared, "You can't fool us any more; you have a white Christ."[66]

Against the missionaries' wishes, black leaders dragged Christianity into political battles. According to Goerner, "radical leaders constantly spread propaganda that Christianity is the religion of the white man, and in some cases loving people are caused to be fearful to attend church services because of intimidation by those who interpret this as a type of collaboration with the Europeans."[67] Political events continued to drive a wedge between white and black in southern Africa, and Southern Baptist missionaries strained themselves in an effort to bridge the crevice.

In early 1963, Goerner announced the establishment of the Baptist Convention of Central Africa, a significant step toward Africanization. It meant that Baptist churches in Southern Rhodesia could operate independently of the Central African Mission, which was staffed by white Southern Baptist missionaries. Goerner said, "The present political situation in Southern Rhodesia lends added significance to the development of this Convention. Recent elections placed in control of the country a government which is committed to racial policies patterned largely after those in effect in the Union of South Africa. This means more rigid enforcement of a pattern of segregation, and development of the European and the African sections of the population into separate communities."[68]

Although the convention theoretically included churches in Nyasaland and Northern Rhodesia, political events made their actual inclusion unlikely. Nyasaland and Northern Rhodesia elected African-majority governments while Southern Rhodesia elected the white supremacist government led by Ian Smith. The elections made the political Federation of Central Africa wholly ineffective. The Central African Mission itself formally split in 1964, allowing the missions in Nyasaland and Northern Rhodesia to operate independently of the problems facing the mission in Southern Rhodesia. While missionaries remained in all three areas, the convention was particularly important in Southern Rhodesia, where missionaries prepared for the day when "it may become impossible for missionaries to work among the African churches." Meanwhile, Baptists could be reassured by the dedication of African Christians in Rhodesia. One Rhodesian minister gained fame for cycling more than fifty miles every Sunday after services in his home village in order to hold another service in a migrant workers' settlement.[69]

In 1964, Nyasaland became Malawi and Northern Rhodesia became Zambia, newly independent nations no longer under the suzerainty of Great Britain. Southern Rhodesia, alone of the former Central African Federation, remained under British control, nominal though it was. Southern Baptists welcomed the two new nations, and *The Commission* ran extensive stories informing readers about the background, people, and culture of both Malawi and Zambia.[70]

In Southern Rhodesia, however, the European minority tenaciously held to political power and denied the Africans the right to vote. Goerner predicted, correctly, that "Southern Rhodesia, alienated from its former partners in the Federation, will seek closer political ties with South Africa." Southern Rhodesia was moving against the grain of world opinion. Goerner noted that roughly one-third of the members of the United Nations were newly independent African nations.[71]

The demand for "one man, one vote" remained quixotic in Southern Rhodesia into the 1970s. Goerner noted increasing racial and political tensions and said that Southern Rhodesia under the leadership of Ian Smith was an unknown quantity. Smith had threatened to declare independence from England, which would make it only the second nation, after the United States, to do so. England's view of the situation, after two hundred years, remained the same: a unilateral declaration of independence would be treason, though they would not send an army to try to prevent the action. The United States, this time, would side with the British, and the United Nations would not recognize an independent, white-ruled Rhodesia.[72]

H. Cornell Goerner arrived in Salisbury on November 6, 1965, to tour the Southern Baptist work in the region. The day before, negotiations between Ian Smith and Harold Wilson, the British prime minister, ended in an impasse. Goerner reported, "I found the country surprisingly quiet." The missionaries were "quite calm and seemed unaware of the apprehension felt for them by those outside Rhodesia." The board assured Baptists that all forty-eight missionaries serving in Southern Rhodesia were safe. As a precaution, however, Goerner discussed the region's situation with the United States Consulate General in Salisbury, who told him that if Ian Smith went forward with his promised declaration of independence, the United States would close the consulate. Goerner then went to the Sanyati mission station, where he was on November 11 when Smith announced Rhodesian independence. Goerner told the Foreign Mission Board that "we now face the necessity of understanding and sympathizing with the indignation of African leaders against the Rhodesian government, which symbolizes a white minority rule determined to deny civil rights to the African majority, while at the same time we avoid making statements which might result in the expulsion of our missionaries from Rhodesia. Their ministry is more needed than ever in that land. We must maintain our neutral position on political issues, even though it might at times involve silence on what some would regard as basic human rights." Silence in Africa would preserve the mission. Yet missionaries found themselves in a dilemma. Baptist leaders condemned the silence of American pastors on racial issues, saying such silence aided and abetted racism. In Africa, they had to face the fact that their silence could be interpreted that way, though they believed it was necessary to achieve the greater good of ensuring that the missions continued operation.[73]

After the declaration of independence, missionaries became particularly concerned with the National Registration Act, which threatened to pull male missionaries, as resident whites, into military service to defend the white-supremacist government. The missionaries, except for Clyde Dotson and Sam Cannata, signed the registration forms, but they sent a letter of protest saying they were not signing voluntarily. They signed only so that the mission could remain open in Rhodesia. They hoped that their letter would minimize the image of their cooperation with the Smith government and lessen the damage that might be done to their work with the Africans.[74]

The missionaries had no intention of leaving Rhodesia. Instead, they prayed for additional missionaries and remained optimistic that a political solution was possible. Goerner related the missionaries' sentiments to Baker James Cauthen, who assured him that he and the rest of the board would pray for the missionaries stationed in Rhodesia. The board took no action toward preparing to withdraw them. Only a "serious" military or racial crisis would prompt the missionaries to leave. Given the situation in Rhodesia during the early days of Ian Smith's rule and the threat of war from several nations, some observers would have already declared the situation "serious." That the Baptist mission-aries did not consider the situation serious enough to leave offered an eloquent testimony to both their faith in God's protection and their belief in the urgency of their work.[75]

In the postwar years, Southern Baptists increased their mission efforts in Africa more than tenfold. While in 1945 they worked in only one African nation, Nigeria, within twenty-five years their work had spread through sub-Saharan Africa. Dramatic changes took place in Africa in those years, but some problems dogged Southern Baptist missionaries no matter where in Africa they went. Foremost among those problems was racism. Racism and the legacy of imperialism left deep wounds in Africa, and American missionaries were associated with imperialists despite their anti-imperialist leanings. This situation was further complicated by the persistent racial problems in the United States in the years after World War II. Missionaries coming from the segregated South appeared, to Africans, to be hypocrites. If they personally were not, then their denomination, the Southern Baptist Convention, with its segregated churches, universities, and hospitals, certainly appeared to be. The missionaries, then, stood against imperialism in Africa and racism in America. Their dedication is evident at several points, but most certainly it was clear in their decision to stay in Southern Rhodesia and work among the African population even after Ian Smith's government issued the Unilateral Declaration of Independence.

4

AN AMERICAN AMOS

Baptist Missionaries and
Postwar American Culture

The years after World War II were particularly good for American religion. The omnipresent threats of the cold war, combined with unprecedented changes in society, led people to look to religion for a sense of grounding and community during the postwar years. Church membership increased from 57 percent of Americans in 1950 to 63.3 percent in 1959. Christian Americans became hostile to any criticism of their society, especially the implication that America was not the Christian nation it professed to be. Those who dared criticize America could easily be branded communists, and the charge could stick with little or no evidence.[1]

During the postwar revival, the Southern Baptist Convention became the fastest growing denomination in the United States, and its members were often considered "hyper-Americans." Baptist missionaries and leaders, however, questioned the direction of their nation. Fortified with impeccable anticommunist credentials, Baptist leaders even questioned the vigor with which the government pursued suspected communists, calling the Federal Bureau of Investigation "a vast army of sleuths." In 1947, Charles A. Wells, who wrote for the *Baptist Student,* claimed that "several pages could be filled with things that Jesus said which would be labeled Communistic by the smear artists of today."[2]

Baptist mission leaders believed that America was "God's chosen vessel" for bringing peace and Christianity to the troubled world of the cold war. For America to lead the world as God wanted, however, Americans would have to forego liquor, gambling, smoking, and "filthy literature." Most important, if America were to be truly Christian,

Americans would have to overcome the dual sins of materialism and racism. Progressive Southern Baptists focused on materialism and racism in their critique of postwar America, a critique that remained consistent well into the 1960s. They realized that they stood against traditions that many southerners considered Christian, but that was no deterrent. As W. E. Denham Jr., pastor at First Baptist Church of Newport, Tennessee, wrote in 1945, "Dishonesty, racial antagonisms, economic injustices, personal and national selfishness, war, etc., all will be placed against the pattern of God in Christ. Those parts which do not fit will be lopped off. Tradition, or any other force, will not prevent the true Christian from an increasing expression of this new life within." Like the prophet Amos, who predicted doom for Israel at the very moment of its glory, Baptist missionaries believed that America had turned its back on God and that God's wrath was inevitable unless America repented. Baptist leaders intended to lead America to that repentance.[3]

Baptist leaders feared that the United States was not ready for world leadership. J. B. Lawrence, executive secretary of the Home Mission Board, told the Woman's Missionary Union in 1948 that the country would clearly become the world's economic leader. He worried, however, that the United States would not provide Christian leadership for the world. Failure to minister to the lost, to minorities, and to the growing "worldly-minded" cities would mean "no matter what else we may do— we are doomed ultimately to fail in our efforts to evangelize and Christianize the nations of the world." To demonstrate how bad the situation was, Lawrence told Baptists that two out of every three Americans were not affiliated with any church and half of those who were affiliated rarely attended services. What frightened Lawrence most, however, were the "twenty-seven million youths under twenty-one years of age . . . growing up in America with no religious training of any kind— growing up to join the already large army of adult pagans."[4]

In 1950 Cal Guy echoed Lawrence's concerns. Guy explained that, by the standards of the minor prophets, America was not Christian. He wrote, "If America is Christian, God has first place in the lives of the American people." However, Guy estimated that only 10 percent of the people in the average southern town attended church regularly. He asked, rhetorically, "Does this show that God has first place?" In addition to breaking the Sabbath, racism was prominent among the reasons America was unchristian. Guy argued, "America will not live up to her Christian

Courts Redford (right) and J. B. Lawrence led the Home Mission Board
through much of the postwar era. Photo courtesy of the Southern Baptist
Historical Library and Archives, Nashville, Tennessee.

name until all races are treated as belonging to God and therefore
deserving fair treatment."[5]

Progressive Baptists realized that many Americans believed they
lived in a Christian nation. One pastor, Harold G. Sanders of
Tallahassee's First Baptist Church, explained that Americans should learn
to see themselves as the rest of the world saw them. He argued, "Others
know that our Christianity is incompatible with [the] personal and
national sins of America—debauchery on a national scale, unprecedented breakdown of marriage vows, unmitigated racial bigotry, and pride
demonstrated in 'white supremacy' and other themes, widespread
disregard for constituted authority and law, sinister steps toward
unification of church and state and disregard for the rights of both
minorities and majorities."[6]

If Americans could see themselves as the rest of the world saw them,
they would also understand the international implications of America's
sins. Baker James Cauthen believed Americans knew how America's
problems impacted foreign missions but simply did not want to face the

facts. Cauthen explained that "America stands on a spotlighted stage with the rest of the world looking to see what we do; they will judge the gospel of Christ largely in terms of our actions and attitudes." In the midst of the cold war, the stakes could hardly be higher. As Cauthen had warned Baptists, "The day in which we live is critical and the outlook for the future is grave. Human freedom is threatened by Communist ideology which is militantly atheistic and materialist."[7]

In the dangerous world of the cold war, Baptists had to act quickly to bring the world to Christianity. Mrs. George R. Ferguson, the executive secretary of the Kentucky Woman's Missionary Union, announced, "Scientists, statesmen, sociologists, editors, and military men, with one voice, are warning us that the world is in a crisis such as history has rarely seen. The United States stands in the awful position of having the major responsibility for deciding the outcome of the crisis. Men of keen minds from all walks of life are saying, almost with one voice, that Christianity offers the only hope for the future. America is known as a Christian nation. Can we meet the challenge? The situation requires action now. The Scriptures and science tell us the time may be short!"[8]

Courts Redford, Lawrence's successor at the Home Mission Board, agreed, pointing out that "all of the people of the world who love freedom look to the United States with hope and expectation." He believed that no other nation had the resources or experiences to meet the world's physical and spiritual needs. Yet time was running short, and failure would be devastating. Communism, atheism, and chaos stood waiting to sweep the world. Redford warned: "we stand only one generation from the evil philosophies, the false religion, and the selfish attitudes that have brought other civilizations to destruction. For us, the call is now or never."[9]

Answering the call meant more than merely building new churches. J. W. Storer, president of the Southern Baptist Convention in 1959, suggested that some churches were more concerned with numbers than with living a truly Christian life. Courts Redford agreed and noted a common problem in America when he suggested that "for many, religion is a sort of adjunct to life that gives some measure of social acceptance and self-respect." He believed that many American Christians placed religion on the same plane as property, security, and happiness—all of which could be purchased with money. As a result, "our church members seem to be impotent to solve the moral and social problems that threaten

Juliette Mather, Young People's
Secretary for the Woman's
Missionary Union and founder of
the *Window*. Photo courtesy of the
Southern Baptist Historical Library
and Archives, Nashville, Tennessee.

our American way of life." True Christianity would permeate all of a
Christian's life and enable him or her to confront and solve America's
social and spiritual problems.[10]

America's problems were spiritual, not economic. After living
through the Great Depression and World War II, people naturally wanted
to provide material comforts for themselves and, especially, for their
children. Nevertheless, Professor W. O. Carver feared that America's
wealth rested on a faulty foundation. In the late 1940s, he told readers
of *The Commission* that America's prosperity was due to its "manipulation
of the materials of power in a depleted world and in the exploitation of
the weaknesses and dependence of the vast majority of our fellowmen."
He argued, "Most of us know, when we are willing to give attention to it,
that such superficial and unrighteous prosperity cannot continue
indefinitely." When Carver wrote in December 1948, however, the
economic boom was just beginning. Bolstered by the baby boom, the
Marshall Plan, and other circumstances, it lasted another decade.[11]

Prosperity exacerbated what Juliette Mather called a "moral let-
down," which she believed always followed a war, a time that was,
ironically, also a time of high church attendance. Mather, the Young
People's Secretary at the Woman's Missionary Union, saw alcohol, the
increase in divorces, and the temptation for "undesirable recreation" —

a vague phrase that probably included everything from dancing to premarital sex—as the main dangers of the postwar era. In the face of these temptations, Mather urged Baptist churches to redouble their efforts to reach out to young women. She had long been in the forefront of those efforts, launching the *Window*, a monthly publication for young women, in September 1929. After the war, she urged Baptists to emphasize the Girls' Auxiliary and the Young Woman's Auxiliary, building on the success that had already made the Girls' Auxiliary, an organization for girls aged nine to sixteen, the largest denominational organization for girls in the world, with over one hundred thousand members. Mather believed that girls were susceptible to "the glamour of recent perfume advertisements" that would "suggest that world problems would all be settled if women and girls just chose the strategic perfume." Mather, however, believed that only when women possessed souls "zealous for truth and salvation to be made known to all people" could they begin to solve the world's problems. Truth and salvation could not be found in makeup or perfume.[12]

Other progressive Baptists agreed that America's materialism contributed to the moral decay Mather feared. Mrs. Taul B. White claimed that "our desire for things adds to the breakdown of Christian observance on the Lord's day. . . . How many times on Sunday do we say, 'fill 'er up.' How many times on Sundays do we have social functions, teas, and showers. We have grown unaware of the Lord's day." Others, including an anonymous writer who claimed his or her college was a typical Christian campus, pointed beyond advertising to smoking and drinking, especially among people who were training for the ministry. Like Mather, the writer put the responsibility for upholding morality on women, as was typical for the early postwar era. The student wrote, "Possibly the most important need of the moment is for the vast majority of those of the fairer sex to win back the respect of the men on campus by changing their numerous bad habits into others that are more fitting to them." However one ranked the evils of postwar America, the net result was the same: "materialism and secularism have brought a let-down in our reverence for things once sacred." Americans clearly needed to return to the basic teachings of Christ, but material comforts blocked the path. Returning to the Christian path was the individual responsibility of each Baptist.[13]

Looking at the ever-expanding selection of consumer goods, Mrs.

Taul B. White argued, "Desperately we need to rediscover the Christian teachings concerning material wealth." America had, she claimed, a moral obligation to help those who suffered. If America did not use its wealth responsibly, its international reputation would be severely damaged. Earl Hester Trutza, who came to the United States from Romania, told Southern Baptists that America's wealth created jealousy throughout the world. She noted, "America will be hated if she continues to live on an economic level so much higher than that of other nations. And hatred leads to war." Trutza believed that "Christian love should prompt us to aid where there is poverty" and also noted that economic injustice and distress encouraged communism abroad.[14]

Writing for *Royal Service* in 1951, Lula Grace (Mrs. Joe E.) Burton worried that efforts to sustain popularity and social status got more time than prayer. She believed that most Southern Baptists were more concerned with their economic livelihood than their spiritual life: "in the field of material progress, our nation has reached an all time high. We become sick at heart when we realize that the things in which we have placed our confidence for securing peace have failed us. It will ever be so. If our nation does not obey the Word of God, if it continues to use the Lord's Day for pleasure and profit, if gold and force are our gods, downfall is inevitable. . . . If our nation sets itself to rediscover Christ and his way of life, to govern our social, civic, economic and international life by his work, there is hope."[15]

Just as racism damaged mission efforts abroad, so did moral decay. E. C. Routh, editor of the Foreign Mission Board's monthly publication *The Commission*, saw America's sins as a special problem for the Baptists' overseas mission efforts. He believed that the "old partitions are falling down" and that the "races of the world, whether we like it or not, are at our doors." The problem, according to Routh, was that "Communists, Roman Catholics, cynical education, sensual materialists, fomenters of racial and religious strife, [and] creators and distributors of filthy literature" were all poisoning the soul of America. Routh warned that "Christian forces of America had better be alert or we shall witness more tragic moral and spiritual decadence not only in our own land but throughout the world."[16]

Though Baptists retained hope for the future, the forces of commercialism were formidable foes. They damaged America's reputation abroad and turned people away from missions and Christian service. Writing for the *Window,* Edith Huckabay told Baptist youth that foreign Christians hardly recognized America as a Christian nation. Indeed, foreign converts and foreign missionaries saw, as Huckabay did, that "young Americans are forever looking for something new, and they continue to hold onto their dates and shows and proms and an inconceivable variety of other activities, some of which are questionable." Huckabay related the problem to the future of missions, saying "young people like these would never discard their luxuries to become foreign missionaries." *Ambassador Life* ran a political cartoon showing a strong Russia planting the flag of communism around the world, while Uncle Sam, whose flag read "Christian Democracy," struggled under the burden of a ruck-sack of "overwhelming materialism." America's mission, and Baptist missions, in the world were clearly threatened by materialism at home.[17]

Foreign missionaries, who tried to plant the flag of Christianity around the world, often voiced their criticisms of America. Virginia Cannata, a missionary serving in southern Rhodesia, wrote that she and her husband were "astounded by the rank materialism in Southern Baptist churches and the lives of American Christians during our recent medical furlough." She pointed directly at the churches, saying, "Everything in many churches is measured in dollars, buildings, and numbers. And apparently the main objective of many of our Christian friends is a life of comfort rather than of service." Cannata saw the materialism around her and realized her own participation in American culture led her to value material comfort. She and her husband then eliminated all nonessentials while packing for their return to Southern Rhodesia.[18]

While Cannata and her husband came to the realization that materialism infected their spiritual life, many were reluctant to see such evidence. T. B. Maston argued that the denomination suffered from an "obsession with success" that was "making the denomination more concerned with our prestige in the world than in our impact on the world." In an insecure world, Maston urged Americans to turn to God, not worldly possessions, for comfort and security.[19]

Mission leaders saw the United States as an island of prosperity in a distraught and economically depressed world. Americans, however, did not always realize just how much worldly comfort they enjoyed. Toward the end of the 1950s, one missionary, Robert H. Culpepper, wrote, "With half the world unable to feed itself and countless millions never know[ing] what it is to have a full stomach, millions of Americans like myself are fighting the battle of the bulge and our country as a whole faces the perplexing problem of what to do with its surplus of agricultural products." Culpepper looked to Christianity for the solution to the world's problems, and that gave him hope. He noted that Southern Baptists were the fastest growing denomination in the United States, and indeed they increased their numbers by roughly two and a half million in the 1950s. In 1957, the year Culpepper wrote, church membership continued to increase, and Billy Graham led a successful crusade in New York City. That year, however, was also problematic. The latter half of the year brought both the Little Rock crisis, in which Eisenhower had to send federal troops to ensure compliance with the *Brown* decision, and the escalation of the cold war into space as the Soviet Union launched *Sputnik*. Still, Culpepper was optimistic. The continuing surge in church membership and the expanding mission program prompted him to argue that "now, as never before, Southern Baptists seem to be recognizing their world mission responsibilities."[20]

There was much to be done. In her program notes for *Royal Service*, Irene Curtis lamented that race remained an excuse to oppress people and keep them in squalor. She explained that World War II "taught us that peoples of every race, color and creed have something constructive to contribute to our way of life." Americans needed to apply the lesson of war to peacetime. Curtis concluded, "We have an obligation to make them feel that they have a place in their community in peace as in war."[21]

Materialism and racism were tied together in economic exploitation after the war. In 1950, Kate Bullock Helms noted that "the right to live is closely related to the right to work." Helms argued that economic exploitation was rampant in America and cited the migrant farm workers as a prime example. She also noted that Indians faced discrimination "in spite of their being the only true Americans." Indians were "not accepted easily in professional positions and the prejudice against them in many sections of the country is as great as against other minority groups." Most southern whites, however, dealt more frequently with blacks, and Helms related economic exploitation to daily behavior in the South. She said, "When we think of the low wages that we have paid Negro domestic servants in years past we wonder that they were ever able to live in any degree of decency." Helms argued that the "economic opportunities open to Negroes are still limited, yet where employed in skilled or professional occupations Negro workers are giving a high degree of satisfaction."[22]

Six years later, and after the Supreme Court's *Brown* decision, Kate Fristos (Mrs. Davis) Woolley cited continuing exploitation. She noted, "Sometimes a Negro is not paid enough—not what a white person doing the same work would receive." She added, "Frequently a Negro does not receive his money's worth for the rent he pays." Woolley related economic injustice in America to the world situation, especially as southerners resisted the desegregation of their schools. She pointed out that "the evil of our treatment [of minorities] is especially serious because it has world effect. Three-fourths of the population of the globe is colored. They are watching to see what we will do with American Negroes, whether we practice what we preach. The Communists are appealing to the other colored peoples to forsake the United States."[23]

Things changed only slowly, when at all. In 1962, a decade after Helms wrote, Jacqueline Durham argued that women were "notorious offenders" in violating human rights. Women, she noted, had requested "good, able-bodied" workers and then paid them less than a fair wage. Marie Wiley (Mrs. R. L.) Mathis, president of the Woman's Missionary Union, argued that in order to solve the problem women needed to act, not just talk. She chastised Baptist women, saying "the plain fact is that we never have taken the matter seriously, or as seriously as we ought." Moving from talk to action proved difficult for even well-meaning Baptists who lived in a society where custom was at odds with the preaching of the Convention's progressive leadership. Tradition proved a formidable foe to a Christianized South, perhaps even more formidable than W. E. Denham had anticipated.[24]

Traditions were intractable in part because many southerners believed that their traditions were Christian and that segregation had biblical sanction. Progressive Baptists, however, believed that racial discrimination was unchristian and that whites were clearly responsible for both creating and solving it. Writing her program notes for "How Christian Is America" in 1950, Kate Bullock Helms argued that the most difficult problem facing America was the treatment of minority groups. She told Baptists, "If we face the issue, we realize that the problem is ours—with us—not the minority group. Our attitude toward people who are different creates the problem." Hermione Dannelly Jackson also blamed white Americans for discrimination. Jackson had been born in 1918 and lived in Birmingham, Alabama, where her husband, Lamar, pastored Ensley Baptist Church. During the 1960s, Birmingham gained the reputation as one of the most segregated and virulently racist cities in America. Jackson, however, challenged segregation on moral grounds even before the Supreme Court declared the practice unconstitutional. In 1950, writing one of her many articles for the *Window*, Jackson told Baptist young women that "we in the South have made the Negro what he is because of our segregation and treatment of him. Then we point to the product of our system and use it to justify the way we treat him. It is a vicious circle that the white man himself could not beat under the same circumstances." The progressive leadership saw, by 1950, that America's race problem was a white problem: white racism, not black "inferiority," lay at the heart of the race question.[25]

Mission leaders understood that Americans had failed to live up to their ideals. In 1951, Jackson told Baptists that segregation was "a major failure of American democracy and one of our greatest handicaps in dealing with the rest of the world." Baptists moved toward overcoming that handicap by ending segregation at Baptist seminaries, which were graduate-level institutions by the 1951–52 academic year. Even so, progress was slow. As late as 1963, only one, Golden Gate in California, had a program for recruiting black students, and none had as many as ten black students.[26]

While the seminaries moved toward a more Christian position on race, Baptists continued to insist that overcoming prejudice was primarily an individual responsibility. Mission leaders offered advice to those who were struggling to overcome their prejudice. A young woman named Wanda wrote to Edith Huckabay looking for advice on how to avoid prejudice. Huckabay's monthly column in the *Window* usually dealt with such teenage problems as popularity, dating, and parents, but in early 1954, just months before the Supreme Court announced its decision in the *Brown* case, she tackled the race question. Huckabay admitted that many of the people who were telling America's youth to avoid prejudice failed to do so themselves. They were, she said, "still in the process of learning." To Wanda's main concern, Huckabay answered,

> I don't think we actually avoid any kind of prejudices—rather we develop beyond them. Prejudices are really over-emphasized

preferences. You prefer popular tunes instead of classical ones because you've heard them more . . . consciously or unconsciously you believe that redheads have high tempers, unless you actually know redheaded people rather well.

Race prejudices are like that too. False ideas about other races dissolve as we come to personally know fine members of that race.

Huckabay stressed developing personal relationships with people of differing backgrounds, reflecting a common theme among Baptist mission leaders.[27]

Personal relationships were one key to overcoming racism. For Baptists, another key was living according to the teachings of the Bible. A. C. Miller of the Christian Life Commission reminded Baptists about fundamental Christian truths concerning race as revealed in the Scriptures. Those truths were "that every man is embraced by the love of God, every man has value in the sight of God and every man is included in the plan of God." When the Supreme Court ruled in *Brown* that segregated schooling was unconstitutional, Miller agreed with the Court. He urged Baptists to accept the ruling as consistent with Christian teachings and to adjust their behavior accordingly. He wrote that under segregation "the colored people of our nation and of the world have come to know that our particular brand of democracy offers to them neither freedom nor social justice. The Christian way would offer both."[28]

After *Brown*, southern traditions stood against both federal law and the Christian path in race relations. Baptist leaders believed that it would take time to overcome the long-established prejudices of the South in part because many southerners continued to believe that segregation was, in fact, Christian. Baptist leaders believed it was necessary to convert southerners to a truly Christian view of race, but many Baptists in the pews, believing that individual Christians approached the Bible on their own, resisted the teachings of the Convention leadership. Nevertheless, the leaders believed that these Christians could mature in their faith and come to a truly Christian understanding of race. The law might help, but a deeper understanding of Christian principles was the only sure way to overcome racism.[29]

Progressive Baptists disapproved of the racism behind resistance to *Brown*, but that very racism validated their view that, while the law could make segregated education illegal, changes in moral convictions could only be won by redemption. In its 1947 report, the Committee on Race Relations urged the Southern Baptist Convention to take an active role in solving America's racial problems. Seminary professor J. B. Weatherspoon argued that "political action, even at its best, cannot do what must be done. Laws create a measure of restraint against injustice and mark out certain producers under sanction of government power. But we are seeing the truth today that law, even the Constitution of our Nation, cannot relax the tensions and resentments nor banish the prejudices and injustices that spring from fallacious thinking and racial feeling." Mission leaders, often optimistic, correctly anticipated the situation in the South after *Brown*. The law did not quickly change thinking, and racism persisted.[30]

Nevertheless, the *Brown* decision was a critical turning point in southern history, and it did provide progressive Baptists opportunities to promote their views. Mary Elizabeth (Mrs. Chester F.) Russell wrote for *Royal Service* in late 1954, noting that "now we are not faced with the question of whether or not racial segregation is right; or whether or not we want to allow it; but rather, how are we as Christians going to adjust to a society in which it is illegal."[31]

Adjusting to a society where segregation was illegal required awareness of the depths of prejudice in southern culture. Charles Prewitt, a student at Hardin Simmons University in Abilene, Texas, related his awakening to the depths of racial prejudice and segregation. As a child he had been playing soldier when he received a "terrific blow to the head":

> when I got to my feet and saw a colored boy bolting for Dixie, I realized what had happened. The mischievous black prankster had slipped up on my back side, raised the helmet a few inches from my head, and then let it drop. Right then I began to develop a dislike for colored people. It never became a hatred, and I would not even admit the ill feelings, but they were there.
>
> Years later I was wearing a real military uniform on a bus in San Antonio. A Negro friend of mine got on the bus. I was glad to see him and greeted him cheerfully. He returned the greeting, and it was evident that he was glad to see me too. I moved over to let him sit down. His dark eyes met mine. He forced a smile. He passed on by.
>
> Another blow. Another state of confusion. Another realization. This blow was echoed by the familiar sign at the front of the bus which

read, "Front Seats Reserved for White Patrons." The confusion was an attempt to justify such discrimination. The realization was that my prejudice had been conquered by love.

Prewitt found his prejudices challenged on a segregated bus, but many southerners continued to justify, at least in their own minds, racial discrimination. Christian love had a long way to go in conquering racism, but just two months after Prewitt's account appeared in *Home Missions*, the Montgomery bus boycott began, forcing the issue of segregated seating on buses into the national limelight, though the Baptist press said little about it.[32]

Mission leaders believed that racial prejudices were learned, much as Prewitt had learned his prejudices while playing as a young boy. Therefore, eliminating racism involved teaching children to have Christian attitudes regarding race. If that were done successfully, the problem could be solved, at least for future generations. Progressive Baptists believed that children were never too young to begin learning Christian attitudes and sought to teach about missions and race in the Sunbeam Bands. The Sunbeam Band program was designed for young children and generally involved teaching Bible stories or telling the stories of famous missionaries. In the early 1960s, over 310,000 children participated in nearly 28,000 Sunbeam Bands.[33]

Local Sunbeam Band leaders found program materials for the meetings in *Royal Service*. Ruth LaTuille Matthews, who wrote many of those programs in the early postwar years, reported being asked, "Why bother to teach correct racial attitudes to our little children? If grown-ups have trouble trying to untangle world problems today, we can't expect infant minds to cope with them." Such attitudes deeply bothered Matthews, who had begun writing the Sunbeam program material with the explicit intent of helping mothers teach their young children Christian attitudes about race. She refuted the question, saying, "If this is our idea, we are passing up golden opportunities. Between the ages of two and five, a child learns not only his own place in the family but also in the neighborhood. More and more, we adults have come to regard the world as a community of neighboring peoples and cultures. We should want our tiny tots to respect the entire family of man."[34] Children learned not only from what adults told them but from watching what adults did as well. Therefore, parents "must be certain that our own racial conceptions are wholesome and free of prejudice." Matthews argued that "much more eloquent than the actual words we use are our attitudes, revealed in our emotional language—in tone of voice or shrug of shoulders. Even a pre-school youngster notices our consideration—or lack of it—in dealing with the yard man, delicatessen owner, sharecropper, or delivery boy who happens to come from another racial background."[35]

Although Matthews was not a lone voice in 1948, she clearly urged parents to teach their children a view of race that conflicted with the segregated world around them. The Sunbeam Band, however, had a positive influence on at least some of the children who were enrolled. The Woman's Missionary Union offered readers of *Royal Service* examples of the organization's influence. Jane Winchester Martin, a missionary serving with her husband in Tanganyika, wrote, "At five years of age I became active in Sunbeams. I attribute an early awareness of missions [and] of God's love for all people to the influences of this organization." Likewise, Mrs. Steve Ditmore told the Woman's Missionary Union that her "dream to be a missionary started when I was a Sunbeam and grew when I became a GA [Girls' Auxiliary]." She realized her dream in 1965.[36]

While the Baptist leaders, through the Sunbeam Band, Royal Ambassadors, and Girls' and Young Woman's Auxiliaries, strove to teach children Christian attitudes regarding race, other organizations offered quite different messages. Competing visions of America reverberated throughout the postwar era. In her "Reflections" for *Royal Service*, Lucy Grace wrote that "one newspaper recently showed a little girl in Klan hood and cape; all the regalia but the mask and the cross were reflected in the dress of the child." Grace asked, though she hardly needed to, "What went into her heart and mind?" When the Ku Klux Klan met in Macon, Georgia, in December of 1948, the Grand Dragon had announced that the Klan was the world's greatest Christian organization. Grace disagreed: "how can intolerance reflect the spirit of Calvary? How can superiority find room at the cross? Has this order . . . any right to call itself Christian?" The Klan rally also provided an opportunity for Baptists to act. Roughly forty students from Mercer University, the flagship educational institution of the Georgia Baptist Convention, "stood on the auditorium steps for the hour and a half in 'silent protest.'" Quiet as the protest may have been, it can hardly be said to have been "silent."[37]

Martha Anne Oakley was one of the Mercer students who protested the Klan. She noted a series of Klan acts, including the burning of a cross—"a well known symbol, especially in the South, of prejudice and terror"—at an unnamed college president's home. When the newspapers announced that the Klan would meet in Macon to initiate new members, Oakley wondered, "What would we do? Would the Mercer University students protest? Or would we join the hosts of others—fearful of this repulsive and malignant growth in our midst—yet unwilling to become personally and publicly identified with the opposition. . . . These students felt that something must be done. There must be no violence, but at least a silent protest must be made in the name of Christian young people who must face the issues of both today and tomorrow." The students carried signs that read "I am here in protest against the Klan and all its principles." Several students told Oakley their reasons for joining the protest, including Bette Ann Kimmel. Kimmel said her "personal experience at the hands of the Ku Klux has taught me just what such ideology must inevitably lead to—terrorism and fear." Another student, Miriam Thurman, turned the claims of the Klan against it. She protested the Klan for two reason: "First, I am a Christian. Second, I am an American. Therefore, I cannot believe in the principles of the Ku Klux Klan."[38]

Baptist leaders believed, clearly, that no one was too young to learn racial tolerance, or intolerance. For children to learn the Christian view of race they had to be taught early and consistently. That required that they be reared in a Christian home. Marie (Mrs. A. L.) Aulick wrote, "The influence of the church is profound, but, at best, worship periods and definite religious instruction given by the church can be only a few hours a week while the influence of the home is present day and night."[39]

The Christian home was not only necessary for a Christian society—it was itself a missionary enterprise. Mary Dobbins wrote for the *Window* that "not only do Christian homes affect the children raised in them, but they can also have a good influence on any neighborhood or community." Any threat to Christian homes would threaten to unravel the very fabric of a Christian society.[40]

Baptists feared that the materialism and corruption of the postwar world threatened to destroy Christian homes. H. Cornell Goerner told Baptist boys that "the shortage of homes is more serious than the shortage of houses, because history proves that the breakdown of home life results in the downfall of a nation." Jewel Chancy (Mrs. Noble Y.) Beall argued that "the home, the most basic of human institutions, is being battered from all sides." Kyle Yates agreed, writing "no other basic relationship in society has been so undermined by modern life. The front page of almost every daily newspaper carries some tragic story of weak and broken homes." Helen Fling, who became president of the Woman's Missionary Union in 1963, wrote that the home was the "soul" of a society, and America's soul was sick. She cited broken marriages, juvenile delinquency, and illegitimate births as evidence that the home was disintegrating.[41]

Some progressive Baptists, like Katharine Parker Freeman, tied the ideal of the Christian home directly to racism. Freeman suggested that prejudices blinded Baptists to the reality around them. She scolded Baptist women, writing, "We think nothing of the disruption of family as when the Negro mother has to go out to work leaving home early and going back late." The reason was simple. Whites employed a double standard. Freeman wrote, "We have one set of standards for our homes and families and another for other races." She related another story to demonstrate her point: "a white woman told a group of friends that she had tried to get a girl from a Negro college to be a baby sitter. The dean refused to let a student go alone on the streets late at night. The white group listening was hilarious at the thought of a Negro girl needing a chaperone or escort for safety." Freeman took exception. She told Baptist women, "Prejudice, ignorance, and inconsistency contrast with Christian maturity."[42]

In the wake of *Brown*, mission leaders urged Baptists to teach their children to accept integration. Mary Elizabeth (Mrs. Chester F.) Russell realized that there would be considerable resistance to integration. She warned Baptists to "steel themselves against the swelling tide of emotional propaganda which will sweep our nation in the wake of the decision by the Supreme Court." Importantly, children had to be taught lessons very different from the messages of racist propaganda. Russell concluded, "We must begin now to condition our children to this new situation. They will need to understand the immensity of the events taking place and the Christian approach to these to be able to make the necessary adjustments in school, on the playgrounds, on the streets and in public places. . . . We have taught our children to love the Negroes in Africa. Now is the time to be specific and teach them to love the Negroes around them."[43]

For parents who wanted to teach racial tolerance, opportunities to do so presented themselves in a myriad of unexpected situations. Zenona (Mrs. Douglas) Harris remembered her family's drive through a "drab section of a Tennessee city," when her son asked, "Daddy, why do brown people have to live in old broken-down houses like these?" While trying to answer their son's question, her husband was "startled into consciousness of his surroundings." Perhaps the parents, jaded by having always lived in a segregated society, learned more from the incident than their son. But their son had learned other lessons in the racist South. Harris noted that a few days after the incident she heard her son tell a playmate, "Get out of my way, niggah." She claimed that he had never heard such an expression at home. He must, therefore, have learned it somewhere else. Clearly, parents had to do everything they could to confront such outside influences. They had to teach their children Christian attitudes about race, and they had to work for racial change in the community.[44]

Parents could teach Christian attitudes by being living examples of Christian teachings. They could also provide positive contacts across racial lines that would teach children to be tolerant in their racial views. Among the children most likely to have such contacts were the missionary kids. One missionary, James E. Hampton, wrote from Tanganyika. There, his two children were "just as happy playing with the little girl who stays with this couple [grounds keepers at the mission] as if her skin were white." Linking materialism and racism, he added, "There seems to be no racial prejudices among children unless their minds have been warped by the greed and selfishness of unthinking adults."[45]

Positive interracial experiences were available to any Baptists who sought them, not just missionaries. H. Cornell Goerner realized that few Baptist youths could afford to attend the Baptist Youth Congress in Stockholm, Sweden, in 1949, but reminded them that the next year it would be in Cleveland, Ohio. Meanwhile, Goerner suggested studying a foreign language, making pen pals from around the country and the world, and going on a tour of home missions or, if possible, foreign missions. Fifteen years after Goerner wrote, one couple in Alamosa, Colorado, found ways to expand their child's horizons without having to leave their remote Rocky Mountain home. Foreign students from the nearby college visited the Hamilton home beginning around the time Layne was seven. Her mother wrote to *Royal Service* that Layne was "a world citizen." Her only prejudice was against people who were prejudiced.[46]

Older youths could gain firsthand experience working with minority groups through Convention agencies. Many became student summer missionaries. For some of these students, the summer experience was their first real opportunity to know people from different backgrounds. These experiences challenged students to confront prejudices they had learned at home, at school, or from the community at large. One student missionary wrote, "At home the Negro residential and business areas were to be avoided, to be ignored, actually. I didn't hate a black face or discriminate in personal association, but the deepness of an ingrown prejudice remained dormant. In this [summer mission] experience of confrontation it has come alive forcing me to evaluate, analyze, and objectively to decide what Christ would have me do in this area of my thinking."[47]

Fred B. Moseley, the Home Mission Board's assistant executive secretary-treasurer, believed that the students' experiences changed them as individuals. Baptist missionaries believed that the only way to change society was by changing individuals, leading Moseley to conclude that the summer experience influenced campuses and churches because the returning students would necessarily affect their environments. Campuses were particularly important because Baptist colleges were the training grounds for future missionaries and ministers.[48]

Many young Baptists found ways to "pioneer" even though the Home Mission Board could appoint only a limited number of student summer missionaries. In 1949, young women in Booneville, Mississippi, helped start a Young Woman's Auxiliary at a black church and participated in various joint programs. That same year, Baptist young men did much the same in Sinton, Texas, where they helped create a Royal Ambassador chapter at a local black church. Three years later, in Houston, youth at First Baptist operated a Vacation Bible School for black children. The pastor, W. Boyd Hunt, wrote to *Home Missions* saying that it "was the greatest experience of their lives." The effort in Houston grew, Hunt wrote, from the realization that "underprivileged groups to whom we send missionaries across oceans are represented right in our own communities." The Baptist youths who initiated and participated in such projects understood their own personal responsibility for improving race relations. They also reflected the internationalism and the belief in the unity of humanity that were mainstays of progressive Baptist thought. They worked within well-defined parameters, to be sure, but their efforts demonstrated that at least some youth took to heart the mission leadership's insistence that Baptists act. The youths also gained positive firsthand experiences—for some apparently "the greatest of their lives"—with members of a different race.[49]

Mission leaders believed that Baptists, individually and collectively, were particularly accountable for America's situation. Acting editor of *The Commission* Eugene L. Hill reminded Baptists that they were the largest group of Christians in the South. In 1956 Southern Baptists prepared for "World Mission Year," a year-long rededication to their already rapidly expanding foreign mission work. Hill feared, however, that "Southern Baptists face[d] a testing through which we could pass and be found wanting." The same message came from John Caylor at *Home Missions*. Since Baptists constituted the majority of the South's Christians, they had considerable responsibility for the nation's ability to see itself through the racially troubled times of the latter 1950s. In July 1956 Caylor wrote about a racial incident on a trolley car and reminded Baptists that "the Christian point of view would lead all of us to examine ourselves and each of us to tell himself what is Christian in race relations." Two years after *Brown* and in the middle of the Montgomery bus boycott, Caylor called only for Christian decorum in race relations. His article hardly amounted to a significant attack on segregated public transportation, nor did he mention the Montgomery bus boycott. Perhaps the reserved nature of the article was an attempt to avoid offending a significant portion of *Home Missions*'s readership by providing them with a request to which they could likely agree.[50]

Even among progressive Southern Baptists, some ambivalence about integration persisted throughout the late 1950s, even after *Brown* and the early civil rights movement had made it clear that segregation's days were limited. In 1957, Mildred Dodson (Mrs. William) McMurry, who wrote mission study guides for the Woman's Missionary Union, outlined a program of action for southern communities. She recommended a service project in cooperation with black community leaders that would ask such questions as "are Negro schools adequate? Are there playground facilities for Negro children?" While McMurry recommended a program to create community interest in public facilities for blacks, she did not call for integrated facilities. McMurry's ambivalence was not an outright defense of segregation, but it was hardly an attack on the institution. She may have been personally ambivalent in 1957, or she may have considered a direct assault on segregation quixotic.[51]

Not all leaders were ambivalent. Hugh Brimm, a professor at the Southern Baptist Seminary in Louisville, Kentucky, attacked segregation directly in "What's Wrong with Racial Segregation?" Brimm argued, "Now a new day is dawning. A concept once held by most white Southerners as being right beyond any question has been declared to be illegal. *Segregation is now a violation of the Constitution of the United States* according to the highest legal authority in the land—the Supreme Court" (italics in original). According to Brimm, segregation was wrong because it was "based upon the false assumption that some people, by nature, are inherently inferior, while others are inherently superior." It was also wrong because it humiliated people who were already oppressed and exploited. Further, it denied people opportunities based solely on the color of their skin. Brimm attacked biblical segregationists, saying: "if any who hold to segregation as a principle want to find the 'greatest' and 'most eloquent' justification for it, they should turn to the book *Mein Kampf* by Adolf Hitler, the madman who plunged the world into World War II."[52]

Christians had to reject the institution on a spiritual rather than legal basis. Brimm told Baptist young women that all "men" were created by God and endowed with basic human rights and created by God in God's image. To allow segregation was unchristian because, in effect, "it says to God 'No, God, you have done wrong in the whole plan and purpose you have had for the world and for man. You can't create all men equal because some are inferior.'" Brimm reminded his readers that "some of us have vast changes to make in our patterns of thinking and practice with respect to the Negro in the South." He was optimistic, though perhaps too optimistic. He concluded his article by saying, "a new South is emerging, and many are ready to welcome it as a South in which the ideals of democracy and Christianity are becoming more and more a reality."[53]

Brimm's target audience was different from Caylor's and McMurry's. Brimm wrote "What's Wrong with Racial Segregation?" for the *Window*, the same journal in which Hermione Dannelly Jackson discussed missions and race in the early 1950s. The majority of the readers would be young, unmarried women. Caylor's audience, the readers of *Home*

Missions, represented more of a cross-section of Southern Baptists in both gender and age. Although *Royal Service*, where McMurry's article appeared, was directed at Baptist women, its readers were generally older than the *Window's*. One historian has suggested that Baptist men allowed women and youth more leeway in discussing racial issues. Women could be excused based on the "sensitivities of the gentler sex." Young people could be excused for the "passing and unrealistic idealism of youth." And T. B. Maston long believed that women, especially at the Woman's Missionary Union, were far in advance of men on the race issue. For G. Frank Garrison, the reason was simple: Baptist women were more informed about missions and therefore more interested in the cause of missions. Such allowances, however, undermined white supremacist beliefs in significant ways. But this is not the entire story.[54]

Male Baptist leaders wrote in all Baptist journals. They promoted progressive views of race in *The Commission* and *Home Missions*, both of which targeted all Southern Baptists, including adult males. Furthermore, Baptist leaders, including Maston, wrote for the *Southern Baptist Brotherhood Quarterly*, which targeted adult men almost exclusively. True, the writings on race were less frequent and less emphatic in that publication, but when articles appeared in it, they echoed the progressive view of other Southern Baptist publications. Moreover, some Southern Baptist men complained that publications for men's classes at Sunday Schools shied away from the race issue. One, John P. Davies of Alexandria, Virginia, wrote Clifton J. Allen at the Sunday School Board in the spring of 1958 with just such a critique. He told Allen, "Fifty years ago that might have been excusable, but now with so much turmoil here and all over the world Christian people must study the question and seek a Christian solution." Two years earlier Allen had written to Maston that the Sunday School Board sought only to "appeal for a Christian spirit" within its publications because more forceful statements would serve to increase tensions within the Convention. He lamented that "there are many areas in which it is next to impossible for anything like a Christian viewpoint to gain acceptance. I think we need to be very careful and considerate of our fellow Christians in those areas." While Allen could be accused of abandoning the role of prophet, he clearly believed it was important not to antagonize his readership. Davies's comments suggest, however, that some Baptist men were eager for more progressive guidance on the race issue and were disappointed in the cautious approach of the Sunday School Board. The literature published by mission organizations was, on average, less cautious.[55]

Nevertheless, targeting youth allowed Baptist leaders to undermine the legitimacy of segregation in the minds of the younger generation. Moreover, Baptist leaders realized that the "new South" Brimm spoke of would be a very different world from the older South, even if many Baptists in the pews did not, or would not, face that fact. By making desegregation, and not segregation, "Christian," Baptist leaders helped youth adjust to the changes taking place in the South. Some Baptists clearly recognized the role of religious teaching in passing racial attitudes to the next generation. Noble Y. Beall wrote "Maintaining the Status Quo: Preserving Our Little Gods," in which he noted that "in the South, one of the most cherished and guarded little gods is the one of 'prejudice against the Negroes.' It does not matter what the occasion or issue, if the Negroes are involved, someone must see to it that the little god is well preserved. If a Christian service is being held, the little god is present, and some of his devotees will assuredly look after him. Our prejudices must be preserved and passed on to the youth." Some Baptist laity also understood the power of religious teaching in shaping the racial views of youth, even if they disagreed with the direction in which the progressive leadership was trying to take the denomination. Mrs. W. L. Mayfield of Louisville, Kentucky, wrote to Porter Routh of the Executive Committee that she did "not know a single Baptist in favor of integration, regardless of what the preachers say." She continued, "We sincerely hope our churchmen will not try to force this thing down our throats, or brainwash our young people so they will accept it in the belief that God wills it."[56]

Despite some ambivalence, writers generally supported the Supreme Court decision and called on Southern Baptists to accept desegregation. By 1963, however, much of the ambivalence had faded from the writings in *Royal Service*. Mildred Dodson McMurry, by then president of the North American Baptist Woman's Union, a confederation of women's Baptist organizations throughout the continent, abandoned her earlier ambivalence. Her stand set off a storm of protest. Her article, "Our Freedoms," appeared in June, after two solid months of protest in Birmingham, home of the Woman's Missionary Union. She offered her version of what the founding fathers meant when they wrote the Declaration of Independence and what the document meant to

Americans in the early 1960s. She noted the truths cited by the founders: that there is a God, that all men are created equal, that each person is endowed with inalienable rights, and that the role of the government is to protect those rights. Focusing on the phrase "all men are created equal," McMurry explained, "Science and the Bible are in agreement that all men have a common ancestor. The unity of the human race is declared in its anatomy, its blood, its pigmentation. There is no difference in mentality due to biological inheritance." She went on to argue that "God is not class or color conscious." She then reminded Baptists that they stood for the protection of First Amendment rights, including the freedom of speech and the separation of church and state, while they "continue[d] to ignore the 13th, 14th, and 15th Amendments which provide for the civic and social freedom of every citizen without respect 'to race, color, or previous condition of servitude.'" She referred to the *Brown* decision and told Baptists, "We all know that we can neither stop nor go back." Pointing to the responsibility of Christians, McMurry asked, "Who should be expected to take the initiative in the bringing about of racial harmony and justice? Yes, who if not Christians in their churches?" Ultimately, however, she put her hope in future generations, who might be able to "rise above the deep-seated prejudices of their elders."[57]

Soon after McMurry's piece appeared, editors at *Royal Service* began receiving letters about it. A letter signed "Mrs. O" said of the issue: "through its pages God speaks." She particularly commended McMurry's "Our Freedoms," adding, "We continue to look to WMU [Woman's Missionary Union] for leadership." "Mrs. O" was not the only person to commend the article. "LB" offered a "sincere thank you" for the article and "REF" said that the "support of the Christian's role in race relations is very heartening." "ED" was grateful to *Royal Service,* but her letter revealed a deep concern for the denomination as a whole. She lamented, "As a Southern Baptist I have deplored the fact that our churches and denomination have given so little constructive leadership in this important area of Christian concern." Here were Southern Baptists echoing the leadership's progressive position on race, the kind of Southern Baptists apparently unknown to Mrs. Mayfield of Louisville.[58]

Royal Service also received hostile responses to McMurry's "Our Freedoms." One writer, "A Member of a Circle," said she had always enjoyed *Royal Service* before the June 1963 issue. She noted: "the article by Mrs. William McMurry could certainly have been eliminated from this or any other issue." Another writer, "AS," was so disgusted that she canceled her subscription and announced that "the major portion of the Negro race would be far happier if left alone and allowed to be with their kind." Such attitudes frustrated progressive leaders' attempts to shape racial attitudes in the Convention and missed the point of the civil rights movement.[59]

Progress on both race and evangelism proceeded at a slow pace. Courts Redford, the executive secretary of the Home Mission Board, provided alarming information regarding religion in the United States. As he prepared to retire in 1965, Redford noted that 37 percent of Americans did not belong to any church, and "more than half of those who are church members have no vital relation with Christ and no part in Christian service." While Baptists had overtaken the Methodists to become the nation's largest Protestant denomination, Redford reminded readers that there were at least twenty-five thousand communities with no Baptist churches. With so many church members being something less than Christian and so many Americans not being Christian at all, the progressive Baptists' message seemed to have a frighteningly small audience.[60]

Despite the odds, Baptist mission leaders continued to have hope. Arthur B. Rutledge, who succeeded Courts Redford as executive secretary of the Home Mission Board, demonstrated the leadership's persistent faith in their vision. When President Lyndon Johnson announced his Great Society program, Rutledge applauded, calling it an "inspiring objective." Rutledge added, "Our Christian faith, however, leads to the conviction that to realize the Great Society we must build the Godly Society." Building a godly society remained the goal, and obligation, of the missionary leadership.[61]

To the dismay of mission leaders, deeply held racist attitudes proved resistant to change among professed Christians. After twenty years of promoting progressive ideas on race, mission journals continued to get letters of protest in the late 1960s. One, written in 1966 to *Home Missions* by Mrs. James T. Higgins of Jasper, Alabama, announced, "How happy I am that we still have freedom! I have no intention of integrating and have taught my children likewise. The day I *have* to, ours will no longer be a democracy" (italics in original). Her letter demonstrated that the Baptist leadership's attempt to reach children with a more progressive message on race could be blocked by unchristian attitudes and actions among parents. Higgins clearly believed that Baptist leaders were changing their views under pressure from the Supreme Court and the federal government. She wrote, "I have yet to read in God's infallible Word where Jesus imposed upon a people socially or where he tried to coerce others to be imposed upon. Jesus never urged a people to 'change with the changes' [the title of a recent article on race] but rather . . . 'be ye steadfast, unmoveable' (in your faith)." Perhaps Higgins herself added "in your faith," but it seems more likely that the editors at *Home Missions* added the phrase. Regardless, Higgins clearly intended to be immovable, but she overlooked the fact that the Baptist missionaries and leaders had been steadfast in both their faith and attitudes. They had been surprisingly consistent.[62]

At the end of the 1960s America had yet to overcome either materialism or racism. L. Dudly Wilson, pastor of Northminster Baptist in Jackson, Mississippi, noted that "constant references to 'the good life' and to materialistic values leave their mark on us." He saw conformity to America's materialistic culture as a serious problem, saying that "the moral demands of the Christian faith collide with popular attitudes and actions." He pointed directly to race relations, poverty, and war as the most serious problems facing the nation and the church and concluded that "doing the usual, following the traditional, or checking the consensus will not allow the church to meet its opportunity or carry out responsibility." His view collided not only with southern cultural norms but also with the views of Douglas Hudgins, another Jackson pastor. Hudgins, pastor of Jackson's First Baptist Church, argued that churches should focus on redemption and not become involved in social problems like segregation. While not expressly supporting segregation, such ideas allowed many Southern Baptists to be comfortable with their own views that segregation was Christian and undermined the more activist and transformative model of Christianity that progressives promoted.[63]

During the postwar boom years the progressive leadership of the Southern Baptist Convention offered a vision of America dramatically at odds with tradition. Despite the rapid growth in church membership, Baptist leaders remained dissatisfied. Americans may have been going to church, but persistent social problems, materialism, and racism showed that they were not living truly Christian lives. Southerners, and Baptists prominent among them, resisted the vision offered by the progressive leadership. Still, the leaders pushed their views, convinced that if they reached enough individuals, and especially enough of the youth, they could change the society. The process was agonizingly slow. After twenty-five years, Baptist leaders still held views at odds with those of many Baptists in the pews. Religious historian Robert Ellwood characterizes 1957 as "all deliberate speed versus Jim Crow in the pew." For Southern Baptist missionaries and leaders, often unable to move their denomination, the characterization fit the whole of the postwar era. In the late 1960s, with materialism and racism still rampant in America, Baptist leaders continued to cry out against such sins. Calling for a rededication to the church's prophetic mission, Braxton Bryant, director of the Tennessee Council on Human Relations, announced in 1968 that "the church is in great need today of a modern-day Amos."[64]

5

THE TOWER OF BABEL

Language Missions and
the Race Question

Central to progressive Southern Baptist thought on race was the idea of the unity of humanity. Racism created divisions in humanity that God had never intended, and progressives viewed issues involving racism in much the same manner regardless of which minority groups were involved. As a result, Latinos, Indians, and other minorities figured significantly in discussions about race and racism. Baptists combined their work among Latinos, Indians, immigrants, and the deaf in the Department of Language Missions. In 1945, Baptists had 136 missionaries working with 1.5 million Spanish speakers, and 83 missionaries working with 250,000 Indians. By 1969, the Home Mission Board had 969 missionaries working in the various language fields, two-thirds of them among Spanish speakers. As Baptists sent increasing numbers of missionaries into the field throughout the postwar years, missionaries and mission leaders remained consistent in their views regarding race. Their guiding principle was that, in the words of Courts Redford, executive secretary of the Home Mission Board, "Christ died for them too."[1]

Baptist leaders saw discrimination as a problem facing all ethnic minorities, including ones not typically considered a "race." Their emphasis on the unity of humanity, based in their belief that the Bible allowed for only one race, led them to write about the problems facing those minorities in much the same way they wrote about other "racial" groups. Indeed, their writings reflect a belief that "race" is a social construct. Predictably, Baptist writers conflated the ideas of "nation," "culture," and "race" throughout the postwar era.[2]

J. B. Lawrence. Photo courtesy of the Southern Baptist Historical Library and
Archives, Nashville, Tennessee.

Baptist leaders emphasized the biblical principles of equality and
unity and urged Baptists to take personal responsibility for the race
situation. The leadership believed that ignorance about ethnic groups
and about the biblical principles regarding race lay at the heart of the
race problem. Missionaries and leaders sought to teach Baptists about
the situations facing Latinos and Indians, much as they sought to teach
Baptists about blacks and Africans. They never offered a substantial
history of Latinos or Indians in America. The issues remained racism
and the unity of humanity. What progressives said about Latinos and
Indians serves to demonstrate the continuity of progressive Baptist
thought on the race issue throughout the postwar period.[3]

The United States Supreme Court added credibility to the Baptist
view with its 1954 decision in *Hernández v. The State of Texas*. The
Court determined that the exclusion of Mexican Americans from juries
violated the Constitution. The Court recognized that Mexican
Americans, like blacks, had faced a history of oppression. Mexican

Americans had been excluded from full participation in civic life and, therefore, subjected to the effects of racism even if they were not an easily defined "race." Howard G. McClain, the executive director of the Christian Action Council in South Carolina, told Baptists, "It is especially important in today's world to have respect for members of minority groups. The particular group may differ—Negro, Mexican, Japanese, and so on, but the patterns of prejudice and discrimination are very similar."[4]

T. B. Maston pointed out that the Tower of Babel explained the existence of multiple languages. Race, however, was different: "there is not the least hint that it is supposed to account for the different races." Maston also noted that Christians of all backgrounds prayed "Our Father" to the same Father. One Father meant one humanity, and there could be only one race. Maston wrote simply, "We are one big family," and noted that theologians and scientists disagreed on the origins of humanity, but they did agree on the fact of a single human ancestry.[5]

Similarly, W. O. Carver denied that God had separated the races. He maintained that, biblically, there was only one race. Still, he admitted, "However they came about, they do exist and they do create tensions," adding that "in America where many races are side by side the problem becomes problems." J. B. Lawrence of the Home Mission Board agreed that discrimination caused problems: "in the homeland we have groups from thirty-seven nationalities. Many of these people cannot speak our language. They are not wanted in our churches. They are segregated by race, tradition, and language."[6]

Baptists worked to overcome barriers of race, tradition, and language, building on efforts stretching back to the early days of the century. In New Mexico, missionaries sought to bring together the three main cultural groups of the state. Miguel A. Lopez, a New Mexico Baptist and missionary who wrote for *Ambassador Life*, explained that by bringing together Indians, Mexicans, and Anglos, missionaries in New Mexico hoped to "make our living a laboratory of race relations."[7]

When the Home Mission Board introduced its student missionaries for 1952, C. W. Stumph, a Baptist missionary in New Mexico, noted that they came from ten different "nationalities." These included "Indian, Chinese, Japanese, Mexican, Spanish, Negro, Italian, Cuban, Russian and Anglo," all of which were, at other times, referred to as races. Baptist leaders like Stumph believed that God intended people of all nationalities to live together in harmony. The people who came together for prayer and study at Inlow, New Mexico, in 1955 demonstrated such harmony. One missionary wrote that the people attending represented several "countries" including Alaska, the San Andres Islands, China, Pakistan, Brazil, Ethiopia, eight Indian tribes, Spanish—not "Spain"—Negro, and Anglo. The writer concluded, "To see them in their colorful clothes and the red, yellow, tan, black and white skin called to mind a true harmony of color."[8]

Harmony was possible because all people needed the presence of Christ in their lives. Lawrence noted, "The problems of sin and vice and ignorance [are] the same in all races, and the process of salvation [is] the same." Student summer missionaries shared his views. In 1959, Anne Garner admitted that she had to face her prejudices when she realized that she was going to spend the summer among people who were different from her, or anyone she knew. She wrote, "They were different in appearance; they thought differently; their backgrounds were different; and they spoke a different language." Still, she was bound together with them in God's plan. Despite the differences, Garner declared, "We had one thing in common that outweighed all the differences—that was a need to know Jesus Christ as Saviour."[9]

Just as all people needed to know Jesus Christ as their savior, Saxon Rowe Carver wrote, God intended all people to live "in one accord." That required mutual respect and consideration. Carver wrote, "For Christians, it means that we seek to see the divine spark in each personality, no matter how unlike our own it may be." Carver's analysis demonstrated the difficulty involved in defining races. She explained that the United States Indian Service had determined that an Indian was a person with one-quarter Indian blood, a recent revision from the one-half requirement passed in the 1930s.[10]

Carver offered a different view, arguing that social conventions defined race. She concluded: "probably the best working definition for us is this: an Indian is a person of Indian descent who continues to think of himself as an Indian and who the community thinks of as an Indian." For Saxon Rowe Carver, as for W. O. Carver and an increasing number of scientists and social scientists, race was a social construct.[11]

Southern Baptists discussed the heritage of Mexican Americans in similar terms. In 1947, Pen Lile Pittard, mission studies chair for the North Carolina Woman's Missionary Union, explained "who is the Mexican" to readers of the *Window*: "he is technically a cross between

Spanish and Indian racial stock." At the end of the 1950s, Congressman O. K. Armstrong, husband of Marjorie Moore Armstrong, offered a similar description of Mexicans to Baptist boys in the Royal Ambassadors program: "the Spanish explorers came into the country soon after Columbus discovered America, and today about sixty percent of the people are mixed white and Indian. Only about ten percent are of the white race." Thus, identifying Mexicans as a "race" had little basis in biology. The only clearly defining traits were cultural and linguistic. Yet Mexicans and Mexican Americans were a socially defined race and were subjected to racial prejudices. Those prejudices were unchristian and interfered with the Biblical mandates of unity and service to "all nations."[12]

Ignorance about minority groups was certainly pervasive, and what people did "know" was often based solely on stereotypes. In 1949, Helen Dale Armstrong, a student summer missionary from Mississippi, pointed out that the Indians were "almost a forgotten people—certainly a neglected one." One Baptist minister frankly admitted, "I had forgotten that there is a tribe of Choctaw Indians in Mississippi." Years later, in 1962, Southern Baptists argued that "few Americans realize that there are still Indians—almost 500 years after Christopher Columbus—in every one of the nation's 50 states." Roughly one-tenth of those Indians were in the Southeast, the Baptist heartland, though few Baptist missions to the Indians were actually in the Southeast.[13]

Latinos and migrant farmers were also a forgotten people. Indeed, the Home Mission Board did not begin working with migrant farmers until after World War II. James P. Wesberry, a prominent Atlanta pastor, chaired the committee that investigated the work and found the migrants' situation to be desperate. The committee recommended starting a mission program among the migrants immediately. The board employed Rev. and Mrs. Sam Mayo to minister to the migrants. After ten years in the field, Hazel Hunt (Mrs. Sam) Mayo wrote of the couple's work, recalling one man who told her, "I never saw the migrants until you came here." She wondered how anyone could have missed them. Upon pressing the man, he admitted: "oh, you know what I mean. . . . Of course, I knew they were there. Our newspaper announced their coming, but I never realized before that they were people, too" (ellipsis points in original).[14]

Even well-meaning Baptists had impressions based on stereotypes that served to reinforce prejudices rather than overcome them. This became particularly apparent to one student summer missionary, who wrote, "When I started out here in June, I must admit that my conception of Indians was far wrong. After working with them these ten weeks, I realized that they are not wild and un-civilized, as we in the East so often think of them." One reason for such misunderstandings was that many Americans got their information about minorities from less than reliable sources. Mrs. Ralph Gwin of the Woman's Missionary Union noted that American Indians were the subject of novels and movies that left them virtually unrecognizable as human beings. Baptist leaders recognized that Hollywood's depictions were often grossly inaccurate. Readers of *Home Missions* learned that "the irony is in the fact that Anglo Americans, who applaud the quiet strength and patience of the Indian, think of him as the cinematized redskin who brutalized the West with aggressive terror, thwarting the peaceful aims of a white man fulfilling his coast-to-coast manifest destiny." Such images could lead to hostility. American Indian Movement activist Russell Means remembered that movies often inspired whites to violence, and white children would attack him and his brother as they left the theater after a Western. Because of Hollywood, Baptists believed that Indians were "probably the least understood and most misunderstood Americans of us all."[15]

Baptist leaders worked consistently to provide different information about Indians to their congregations. At the Glorieta Baptist Center in New Mexico—which attracted Baptists from throughout the South for retreats—sessions frequently focused on the problems facing the Indians. While Baptists offered a vision of American Indians vastly different from the one offered by Hollywood, they stressed the need for Indians to convert to Christianity and to abandon their "pagan" traditions. In America, as in Africa, the missionary message was laced with cultural imperialism. Still, they did call for fair treatment for all minorities, Indians among them.[16]

Indians had rarely been treated as Americans ought to be treated. Baptists noted that "the history of our government's relationship with these people who are in fact the original Americans has not always reflected credit to the high ethical standards we ascribe to our country." As one North Carolina Cherokee, Robert Bushyhead, pointed out, "Treaty after treaty has been made and broken with us. We have crawled along in progress, but never have been allowed really to walk. Each time we get to the walking stage, the white man clips our strength."[17]

The Citizenship Act of 1924 changed the legal status of Indians in

America by making them all United States citizens. Still, some states denied Indians the vote until 1948, when three Navajo Indians won their lawsuit against New Mexico. New Mexican authorities had argued that Indians, and the Navajo specifically, were not residents of the state since all reservation lands had been ceded to the United States. J. B. Rounds pointed to Navajo service in World War II and said, "Why call on Indians for services required only of citizens, if they are not citizens?" The Navajo made up a significant portion of the nearly twenty-five thousand Indians who served in World War II. Furthermore, to New Mexico's claims that Indians were only United States citizens and not New Mexicans, he retorted, "New Mexico reaps large financial returns from Indians as show people, and if the Indian is denied state privileges, the financial profits accruing therefrom should be awarded to federal, rather than state treasuries." Even Rounds did not consider the possibility that, perhaps, that money ought to go to the Indians themselves.[18]

The vote was not the only civil right Native Americans were denied. Baptists also cited the lack of constitutional protections for religious freedom on Indian reservations. In 1951 C. W. Stumph wondered why the First Amendment was "only a farce in New Mexico." The main question was the freedom of religion, but Stumph was adamant that New Mexico's Indians should insist on all of their First Amendment rights. President Truman's Civil Rights Commission disappointed him. Stumph said the commission "either ignored or white-washed" the problems facing Indians and noted that Americans had no idea, or refused to believe, that religious persecution was happening in the United States.[19]

Baptist missionaries believed that reservation governments resisted the "Jesus way" because they, like many Africans, viewed it as the white man's way. Indians who became Christians were persecuted without the First Amendment protections that most Americans had. One case involved the Hererra family from the Zia Pueblo in New Mexico. The Zia Pueblo had begun expelling Christian Indians in 1932. In 1939, Viviano Hererra, lieutenant governor of the Pueblo, "took a firm stand for Christ." He was banished from the reservation on March 31, 1940. Hererra took his case to federal court in 1948, arguing he had been unlawfully denied his rights. Several missionaries attended the trial in Santa Fe where Hererra "avowed his faith in Jesus Christ, in contrast to idol worship." The trial judge, however, dismissed the case "without prejudice" for lack of jurisdiction. The Zia Pueblo leaders then banished several people. C. W. Stumph reported that "it was a case of 'choose ye this day whom ye will serve.'" He noted that the Christian Indians "chose Jesus, 'choosing to suffer affliction with the people of God, rather than to enjoy the pleasure of sin for a season.'"[20]

Christian Indians faced prejudices even when they did not face official persecution. Eva Inlow, secretary of the Woman's Missionary Union in New Mexico, reported that a Christian Indian named Rolling Cloud faced only increased troubles in his life after his conversion: "To his associates in the theater he became a 'crazy Indian.' His white employers were angry and scornful, worried that his conversion might jeopardize their profits. His Indian friends and relatives had no respect for this one who had forsaken his tribal ways. Some whites doubted Rolling Cloud's ability to withstand the pressure, saying: 'let's just wait and see,' or he's just an Indian. He won't hold out. His people won't let him." Rolling Cloud, however, held out. Eventually some white people began to help him and pray for him. Though Inlow never explained exactly how his conversion might damage the show's profits—perhaps the show manager was worried that Rolling Cloud would cease performing after he converted or cause disruptions by trying to convert other performers—she implied that the employers were more interested in their own profits than in Rolling Cloud's well being, and that they considered the spread of Christianity to Indians a threat to their profits. She offered an example of how white greed—that cardinal American sin of materialism—damaged missions in America by making the conversion to Christianity unnecessarily difficult. Alcohol provided yet another example.[21]

Alcoholism complicated the situation facing Indians. Baptists had protested when New Mexico put the question of liquor sales to Indians on the ballot in 1951. They also protested when it became legal under federal law to sell alcohol on Indian reservations in 1953. Baptists had reported that a large majority of Indians opposed liquor sales, even as the Indian Congress at Phoenix wanted the repeal of the "antiquated" law prohibiting the sale of alcohol on reservations. Doris Roebuck, a missionary in Bernalillo, New Mexico, told Baptists that missionaries were "ashamed that the white man has taught the Indian to drink, and continues to work to keep him drinking." In the missionaries' view, whites who bootlegged alcohol to Indians needed Christ as much as the Indians themselves did. Gilbert Sears, a summer missionary from Murray State

College in Kentucky, noted that "a large portion of the meager income is spent in liquor stores and taverns, owned by greedy and godless white men." Clearly, alcoholism was tied to the materialism and ungodliness of American culture.[22]

C. W. Stumph, who opposed the repeal of laws prohibiting the sale of alcohol to Indians, addressed the accusation that the laws were discriminatory, writing, "The plea that Indians are citizens and that we should not discriminate against them, is simply playing into the hands of the liquor industry. We are not convinced that those who are advocating liquor for Indians are much interested in the Indian and anti-discrimination, as they are in their getting elected to office, or in the liquor industry. Otherwise they would include some of the other . . . discrimination in their plans." Stumph also pointed to plural common-law marriage, immunity from state law while on reservations, and discrimination in education as evidence that it was greed, not concern, that promoted ending the liquor prohibition. Stumph's position was, in some ways, self-contradictory. He argued against special laws for New Mexico's Indian tribes, except in the case of alcohol sales. He claimed to look at the motivation behind the efforts to repeal the anti-liquor laws, where he saw only greed. He noted that if the supporters of repeal really wanted full citizenship rights for the Indians, they would address other issues as well. He was probably right. However, he too favored selective discrimination by wanting other laws changed to allow Indians fuller citizenship while retaining the prohibition on liquor sales.[23]

Baptist missionaries believed that alcoholism undermined the family, the cornerstone of a Christian society. Gilbert Sears wrote, "As a result of the alcoholism among the men and women, children are neglected, poorly clothed, and undernourished." Baptists insisted that alcoholism, and the disintegration of home life that went with it, led to a dramatic increase in juvenile delinquency. Even children were becoming alcoholics. In the Baptist worldview, young women represented the future of a society since they would be the next generation's mothers. Mrs. E. C. Branch noted that among the Apache of Arizona, "thirteen- and fourteen-year-old-girls are being sent to a delinquent home for habitual drunkenness." Future generations could hardly hope for advancement if future mothers were alcoholics.[24]

Christian Indians, at least according to Mrs. Russell Bowren, were less likely to drink. A "Christian doctor from Santa Fe" spoke to a group of Baptist Indians and concluded, "The best way to help a person stop drinking is to win him to the Lord. When he has a new heart, old desires will pass away." For Michael Naranjo, conversion led to overcoming drinking and gambling. After becoming a Baptist minister in 1950, Naranjo remembered, "I used to drink and gamble I am so ashamed [sic]. But I am not ashamed of the gospel of Christ; for it is the power of God unto salvation to everyone that believeth." Baptists, however, had much work to do. As alcoholism brought the "degradation of a wonderful people," Sears wrote that the "first Americans" were being destroyed and "few of their conquerors care enough even to learn of their problems."[25]

Many of the conquerors, or at least their descendents, believed that Indians were some sort of archeological relics rather than people. Baptist missionaries confronted the belief that, as they phrased it, "the Indian belongs to the land. He is happy and useful only when he remains there. To uproot him is to destroy him. . . . Let the Indian be the Indian—a beautiful, childlike specimen of humanity which is practically extinct." Marjorie Moore Armstrong countered, "Is not this a violation of both the Christian principle of the supreme value of human personality, and the democratic principle of 'life, liberty, and the pursuit of happiness'?" She believed, instead, that Americans should "let the Indian be a full-fledged American, receiving the full benefits of citizenship and contributing his resources and skills where needed." By 1956, she saw the "old paternalism" as outdated and insulting.[26]

Armstrong apparently agreed with the principles behind the Eisenhower administration's policies as set forth in 1953. Those policies, often collectively called Termination, transferred jurisdiction for criminal and civil suits involving Indians from federal to state courts and declared that the special relationship between the Indian tribes and the federal government should come to an end "as soon as possible." Armstrong noted that Indians were becoming educated, acquiring jobs, and striving for adequate living. Her husband, Congressman O. K. Armstrong, believed that the Eisenhower policy would offer the Indians freedom and would lead to their integration into American society. Some Indians, like Russell Means, had quite different views of policies supposedly designed to help them integrate into American society. He believed instead that the government hoped Indians would merely disappear into a permanent underclass.[27]

Nevertheless, the Armstrongs' ideas were in keeping with progressive Baptist thinking on race. As with First Amendment issues regarding religious freedom, Baptists generally saw the rights of individual Indians as taking precedence over tribal rights. Progressive Baptists had, by 1956, abandoned the idea that segregation and equality were compatible in the case of blacks. Their vision of a single humanity meant that segregation and equality must therefore be incompatible for any group, and they related the reservation system to segregation.[28]

The effects of Indian Termination, however, were not so simple. The relationship between the government and the Indians certainly needed to be rethought in the 1950s. Paternalism angered Indians as much as anyone, and it was certainly outdated. Many Indians, however, saw Termination as forced assimilation. They were not of a mind to give up their culture. Further, the government's promised efforts in job training and placement did not do much to keep Indians, including many veterans, out of poverty. Finally, in 1958, the Eisenhower administration allowed tribes to choose Termination if they wished but no longer forced it upon unwilling tribes.[29]

Indians who resisted the "Jesus way" often saw it as the "white man's way" and associated it with white racism and assimilation. A. C. Miller, secretary of the Christian Life Commission, noted that "another door of opportunity is closed to our missionaries among the Indians because of our American brand of racism." He explained, "The Indians of America have had to endure much oppression because of the white man's general belief that racial advantage brings racial supremacy."[30]

The Navajo were among those who resisted the "Jesus way" because of its association with white Americans. Navajo elders warned the tribe's youth to "learn the white man's ways, but don't take his religion." Many of the elders believed that accepting Christianity would cause the next generation to abandon traditional Navajo practices and customs. Southern Baptists, whether in Africa or in America, realized they had to sever Christianity from the oppressive and racist legacy of white domination if they were to spread the Gospel among the "natives." And yet Baptist missionaries did insist that "pagan" practices, no matter how meaningful to a culture, had to be abandoned. While Baptists promoted Christianity for all Americans, most white Americans would not face such a loss of their cultural heritage in becoming Baptist.[31]

The evangelism of Latinos foundered on cultural differences as well.

To many Southern Baptists, Catholicism was practically "pagan" and a menace nearly as bad as communism. Indeed, W. O. Carver commented that both Catholicism and communism sought "the mastery of the minds of domination of the social orders of humanity." Other cultural differences and the language barrier also hindered evangelical efforts. Although language barriers stalled their work, Baptists believed prejudices were far more damaging. People could learn languages if they tried. By pointing to prejudice, however, progressive Baptists pointed at white America. Racists found fault with minority groups, believing that they, for one reason or another, were unfit for first-class citizenship. Baptist missionaries, however, blamed the problems of racism and discrimination on unchristian attitudes about race. In other words, they blamed the racists.[32]

Mission leaders believed that some Baptists held prejudices of which they were unaware. Raul Solis, a Mexican American pastor in Texas, noted, "I do not hold any grudge or hate against the discriminators. I know that they do not know what they do." T. B. Maston instructed Baptists that they needed to face their prejudices. Immediately after World War II he wrote, "One of the first steps in reducing racial tensions is for us to realize that we have some racial prejudices." A person could be prejudiced against one group but not another. Still, "we may differ in the subject of our prejudices but we have them, unless we are very, very rare individuals."[33]

Despite Baptist efforts, Anglo prejudice against minorities continued to damage mission efforts throughout the period. In 1953, Raul Solis wrote, "I stand against the sin of racial discrimination not only because I am a Latin-American, but also because it hinders the ministry." Progress was slow. Over a decade later, Helen E. Falls cited bigotry as a barrier to witnessing: "a barrier to effective communication with someone of another language is prejudice. It is expressed in many ways. Perhaps the most evident is attitude. Sometimes English-speaking people feel superior to anyone who is different and who does not speak the language. Prejudice closes doors to effective witnessing. A YWA [Young Woman's Auxiliary] member must recognize and seek to remove her prejudices before she can see the opportunities for witnessing to language groups and respond to them." Falls believed that one way to overcome prejudice was through personal contact with minorities. She reflected one of the constant themes of postwar Baptist thought, the idea that personal contact would help people overcome their fear and prejudices toward different people, including Mexicans, migrants, Indians, blacks, immigrants, and people in foreign lands. Falls told Baptist young women, "When you meet these persons socially, cultivate their friendship." To do that, she reminded readers, they had to learn about and respect the customs and religion of their new friends.[34]

In order to encourage Baptists to make friendships across racial or ethnic barriers, home missionaries, much like their counterparts in Africa, stressed the similarities of people of different backgrounds. William Russell of La Vida Baptist Chapel in Redlands, California, wrote that the Mexican children at the chapel were "as American as the children of any average Southern Baptist family." Southern Baptists also argued that the children of migrant farmers had essentially the same hopes and dreams as other children in America. Young women in the auxiliary studied the problem, using materials published in the *Window*, including a dialogue created by Jacqueline Durham. In that dialogue, the character of Maria, a seventeen-year-old migrant, says, "I have the same dreams that other girls have—of school, of a job, and someday a home with a husband and children." The difference, however, lay in the reality of the dream. Maria's character continues, "but for me, that's like wishing for the moon."[35]

C. W. Stumph made a similar point regarding Indians: "our white friends might not realize that Indian boys and girls are just 'boys and girls' like others are the world over." Whites would realize this if they got to know members of various minority groups personally. Edith Marie (Mrs. Ned P.) King, who wrote the program for the Woman's Missionary Union in January 1961, offered direct advice on befriending Indians. King told Baptist women that "Indian children are as bright as copper pennies" and suggested that they invite Indian children to the zoo or on picnics with their own children. She concluded, "It will thrill all concerned," but, most important, it would help children learn tolerance instead of prejudice. King's suggestions were certainly tinged with paternalism and reflected a belief that Indians ought to be assimilated into the mainstream of American society. Still, despite such shortcomings, her main motive was to help children overcome their prejudices and learn tolerance.[36]

Baptists believed that personal relationships across ethnic barriers would do much to overcome the ignorance that was at the heart of prejudice. Pen Lile Pittard wrote, "Many people consider [the Mexican] sad, lazy, dirty, and no good, but if you will know him you will find that he is not always somber by any means." Like most of the Baptist leadership, Pittard believed that the root of intolerance was lack of understanding. She admitted the Mexican was "hard to assimilate into society because of his language, culture, religion, color, and our intolerable [sic] narrow prejudice." Pittard added, "It is hard to win Mexicans to Christianity when Christian Americans are so superior and unchristian in their attitudes toward them. It is also hard for Christians to work among them when they realize that many of the Mexicans resent them because of unchristian attitudes of others who are not trying to win them to Christ." Pittard, like many progressive Baptist leaders, never questioned assimilation itself, or her underlying assumptions regarding assimilation's benefits. Thus progressive leaders like Pittard overlooked these issues and focused on white American ignorance of minorities, which progressive Baptists saw as the primary cause of the racist beliefs that prevented minorities from fully participating in American society.[37]

To learn about minorities, missionaries and leaders encouraged Baptists to study missions and the needs of minority people. They believed that such a study would lead to increased awareness and, therefore, understanding and tolerance of minorities. Edith Stokely, who had directed the Primary Club at the Mexican Good Will Center in Dallas before becoming the Community Missions director for the Woman's Missionary Union, wrote, "After studying the Home Mission Series, your women and young people should be interested in personally ministering to those of other nationalities who live among them."[38]

In Georgia, Terrell Smith of Cordele acted. Smith, a Royal Ambassador, organized his project for promotion to Ambassador Extraordinary by working with the migrant workers in the area and showing them the "true plan of salvation." Though his views were laced with paternalism, Smith's efforts demonstrated that some Baptists took seriously their personal responsibility and believed that evangelism held the key to solving racial problems through the promotion of Christian attitudes about race. Baptists continued to place their faith in personal interactions across ethnic barriers as a way of overcoming ignorance about different peoples, despite the limitations of such a solution to racism.[39]

Racism prevented Anglos from considering Mexican Americans, Indians, and other minorities their social equals. Racism proved a barrier even when whites were "friendly." According to Maurice Norton, pastor of First Baptist in San Francisco, California, "the member of a language group must be introduced to the church as a friend of equal level, and a person of equal social acceptability." However, focusing on personal friendship obscured structural problems in race relationships that often contributed to the lack of understanding at both personal and broader cultural levels. Civil rights leaders have frequently pointed to skewed or insignificant treatment of minorities in history classes as contributing to misunderstandings and thereby preventing whites from seeing minorities as equals.[40]

The Baptists' belief that ignorance lies at the heart of prejudices led them in 1963 to establish the last week of August as "Language Missions Week." They hoped to encourage churches to hold special services for language minorities in their communities. More important, they hoped that people would get to know their foreign neighbors on a personal level. Margaret Bruce, the Young People's Secretary at the Woman's Missionary Union, wrote, "Families will be asked to invite them [foreign language speakers] into their homes to get acquainted on a social level." Baptist leaders hoped women would continue to work in missions throughout the year, not for just one week, and would recognize their responsibility for breaking down barriers of race, language, and class.[41]

Personal contact could not always overcome social barriers. A young woman, identified only as "a student," wrote the *Window* about Pepe Ramirez, a Mexican American. Ramirez attended the youth functions at the local Baptist church and excelled in sports at school, but that did not win him social equality. The student noted that Ramirez began to feel uncomfortable with the church youths as they grew older and the social and economic distances grew more acute. The student wrote, "Pepe became infatuated with several blond girls at church. They were always kind, willing to be friends, but unable to become romantically involved with a Mexican who, though accepted at church, would never be accepted in their secular social groups. One girl did accept his invitation to a movie, but her parents objected — understandably, perhaps." As a result, Ramirez attended church less frequently. The student told other Baptist young women, "Christ's church should be overjoyed to accept him. Yet, for many reasons, Pepe Ramirez did not feel that he was accepted by the church in the past." She admitted, "I do not know how to remove these reasons. I do not know how we can help ourselves accept people who are different, [or] how we can help different people accept us." The writer, however, realized one of the main messages of the Baptist leadership. The central problem was whites' inability to accept people who were different.[42]

While the relationship between the Baptists and Ramirez represented failure on an individual level, anti-Mexican sentiment damaged American relations with Mexico and all of Latin America in much the same way that antiblack discrimination damaged American relations with newly emerging African countries. Throughout the postwar period, Baptist leaders reminded their readers about the international dimensions of America's race problems. In *"Of One,"* T. B. Maston told Baptists about an incident involving two government officials from Mexico, one a senator, who visited the United States on a goodwill tour. A Texas cafe refused to serve the two officials because it did not serve Mexicans. Maston asked Baptists, "What would have been the reaction of the citizens of the United States if two of our prominent officials had been refused service in Mexico? Is it any wonder we have difficulty convincing Mexico and other Latin American countries of the sincerity of our 'good neighbor policy'?"[43]

The situation persisted throughout the postwar period. In 1953, Raul Solis noted, "Western Texas has a great deal of racial prejudice." He cited cafes, drug stores, fountains, and beauty shops that blatantly refused Latinos service. Aside from being unchristian, Solis argued, "Racial prejudice is an irrational way of thinking, an irrational way of reasoning. It can be described as social blindness, social ignorance." Solis described the situation facing west Texas Mexicans as being quite similar to the situation facing southern blacks: "the discriminators do not mind having Latin American . . . women as maids in their homes to prepare meals, wash dishes, and do the laundry; but try to get such people to eat in a public place next to a Latin-American and they will never do it." Personal interactions regularly took place in employer-employee settings, but these interactions did not result in greater cultural tolerance.[44]

Social acceptability depended upon several factors, including the two closely related issues of economic class and race. Poverty was a constant condition in the lives of many Indians and Mexicans, as it was for many blacks. This poverty horrified those Southern Baptists who witnessed it. One Royal Ambassador, George Marshall Rix, reported his amazement at the destitute poverty many Indians faced. After visiting a

Navajo home he wrote, "Upon going inside what had been fascination turned to amazement and pity as we saw their crowded living conditions: a large number of people, animals, and a million mosquitoes packed in together, all sharing the same drinking water." Such living conditions also contributed to the extraordinarily high rate of disease among Indians. In the early 1950s, the death rate among Indians from tuberculosis was five times that of the general population. Indians' economic position improved only slowly in the postwar years. In the decade after Rix wrote, an increasing number of Indians moved to cities and gained more formal education. Yet in 1968 the average American Indian still lived below the poverty line.[45]

According to A. C. Miller, Indian poverty resulted, at least in part, from white racism. Many Indians finished their education at boarding schools and returned to the reservations because they could not find employment in the "white man's world." Whites turned "the back hand of legal discrimination" against Indians. With few employment opportunities on the reservations, many Indians were forced onto government relief. Missionary Tom Trent noted that this led whites to hold the mistaken belief that Indians were lazy. He offered several examples to remind readers that Indians excelled at a variety of activities when given the opportunity.[46]

Half of the 445,000 Indians in America were under the age of twenty at the end of the 1950s. Even though more and more of them attended public schools, many still had to leave their homes and attend government or religious boarding schools like Haskell in Lawrence, Kansas. Norma and Bill Crews, missionaries stationed at Haskell, noted that Haskell was "sometimes called the Red Man's Harvard." But Haskell was no Harvard. Haskell offered two to six years of vocational training, with the stated goal of bridging "the gap from the Indian young person's home on the reservation to a place of economic security in the world." Whatever the need for such an institution, the message was clear: education for Indians, even at the "Red Man's Harvard," would be vocational, a similar message that had long been sent to blacks in the American South. The boarding schools, which were explicitly assimilationist and which had a heritage of explicit racism, were more problematic than Baptist missionaries—who focused on each individual and shared the general assimilationist views—were able to see.[47]

Indian schools like Haskell and Chilocco all strove to reduce the cultural distance between Indians and whites by training Indians in the ways of the whites. The schools, often far from home, aimed to break tribal customs by taking students away from the reservations and their parents and mixing students from a variety of tribes. Promoting such changes reflected the government's policy more than it did the hopes of the Southern Baptists because it did little to address the problem of racist attitudes among whites. While Indians confronted those racist attitudes, many tried "to weave two cultures together." The process was, at best, difficult. Carl Todochene, a Navajo councilman from Shiprock, noted simply that "our people want to maintain their identity as Navajos and it's pretty tough." Southern Baptists, even missionaries and leaders, tended to overlook those problems.[48]

A college education was out of reach for most Indians, but Fannie Lou Ben, a Choctaw, managed to obtain one. When she graduated from Blue Mountain College on June 2, 1952, she became the first Choctaw to graduate from any college in Mississippi. Ben's road to college was difficult. She had finished grade school in 1941, but at that time Mississippi had no high schools for Indians. She went to Chilocco Indian School in Oklahoma and graduated in 1945. She then attended the Haskell Institute. After Ben met Mitchell Beckett, the superintendent of Ellard High School in Calhoun County, Mississippi, she began teaching on the faculty of a white school. She left the position after one year to finish her bachelor's degree. While attending Blue Mountain, Ben worked as a Baptist student summer missionary among the Choctaw. By 1952, when she finished at Blue Mountain, Mississippi had opened one high school for Indians, but it only went through the eleventh grade.[49]

Yet Ben had broken into new territory, and others followed. While New Mexico had more Indians who had obtained a higher education than Mississippi, they were still only a small minority. Things were changing, however. Andrea Jojola wrote, "No longer is the average graduate of Albuquerque Indian School, or our other Indian Schools, content to consider their education as complete on graduation from the twelfth year. We have been inspired by the personnel who work with us and also by our parents, to continue to work to develop whatever talents we may have." Jojola's parents were themselves Baptist missionaries in New Mexico. Another Indian who broke new territory was Louise Cata, an honor graduate from Espanola High School near Los Alamos, New Mexico. In 1951, after local Baptists, led by Mrs. John Tucker, made the arrangements for her to attend, Cata became the only Indian at Southwest Baptist College in Bolivar, Missouri.[50]

Fannie Lou Ben, Andrea Jojola, and Louise Cata were clearly exceptional. Most Indians found that, even when they had the opportunity to obtain a mainstream education, it was limited. Jacqueline Durham, who was concerned about the problems facing Indian students, told Baptist women in 1962, "We can help these young people by inviting them into our homes and with extra coaching in new subjects." Her views were paternalistic, but few Indians had parents with a high school education, even though many parents were supportive of their children's efforts to get a mainstream education. Missionaries reported, "Some of these parents are seen on graduation occasions, dressed in their Indian reservation costumes, and in some cases though they know no English, wear smiles equal to those of any other parents." Indian school attendance had steadily increased since 1947, when the Navajo adopted a compulsory school law, but the Indian Bureau was unable to provide enough schools. In 1950 only half of Navajo children were in public schools, but by 1966 that number had swelled to 90 percent.[51]

More and more Indian youths, like other Americans, were attending public schools by the end of the 1950s. This involved—as can be seen at Dulce, New Mexico—the replacement of Indian schools with integrated public schools. However, Norma and Bill Crews at the Haskell school focused primarily on the spiritual well-being of those with whom they worked. They insisted that their role was "to bridge the gap between the pagan, and often neglected spiritual needs of the young Indians' home experiences, to a place in the kingdom of God, and as a servant in the local Baptist church when his education is completed at Haskell."[52] The Crewses' efforts at Haskell represented the widespread belief that the key to evangelization, in America and around the world, was to spark the desire to evangelize among the converts. As Southern Baptists continually stressed the importance of missions among the predominantly white churches of the South, they also stressed mission activity in the minority communities. There were successes. In 1951, Frank Belvin, who was half Choctaw, had replaced J. B. Rounds as field secretary for Indian Work. Belvin had grown up in a Christian Indian home. His father had tried to cooperate with whites, believing that it would be better for the Choctaw, but whites had still ravaged his farm and burned his home. Despite such treatment by whites, Belvin remained a Christian and worked as a missionary among the Creek and Seminole Indians before becoming field secretary.[53]

In the mid-1960s, the Home Mission Board hoped the Navajo Training School near Farmington, New Mexico, would provide "Navajo leadership training without taking the individual out of his environment." The school offered a combination of half fieldwork and half coursework, with a strong emphasis on Bible study, and paid the students for their work in the field. The program provided opportunities for Navajos who had neither the formal schooling nor the economic means to attend the Southern Baptists' seminaries. Indeed, in 1965, the Indians working with Southern Baptist missionaries had, on average, a sixth-grade education. The institute at Farmington, then, was vital to both their education and their mission work, much as the seminary at Ogbomosho was in Nigeria.[54]

Latinos also faced problems in attaining an adequate education. Pen Lile Pittard wrote that the Mexican was illiterate, at least in English, "because he has no chance for education and partly because when he is educated he is still discriminated against so that he cannot obtain any different work from the illiterate laborer, nor live any better." Pittard overstated the case, but Latinos did face significant barriers in their efforts to gain a formal education. Migrants had difficulty getting any education at all, and the more settled Mexican community was often forced into inferior segregated schools. Segregated education for Latinos was declared illegal in several federal district court decisions, beginning with the 1945 California case of *Méndez v. Westminster School District* and continuing through the 1957 Texas case of *Hernández v. Driscoll Consolidated Independent School District*. Still, school districts managed to avoid the integration of Anglo and Mexican students throughout most of the 1950s and 1960s. The system stifled Latinos, denying them hope of advancement even if they obtained an education.[55]

Dallas M. Lee, associate editor of *Home Missions*, recognized that years of educational discrimination had left a legacy of poverty that prevented Latinos from taking some of the opportunities that were ostensibly open to them. The average Mexican American in Texas at the end of the 1960s had completed just over four and a half years of school, while blacks averaged eight years. Poverty also led to incredibly high rates of disease. Lee cited Dr. Ramiro Casso as saying, "By and large, the mass has been chronically ill for so long, it doesn't know it's sick." Indeed, the rate of death from tuberculosis in Texas was four times higher among Mexican Americans than it was among Anglo Americans. Housing conditions clearly contributed to the problem. Over one-third of Mexican Americans living in Texas cities had substandard housing.[56]

Housing conditions were even worse for migrant farmers. Hermione Dannelly Jackson told Baptist girls, "We have known about the migrant worker for a long time, but have done little to improve his condition." Jackson argued that the migrants' lack of organization meant that they were invisible and their problems were not addressed. She was particularly concerned about the children of migrant farmers: "their schooling is interrupted by the constant moving of the family. They arrive in communities at the same time as other families to harvest the crops. According to law, room must be made for them in the classroom. The teacher knows they will only be with her a few weeks, and the children of the town scarcely learn their names before they are gone. . . . The migrant child feels unwelcome in school, but it is even sadder that he does not feel welcome in many churches."[57]

Some churches did not welcome the migrants, knowing there was little chance that they would ever become fully participating members. J. Ed Taylor, a missionary among the migrant farm workers of the Southwest, noted that "many of these harvesters are of another nationality and some church members draw the line there!" Taylor, writing for *Royal Service*, reminded Baptist women how much their lifestyle depended on the work of migrant farmers: "it probably never occurs to you as you drink your morning orange juice, put sugar in your coffee, enjoy your tossed salad for lunch . . . that some of the agricultural migrant workers . . . may deserve a 'thank you' from you." Taylor told Baptists that in one Oklahoma farming region migrants lived in a large barracks where families of six to ten people crammed into one room and had a two-burner gas hot plate for both cooking and heating. He pointed to the work of the missionaries as integral to bettering migrants' well-being: "worn, tired, away from home, they need the friendship which our missionaries can supply."[58]

Toward the end of the 1960s, Walker L. Knight, editor of *Home Missions*, wrote about the plight of Mexican Americans in the Southwest, noting that they constituted the second largest "disadvantaged minority" in America and that the language barrier complicated their persistent problems of poverty and racism. In 1966 these problems came together in the Rio Grande Valley to create an explosive situation. Melon workers went on a strike that lasted over a year. While Anglos claimed that Mexicans could "live on less," Knight argued that that point was simply absurd. Mexican farm workers went on strike to improve their wages, which were a dismal eighty-five cents per hour, and to gain coverage under minimum wage legislation. Mexican American farm workers from the Rio Grande Valley marched to Austin to pressure the governor, John Connally, to pass legislation guaranteeing them at least one dollar and twenty-five cents per hour. Knight wrote of the situation, "No one but the Mexican-American laborer is forced to live below poverty level. No one but the Mexican-American laborer works all week, from sunup to 'can't see,' with nothing more to show for it than that he is still alive." Knight realized that there were larger forces at work, saying, "Most likely the culprit is the economic situation fed by man's natural desire to make the most profit in any given situation," which was complicated by the more than adequate labor supply. Economic factors and flat-out greed came together with racism to create a truly "ugly situation."[59]

Eugene Nelson, who had worked in California with Caesar Chavez, helped organize the strike and the Minimum Wage March, which arrived in Austin on Labor Day, 1966. Among the clergy who were involved in the march were Father Anthony González, a Catholic priest from San Antonio, and Reverend James Navarro, a Baptist minister. Although the strike certainly highlighted some of the problems faced by Mexican Americans in Texas, it failed in its ultimate goal when the Texas legislature refused to pass minimum wage laws for farm workers in 1967, and Texas melon pickers never got a contract.[60]

The coverage of the strike by *Home Missions* brought responses from many Baptists. The majority of the correspondents approved of its articles. Milton L. Rhodes of San Antonio wrote, "I concur in the position you have taken" and noted that the photographs, taken by Walker L. Knight, covered the plight of Mexican Americans in a "more realistic and honest way than any I can remember reading [*sic*] in any Baptist publication." He concluded, "Let us hope that we will not only read but act, and that right early!" Larry D. Farrell of Virginia simply said, "bravo," while Jimmy Allen of Dallas said, "All of us are excited about the direction of the sharp reporting and conscience pricking which *Home Missions* has evidenced in the past few months." He specifically cited the articles on Mexican Americans.[61]

Not everyone was pleased. Raul Solis, who had written for *Home*

Missions concerning the plight of Mexican Americans in Texas, worried that the articles implied that all Mexican Americans were impoverished. He noted the growing middle class and the fact that Mexican Americans were gaining in education. He also worried that the articles displayed too much anti-Catholicism. He said, "There is only a minority of Mexican-Americans who are illiterate, etc. The Church is not to blame, but rather the Anglos of Texas, and unfortunately some Anglo Baptists." Finally, Solis told Baptists, "we are not just 'beginning to stir.' We have been stirring for over 25 years." The editors apologized for any misleading statements and assured Solis that "we did not intend to imply that all Mexican-Americans face the dire situation that they face in the Rio Grande Valley." The editors also assured him that most readers had not seen the article that way.[62]

Solis supported the strike, but other critics did not. One, R. L. Kurth of Lufkin, Texas, wrote, "The union [United Farm Workers] has come into the area as an outside source and has literally stirred up trouble." His view reflected one of the most typical southern responses to the civil rights movement: to blame outside agitators. Kurth was also typically Baptist in seeking biblical justification for his stand. He claimed, "Romans, Chapter 13, verses 1-4 tells us that the law in our country was ordained of God. The Texas Rangers are enforcing the law; and verse 3 tells us they are not a terror to good works, but to evil." The Rangers, he believed, were protecting private property against violence perpetrated by union members. Mexican Americans, however, had long held different views of the Texas Rangers, considering them agents of Anglo racism and harassment.[63]

Indians, too, were actively fighting for their civil rights in the late 1960s. Indians were so far removed from the consciousness of many Americans in the 1950s and 1960s that segregationists claimed, "If anyone has a right to complain, it's the Indians, but you don't see them marching and rioting, do you?" In 1968, when the Baptists pointed to that claim, Indians were continuing a long struggle for civil rights, though the shape of the struggle was often, but certainly not always, quite different from the black or Latino freedom struggles. Walker L. Knight and Dallas M. Lee, who cowrote "The Incredibly Quiet War," understood that "despite the stoicism of the American Indians . . . they are an intensely proud race. . . . and they do have bitter grievances."[64]

Indian actions were not as quiet as segregationists, or even progressive

Baptists, implied, but they were largely outside the traditional Baptist heartland. In the early 1960s, a group of young, college-educated Indians created the National Indian Youth Council. The council dedicated itself to instilling a sense of pride among Indians and held numerous "fish-ins" in the Northwest, similar to the "sit-ins" in the South. Indians had also been active in antiwar protests from the beginning of American involvement in Vietnam. Indeed, Indian leaders like Wallace Anderson, a Tuscarora, and Cherokee anthropologist Robert Thomas spoke out against the war beginning in 1963, before the major campus protests. In 1968, Indians formed the more militant American Indian Movement. That same year Congress passed the Indian Civil Rights Act, which extended protection from unconstitutional policies of tribal governments to individual Indians.[65]

While mission leaders were sympathetic to political and social action by Indians and Latinos, spreading Christianity remained the basis for their work. Racism continued to stymie their efforts, as some churches refused to welcome minorities. Missionaries on the Indian reservations worked hard to introduce Indians to the Baptist faith, but in the postwar years an increasing number of Indians were moving to the cities. Jacqueline Durham wrote in 1962 that "In many places, they [Indians] are not being welcomed into churches and schools." Fundamentally, the problem was a lack of Christian spirit. Durham believed that the proper spirit could break down prejudices.[66]

The cultural chasm between the average Southern Baptist home and the Indian reservation shocked student summer workers throughout the postwar period, and the chasm decreased only slightly over time. As Jane Geiger, a summer missionary, remembered, "I felt I was a real pioneer. . . . I came in contact with a different culture, having unusual customs and traditions." Furthermore, Geiger said, "I pioneered within myself. I pulled out long-forgotten facts and experiences to meet the unusual situations that faced me. I added new facts to my mind by the experiences I had with the Indian people."[67]

Throughout the postwar era, Baptist young people experienced the same awakening Geiger described as they encountered America's minority cultures. Two, Elizabeth Ann Allen of Liberty, Missouri, and Barbara Sue Johnson, a student at Meredith College in North Carolina, wrote to the *Window* about their experiences. Allen went to a Baptist retreat in New Mexico and saw the mission work with the Chinese,

Mexicans, and Indians along the way. She said, "For the first time I realized what a great mission field we have in our own United States." Johnson had a similar experience after working a summer in Texas, reporting, "I never knew how blindly I gave before my summer mission work with the Spanish people of Texas." Her interpretation of the situation clearly reflected the persistent anti-Catholicism in Southern Baptist thought. She wrote, "I have seen a people dominated and oppressed by a religion that denies the freedom of the soul."[68]

The summer experience could reinforce the Baptists' religious prejudices as much as it might challenge ethnic ones. One student missionary, Anne Keelin, wrote that "these people are still very superstitious. Yet they do not worship the true God." She reflected Baptist cultural imperialism, saying, "They seem to think their religion is as good as the white man's." Indeed, some thought it was better. Vine Deloria, who had seminary training, believed that Christianity was inferior to Indian religions, and he feared that missionaries hoped to make Indians into white Christians. Deloria hoped to combine Christianity and Indian religions in a syncretic Indian Christian Church. Russell Means merely hoped the missionaries would pack their bags and leave the reservations, admitting that they had failed and that their efforts had served "only to colonize further Indians and rob us of dignity and self-worth." But Keelin, and Baptist missionaries in general, were not open to such ideas. Nor were they open to similar ideas concerning Catholicism in Mexico. Selma Crawford, a Young Woman's Auxiliary from Texas, spent six weeks in Mexico in 1949. She wrote to the *Window*, "I had come to know Mexico and its people by associating with them." Yet her views of Mexico were not challenged: "I found the land very much as it had been pictured to me, a land of economic contrasts, a pagan Catholic land, a land that knew not Christ as its Saviour."[69]

Keelin and Crawford demonstrated a problem in Baptist thinking on race. If overcoming racism meant overcoming attitudes of superiority, belief that one's own religion is superior to another person's presented a difficulty. Baptist missionaries maintained that all people needed to turn to Christ and that Christ welcomed all people equally. Baptist missionaries, like Lee Roebuck at Bernalillo, New Mexico, argued, "It is not the missionary's purpose to change the age-old culture and customs of these ancient peoples. It is our purpose to tell them of the love of God for them in Christ Jesus." Missionaries believed it was their duty to "deal with man where man is, not where we would have him to be." That way, the man and the missionary could "walk down the same road together." Yet conversion necessarily meant some changes in the age-old culture and customs. This was true in the American Southwest just as it was in Africa or Asia. Progressive Baptists also called white American society "pagan" and demanded that it change in order to follow Christ. Yet white America had only to overcome its sins, not abandon its cultural heritage. Missionaries claimed that "Baptists have no interest in making *white men* out of Indians, but they do have [a] deep interest in making *better Indians* out of Indians" (italics in original). While one Baptist writer, Jack U. Harwell, suggested that "some Indian teachings could profitably be accepted and practiced by Christians today to the betterment of all," later analysts would suggest that, of all Christian missionaries, Baptists were among the least tolerant of Christian Indians' retaining their cultural traditions.[70]

Bringing multiple ethnicities together in one church could be difficult, even when everyone agreed on issues of faith. But, in Poplar, Montana, A. L. Davis succeeded. His congregation, mixed Indian and Anglo, was growing in the late 1950s. Davis noted, "Often race prejudice has proved a barrier; also the Indian's distrust of the white man due to past experiences with them has been a problem." His congregation was, in some ways, the Baptist ideal: members worked together, regardless of race, to spread the Gospel. Indian converts were active in the church, serving as pianists, Sunday School teachers, and mission leaders in the Woman's Missionary Union. Davis noted, "The members of the church realize that they are truly missionaries, white and Indian alike." All "nations" were working together in God's plan. Davis believed, however, that separate churches would be necessary in some locations. He wrote that work needed to be started among Indians in other towns and said, "In some cases this work will have to be in addition to white churches because of prejudices of various kinds." Although Davis had managed to overcome prejudices in building his church, he believed that evangelism would have to proceed even in the face of discrimination.[71]

Davis's church in Montana was one of many integrated churches in the West. In Los Angeles, the Berendo Street Baptist Church was "about as international as a church can get." Of the 160 members, some were "Americans, American-Indians, Koreans, Japanese, Chinese, Spanish, Filipinos, and Hungarians." That did not include the regular visitors from Poland, India, Iraq, Congo, Nigeria, Egypt, and Mexico. In the Southwest, many churches had integrated, if not quite so diverse, memberships. For example, the Baptist church at Shiprock, New Mexico, was "mixed Indian, Negro, and Anglo Saxon." The church was responsible for the mission to the Navajo-speaking Indians around Shiprock and, in particular, the Shiprock Indian School, which attracted some twelve hundred Indians and was the largest of the Indian Bureau's schools. Perhaps even more promising, in Oklahoma fifteen predominantly white Baptist churches had Indian preachers. According to Bailey Sewell, a missionary in Oklahoma, several Indians, including those fifteen preachers, were among the state's leading citizens.[72]

Some churches integrated hesitantly. In Lubbock, Texas, Parkdale Baptist Church opened in the late 1940s in a predominantly white neighborhood. By the mid-1960s, however, it was in a predominantly Spanish-speaking neighborhood. The situation was similar, certainly, to that faced by many churches in the South that found their formerly white neighborhoods were suddenly black. In the West, as in the South, many of the original church members had moved to other areas of Lubbock, and Parkdale had to decide whether to stay or move with them. Sara Hines Martin reported that the church struggled. First, it decided to stay and open a mission for the Mexicans in the area. Yet it refused to accept the Mexicans into full church membership. Martin noted that "the church continued to pray, to survey the area, and to deliberate on courses of action. There was too great a need in the immediate area to be ignored." Ultimately, however, "the final decision was of the Lord. The church decided to stay and to open the doors of the church to the Latin Americans." While Baptists professed that Latinos were "brothers and sisters" in Christ, some apparently found it difficult to sit next to them on Sunday.[73]

The issue of opening a church to Latinos should not have even arisen in Texas when Parkdale Church struggled with the question. Texas had had two Baptist conventions, one Anglo and one Mexican, since 1910. In 1960, several years before Parkdale integrated, that changed. The two conventions voted to merge, even though all Mexican Baptist churches were already members of both conventions. The two formally joined together on November 2, 1960, with no dissenting voices. Meanwhile, in California, a Mexican American, Leobardo Estrada, was elected first vice president of that state's convention. Estrada, who was pastor of First Mexican Baptist Church of Los Angeles and a preacher on *La Hora Bautista*, the Baptists' Spanish language radio program, was the first "foreign language speaker" to hold an office in the California Convention. Nevertheless, resistance to integration persisted at the local level, frustrating the missionary leaders, who believed it damaged their overall efforts.[74]

Baptist writings about the Latinos and Indians demonstrate the fundamental consistency of Baptists' views of race and discrimination. The situations differed from one people to another, but the issues were essentially the same: racial prejudice and discrimination were unchristian and prevented whites from being good Christians, in part because racism hindered mission efforts among minority peoples, whether black, Latino, or Indian. Christians would have to overcome their racism by looking at themselves, examining their racial views, and eschewing those that were unchristian. Once Christians recognized their racism and worked to overcome it, they could begin effectively to spread the Gospel to other people. This would help break down the barriers of racial and economic discrimination and personal antagonism that had risen over the centuries. While clearly optimistic, Baptist leaders continued to believe that, through the Gospel, America could overcome racism and build a nation of peace, harmony, and freedom. Clearly, the greatest racial barriers in America were between blacks and whites. There the Gospel was needed as much as anywhere—perhaps even more.

6

"LIVING OUR CHRISTIANITY"

Southern Baptist Missions and Blacks in America

Between 1945 and 1970 the progressive leadership of the Southern Baptist Convention stressed the biblical principles of equality and unity, the international dimensions of the race question, and the responsibility of each individual to work for better race relations. Missionaries and mission leaders focused on promoting Christian attitudes regarding race. They said little, directly, about the civil rights movement. Instead, they expounded on the Christian principles regarding race. Although their central message did not change dramatically, before 1954 some progressive Baptists hoped to create racial harmony without attacking segregation directly. From 1954 to the mid-1960s Baptists came to understand more clearly that racial harmony was impossible within a segregated society and called for an end to racial segregation as well as discrimination. In the latter 1960s, progressive Baptists more consistently and directly attacked the persistence of racism and discrimination, which they believed had become an embarrassment to the country and to Christianity. Progressive Baptists believed that achieving their vision of a transformed, Christian America required Baptists to be living examples of Christianity.[1]

The Christian Life Commission helped set the tone for the Southern Baptist Convention's postwar teachings on race. In its 1946 report, the Commission recognized that blacks faced discrimination and urged the Convention to assure blacks the right to "share the common privileges of citizens." Discrimination included unequal education, housing, and economic opportunity, and an inability to obtain justice in courts or to vote. The next year, the Southern Baptist Convention officially repudiated prejudice, contempt, and ill will toward blacks. It adopted a program designed to educate Southern Baptists about the racial situation in the South and around the world and determined to "protest against injustice and indignities against Negroes, as we do in the case of people of our race, whenever and wherever we meet them." The Convention called for the "application of Christian Principles of Justice and love at all points of racial contact."[2]

The next year, 1948, J. B. Lawrence, head of the Home Mission Board, told Southern Baptists that they were "in a great Kingdom campaign": "those men who fought side by side with our boys in World War II to win our liberties will expect to have an equal place in our consideration now that these liberties are won." Lawrence was, however, unwilling to broach the idea of social equality. Southern Baptists needed to "recognize here in our land the difference between social equality and racial rights!" Racial rights, as Lawrence conceived them, would guarantee blacks civil and legal rights and educational opportunity but would not necessitate integration.[3]

Reflecting the internationalism that dominated the mission boards, Lawrence tied American race relations to the foreign missions, saying, "If we hope to have an open field and a clear way to win the races of the earth to Christ in the world of tomorrow we must recognize their rights in our land and give the gospel to them here. Our Home Mission work must not only include the preaching of the gospel to these various races here in the homeland, but it must also touch and change the attitude of our people toward these races." Lawrence recognized that the white attitudes about race had to be changed, and he believed that could be done through evangelization. The spread of Christian attitudes about race would lead to racial harmony. Yet Lawrence, and a number of other progressive Baptists, failed to see the elimination of segregation and a dramatic change in the South and America as necessary to bringing true racial harmony.[4]

Other Baptist leaders more directly defended segregation in the immediate postwar years. Myrtle Robinson (Mrs. C. D.) Creasman, who had been born in 1887 and lived her life in a segregated and racist society, warned about demands that were "revolutionary and unreasonable" — mainly integration. Creasman feared that integration would lead to "amalgamation of the black and white people [and that] is not according to the teachings of the Bible or according to God's will for the races."

Nevertheless, Creasman realized that such demands as integration and social equality "have power because they grow out of situations fundamentally unjust." She believed that "if all injustice toward the Negroes could be removed, then all demands necessary for the happiness and welfare of the Negro race would be thereby granted."[5]

Progressive Baptist efforts to build racial harmony and to transform society in the early postwar years focused on working cooperatively with black Christians in the South. By bringing white and black Christians together as Christians, they hoped to build bridges across the racial chasm in the South. To do this, the Home Mission Board actively pursued a program of "Negro Work" in the late 1940s. James P. Wesberry, a prominent Atlanta pastor and chairman of the Committee on Cooperative Negro Work at the Home Mission Board, urged Baptists to expand their teacher-missionary program. Through the program the board supported religious teachers in participating southern black colleges. The program began in 1946 after Dr. Noble Y. Beall surveyed black religious organizations and discovered that only 5 percent of black ministers had any college or seminary training. As a response, the Baptists expanded their efforts to help with black ministerial education. Coincidentally, that same year southern Presbyterians took the same action. Beal, who since 1937 had supervised the Department of Cooperative Work with Negroes, retired in 1945, before the program he had helped develop was underway.[6]

L. S. Sedberry, secretary of the American Seminary Commission (a joint endeavor between the Southern and National Baptist Conventions), noted that "the Negro Baptist church is the one institution in the community run and controlled by Negroes." He believed, however, that many black ministers lacked sufficient training to run their churches effectively. Prominent black Baptist educator Benjamin Mays agreed. While doing research for his book *The Negro's Church*, Mays saw the desperate need for a trained ministry. The Home Mission Board's teacher-missionary and extension programs could help meet that need. For example, twenty-five thousand students, including twelve thousand ministers, took courses from the teacher-missionaries during the 1949–50 academic year. Such efforts were certainly paternalistic, and they did not directly challenge segregation or the South's racial hierarchy. Yet the intent was clearly to build lasting interracial goodwill as well as to help train black ministers.[7]

The Southern Baptists also hoped to build bridges through their "Negro Centers," including the centers in Birmingham and Montgomery (which opened in 1948 and 1951, respectively). Lawrence believed Baptists needed a center in every large southern city and estimated it would cost more than $250,000 to establish and maintain them, an investment that suggested the seriousness with which Southern Baptists approached the situation. By 1968, the board supported sixteen centers in the South.[8]

The model center was in Louisville, where black and white Baptists "mingle[d] together as Children of God." According to Carrie U. Littlejohn of the Southern Baptist Training School, the black children served by the center were "most polite and very clean; they would welcome you as their guest and you would be surprised to hear them say: 'Yes Ma'am,' 'Thank you,' 'Excuse me.'" Littlejohn thus attacked the widespread beliefs that blacks were dirty and rude, stereotypes which reinforced a wide range of prejudices. Positive experiences in such Negro Centers undermined the South's racial norms, intentionally or unintentionally.[9]

The Home Mission Board also tried to build bridges by assisting in the founding and funding of Baptist Student Unions at black colleges. William Hall Preston, assistant editor of the *Baptist Student*, announced that Student Union work at black colleges "opens doors that afford a vista that is staggering in possibilities." Courts Redford, then assistant secretary-treasurer at the Home Mission Board, believed the program would undermine racism. He told Baptist college students, "We must destroy race prejudice." Yet the new Baptist Student Unions were founded at segregated black colleges, clearly limiting the challenge to the South's racial system.[10]

Similarly, Baptist women worked toward greater racial understanding without directly challenging segregation. In 1951, Edith Stokely, a graduate of the University of Tennessee and Community Missions director at the Woman's Missionary Union, encouraged Baptist women to sponsor Vacation Bible Schools, but did not explicitly suggest they be integrated. She reminded readers, "As long as there are children in your community, no matter what their color, who are without the opportunity to learn about God, then there is a job that the Master is depending on you to lead the women to do." Baptist and Methodist women of Cedertown, Georgia, realized that there were five nursery schools for white children but none for blacks. They felt called to do something for the black children and established a separate black school. Clearly, some southerners were willing to do something for blacks, demonstrating their paternalism and still accepting segregation itself.[11]

Even as modest as their efforts were, progressive Baptists encountered resistance, and many southerners resisted believing that racial equality constituted God's will. H. Cornell Goerner admitted that blacks' striving for racial equality met "with stubborn resistance in some quarters." Many southerners associated racial progressivism with communism and called progressives, whether Baptist or not, "dirty reds." W. O. Carver admitted that it was difficult to approach the race situation from the "Christian standpoint": "instincts, traditions, prejudices, emotional urges blind our eyes and harden our hearts and dull our ears to Christ's spirit and words." Indeed, between 1948 and 1955, nearly six hundred segregationist organizations, including the White Citizens' Councils, had formed. Baptists, and even Baptist ministers, joined and led many of them. Some pastors found widespread community support when they joined the councils. When they opposed the local council, they suffered financial reprisals.[12]

Baptist leaders recognized the resistance to their message and searched for a middle ground where they could make progress in solving the racial problem while maintaining the allegiance of the congregations. In 1947, J. B. Lawrence offered an analysis of blacks' demands as articulated by Dr. Rufus Clement, president of Atlanta University. Clement demanded equal schools, justice in the courts, equal employment opportunities, equal access to civic improvements, equal protection of the law, and the right to vote. Once again, Lawrence made the distinction between rights and equality. He explained that Clement had made no claim for "social equality." Even though in 1947 many southerners would disagree with him, especially on the issue of voting, Lawrence wrote, "These seem to be reasonable things to grant the Negroes in our midst." Lawrence, apparently, still saw it as the right of whites to "grant" rights to blacks, which would mean whites could also deny those rights to blacks, as, in fact, they did.[13]

In the late 1940s, some Baptist leaders also believed that the tactics used by blacks to gain their rights were "reasonable." The Social Service Commission commended blacks for their "patience and gracious spirit" in the face of indignities. For such, the commission said, "they stand high in the praise of their fellow Americans." Much of the activity in civil rights in the late 1940s and early 1950s focused on court cases that did not involve large numbers of people or attract significant attention. Still, some Baptist leaders, like Charles A. Wells, lauded the "direct Christian action" undertaken by the Congress of Racial Equality (CORE), "a group of young Christians in Chicago." Wells agreed with CORE that "persistent and unnecessary Jim Crowism is the cause of growing bitterness among hundreds of thousands of well-educated and well-behaved Negroes." Yet Wells's comment seemed to indicate that blacks had to be well educated and well behaved to be served in the same institutions where whites would be served regardless of their education or behavior.[14]

Wells's and Lawrence's statements reinforced, if unintentionally, the idea that blacks needed to earn their basic rights — rights whites had by virtue of being white. The standard in society would remain "white," and the Home Mission Board, to some extent, reinforced that standard in the late 1940s. Lawrence announced that the Home Mission Board stood "ready to help them in every way possible to attain the cultural, educational, and religious standing which will demand and secure respect and consideration from all races."[15]

Such ideas allowed white southerners to continue to support segregation while still calling for better race relations. Progressive Baptists were not alone. As Baptists sought to increase interracial cooperation in religious activities, other southerners began secular organizations with much the same goal in mind. The Atlanta-based Commission on Interracial Cooperation tried to find a middle ground between the racism of the Klan and the activism of the National Association for the Advancement of Colored People. As historian Grace Elizabeth Hale notes, "While the CIC sought improvement in southern race relations, the committee never questioned the racial separation at the heart of both modern southern society and modern white identity." Some Baptists, like T. B. Maston, did question segregation, but the mainstream of progressive thought in the 1940s hoped to end discrimination without ending segregation.[16]

Baptists assured themselves that "worthy" blacks could live up to the standards whites had set for them despite segregation. They often recognized the contributions of black Baptist leaders like Walter H. Brooks. Brooks had been born a slave and eventually took a powerful pulpit in Washington. When Edward Hughes Pruden, who happened to be President Harry Truman's pastor, wrote about Brooks after his death, he noted that Brooks's master had been a "devout Christian" who had kept slave families together. Baptists also lauded George Washington Carver, who despite his humble origins had made significant contributions to science. Such stellar individuals allowed southerners to believe that blacks had opportunities despite segregation and even slavery, but by the early 1950s some progressive Baptist leaders were attacking this belief.[17]

Hermione Dannelly Jackson, writing for the *Window* in 1951, recognized the catch-22 employed against blacks, which allowed a few "worthy" blacks to succeed. She noted that, overall, "qualities that are considered 'good' in a white person are 'bad' in a Negro. He does not know 'his place' if he is ambitious, aggressive, independent, or proud." According to Daniel R. Grant, a professor of political science at Vanderbilt and the former director of the Arkansas Baptist Student Union, that meant that blacks did not have real equality of opportunity, despite a few successes. Grant reminded Baptists that "the Negro's choice of school and occupation continues to be limited because of his color."[18]

Discrimination hurt the entire country. R. Orin Cornett of the Education Commission cited United States Secretary of Labor James P. Mitchell, who claimed that discrimination against blacks cost the country over a billion dollars a year in productive capacity. Cornett believed that "this is of little consequence, though, in comparison with the larger issues of justice and human rights and to the waste in human personality." He cited the all too typical example of Neva Conner, a black girl who was eager to make a significant contribution to the world. Her family, living in Alabama, had no car, refrigerator, or running water. The gross family income averaged $980 per year, well below the poverty level. As a result, she would be unable to continue her education and to contribute her full potential to American society. Cornett believed that people like Neva Conner should have the chance to go to college, and that the decision of whether to attend "Negro colleges, state colleges [or] church colleges" should be left up to them.[19]

Racism and economic discrimination kept most blacks out of college. Whites accepted the accomplishments of a few outstanding blacks, but they prevented the vast majority from having the opportunity to succeed. The more progressive Baptist mission leaders attacked the double standard, seeing its harmful economic consequences. Moreover, they believed that the double standard was unchristian. Baptists were moving, if slowly, away from their earlier beliefs that racial harmony could be achieved within a segregated society. Yet barriers to racial harmony persisted, and progressive Baptists sought more ways to bridge the chasm. Margaret Culpepper Clark, former associate secretary of the Southwide Department of Student Work, argued that crossing barriers was essential because "racial prejudice is always a product of fear; of ignorance; and of poverty."[20]

North Carolina Baptists took a more direct approach. In 1946, North Carolina's Committee on Social Service and Civic Righteousness advocated federal anti-lynching laws, legislation ensuring equal employment opportunities, and equal pay for equal work. The committee also condemned segregation in churches as "unchristian." If segregation in churches was fundamentally "unchristian," it would be difficult to justify segregation in any part of Christian society. Thus, North Carolina Baptists offered a considerably stronger challenge to the southern racial system than other Baptists were yet willing to make.[21]

In 1946 a group of twenty women gathered in Raleigh, North Carolina, to discuss the problems facing blacks. They were part of an emerging pattern of racial progressivism among Baptists. Katherine Parker (Mrs. L. E. M.) Freeman, who wrote to *Royal Service* about the project, noted "we were finding out all the time that there is a contemporary civilization in Raleigh of which we were utterly oblivious. We found those women had the same interests we had." Perhaps more important, the women also realized that "in the heart of God, black is as beautiful and dear as white."[22]

Lucie Yates (Mrs. Edgar) Godbold, Community Missions chair at the Woman's Missionary Union, encouraged other Baptist women to follow the example of those in Raleigh. Godbold noted that "studying about racial relationships always wakes Christian women with a guilty start and we ask 'What can we do for the Negro?'" Although she reflected the paternalism prevalent in the early postwar years, Godbold remembered that before she got involved in interracial work, "I had the average American woman's conception of colored people. They were all right in their place, but I had never thought much about where their place was. . . . today I see the American Negro as a member of a talented race, usually living under hard and harsh conditions which whites can never know."[23]

Despite barriers, Baptist leaders argued that blacks and whites, especially when both were Baptists, had "more in common than many realize." In Florida, Patricia Jordan attended an integrated Young Woman's Auxiliary camp. The young women discovered that "the same things are funny to girls of the same age . . . the same things inspire us and touch our hearts and make us feel near to God," reinforcing the persistent belief that personal contact could bring down racial barriers. The young women worshipped and prayed together and sought to "leave far behind not only for this one week, but for always, racial prejudices and restrictions."[24]

Breaking down barriers between the races challenged prejudices, which eventually could undermine segregation itself. As Baptists, especially youth, found their prejudices challenged, they often expressed ambiguity about segregation. In 1952, Leo Green of Columbus, Mississippi, wrote about race for his project in the Royal Ambassadors program. He believed that "young Christians at schools and colleges are ready to down prejudice [sic] and accept a man for what he is worth, or worthy of becoming." He saw the contradiction in the fact that "we Americans boast of our democracy and then we insist on white supremacy." Green was, however, willing to accept segregation "if all races are given equal opportunities for advancement."[25]

Green was socialized in a society that sanctified segregation, but also in a religious tradition increasingly calling for equality and justice. He tried to reconcile the two but saw that, in places, they were irreconcilable. Green rejected white supremacy but believed that if equality could be achieved within segregation, then segregation should be preserved. Nevertheless, he seemed open to the possibility that segregation might prove incompatible with equal opportunity and, therefore, with the goals of American democracy. Green did believe, however, that southerners were capable of solving their own race problems without the interference of outside agitators or the federal government. Similarly, the Social Service Commission argued that the South was moving "of its own volition" toward better race relations. The commission claimed, "As Baptists we are forging ahead, we are making progress in the name of the spirit of Christ."[26]

Some Baptist leaders, however, understood that racial progress in the South had largely been forced by lawsuits and the federal government. In 1950, Hugh Brimm of the Social Service Commission told Baptists, "You and I have witnessed during the last ten years, a decade of progress and improvement in interracial understanding and co-operation." Brimm cited better schools, health facilities, and job opportunities as examples of progress. In 1952, Margaret Gooch Kiser added to this list the opening of public libraries and some college and post-graduate programs. Unlike Green, however, Brimm and Kiser admitted that federal court decisions had forced much of that "progress" on the South.[27]

While Baptist leaders cited examples of progress, they also reminded Baptists that each individual had a role in solving the race problem. Hermione Dannelly Jackson told Baptist youth that discrimination haunted blacks every day of their lives. It was up to whites, not blacks, "to take the first step in the right direction." To help Baptists take that first step, Hugh Brimm suggested avoiding jokes that "belittle members of minority groups and perpetuate stereotypes" and using proper titles such as Mr. and Mrs. when addressing blacks. Brimm encouraged Baptists to "accept individuals on the basis of their ability and as persons not on the basis of their color or class." He noted that ignorance undergirded prejudices and recommended that Baptists learn about minority leaders, history, and achievements as a way of changing their attitudes about race. Typical of Baptist thought on race, Brimm urged Baptists to get to know members of minority groups as people, a common recommendation. Stressing the unity of humanity, he concluded, "They are just like you and me in their hopes and dreams for the future. They want to be respected, they want to be secure in their jobs. Each wants a home, a family, and a church. You will find all these things out when you get to know them personally."[28]

Baptists did make progress toward integration in the early 1950s. The Southern Baptist Theological Seminary in Louisville, Kentucky, the denomination's flagship institution, removed racial restrictions from its admissions policy in 1951. By 1952 all of the Southern Baptist Convention's seminaries accepted blacks to their degree programs. Baptists also eliminated racial barriers to its newly renamed Carver School of Missions and Social Work in Louisville. That was not typical of southern denominations. A decade later, the Fund for Theological Education determined, according to Charles Shelby Rooks, that it should "revolutionize the prevailing practices of segregated theological education." Rooks noted that seminaries in the South, like the rest of higher education, were still segregated almost a decade after the last Southern Baptist seminary officially desegregated.[29]

According to Charles Hamilton, the desegregation of the Southern Baptist seminaries was "no sudden change, but rather the culmination of a policy of aiding in the education of Negro Baptist ministers which has been in progress for years." It was the logical extension of the ministerial education program that the Home Mission Board had built in the years immediately following World War II. Hamilton, rector at the Episcopal Church of Aberdeen, Mississippi, wrote as an outsider. He saw that the Southern Baptist Convention, or at least its leadership, was more progressive than its reputation suggested. Furthermore, he argued that the desegregation of Baptist seminaries preceded similar action by other "louder" and supposedly more tolerant denominations. Seminaries were particularly important because they were the training grounds of future missionaries and ministers. By desegregating the seminaries, Baptists believed they had acted while others talked.[30]

The Southern Baptists' desegregated seminaries were incongruous with the Convention's reputation for racial conservatism. Thomas E. McCollough of the Sunday School Board was traveling in London when he encountered an angry crowd in Hyde Park. A man from the West Indies questioned McCollough about racial segregation in the churches, but McCollough avoided the question of churches. Instead, he told the skeptical man that 93 percent of the students at the Southern Baptist Theological seminary supported integration and that students of all races attended the school and lived together on campus.[31]

McCollough realized, however, that the world demanded action. He said, "Somewhere they have gotten the idea that many of the actions and attitudes of Christian people are *unchristian.* That's encouraging. It means that they recognize the Christian standard and ideal. It is also painful. It puts us on the spot." Baptists had acted on their decision to desegregate the seminaries, but racism and segregation continued throughout the South and in the Convention, demonstrating that the South still needed a more complete Christian transformation. Indeed, most Southern Baptist institutions had not caught up with the seminaries. This was due, in part, to the fact that the seminaries were controlled by the Southern Baptist Convention, while state conventions or local associations controlled other institutions. Progressive ideas did not always spread from the mission board and Convention leadership to the local leadership, much less to the congregations.[32]

When the Supreme Court outlawed segregation in public schools,

Baptist leaders recognized the essential justice of the decision. They joined the nation's other major denominations in supporting the *Brown* decision. The Christian Life Commission's report to the annual convention confirmed that the Court's decision was "in harmony with the constitutional guarantee of equal freedom to all citizens, and with the Christian principles of equal justice and love for all men." Only a handful of the estimated nine thousand messengers attending opposed the resolution, and an effort to amend the report to avoid the integration question was easily defeated. J. B. Weatherspoon, who had been born in North Carolina in 1887, won applause in his speech supporting the resolution and declaring that "if we withdraw this from our consideration tonight, we are saying to the United States of America, 'count Baptists out in this matter of equal justice,' and I do not believe we want to do that."[33]

Despite the apparent support for the Supreme Court decision, messengers had applauded opposition speeches like the one given by Reverend W. N. Nevins, an eighty-one-year-old minister from Lexington, Kentucky. Nevins claimed, "I believe in emancipation . . . I believe in equality, the Negro ought to have equal rights." However, Nevins believed that "the Bible does not preach . . . amalgamation of the races." Nevins saw public school integration as a step beyond equal rights and toward social equality, a move that would lead, he believed, to interracial sex. He was not alone. T. J. Preston of Georgia wrote about the Convention's acceptance of desegregation, noting, "Common sense would teach us if we mix them [the races] in schools and churches, they will mix socially— they will intermarry."[34]

The Southern Baptists, then, faced a situation similar to that of the southern Presbyterians, who, as it happened, had been the first major southern denomination to meet after the *Brown* decision. The General Assembly voted to condemn segregation. Like the Baptists', the Presbyterians' statement was argued on theological grounds, not legal grounds, and, like the Baptists' statement, it drew considerable criticism from members throughout the South.[35]

In the years immediately following the *Brown* decision, southern politicians moved to resist integration, and extralegal organizations like the White Citizens' Council spread. Politicians, like Herman Talmadge of Georgia, a Baptist, used the pervasive fear of interracial relationships to whip up resistance to integration. In that climate, Convention president C. C. Warren warned Baptists about the resistance movements that proliferated throughout the South: "open defiance of the constitutional principle will endanger our foreign mission work . . . and play right into the hands of the Communists who will welcome the privilege of ridiculing, not only our democratic form of government, but the type of Christianity which seeks to win the world."[36]

Still, southern politicians found support for massive resistance among Baptists. Vernon I. Tillar, chairman of the board of deacons at Main Street Baptist Church in Emporia, Virginia, wrote the state's governor, J. Lindsey Almond, supporting his stand against integration. The church had voted overwhelmingly to "express to you that we are in full support of your efforts to maintain separate but equal schools for the white and colored races." The letter also represented the persistent rift between the congregations and the leadership. Tillar noted, "We also want to make it known to you that we do not concur with the Virginia Baptist Association in it's [sic] recent refusal to back the governor on said issue."[37]

Baptist leaders realized that many southerners resisted change and retained long-standing prejudices against blacks. Mary Elizabeth (Mrs. Chester F.) Russell wrote in Royal Service admitting that "transition will not be easy." "We have been trained by practice and precept in society, in the home, in the school and even in the church that we are superior and the Negroes are inferior in intelligence, culture, cleanliness and civility. We will need personal preparation and continued effort to begin to overcome these fallacies which have been ingrained into our habitual thinking and mores." Russell reminded readers that blacks "have not had equal educational, religious, social or financial opportunities." She asked Baptists not to be discouraged if blacks "forget to be humble, or when they flounder in their newly given freedom." Whites had to overcome their prejudices, but the task facing blacks, that of overcoming years of oppression, was, she believed, far greater.[38]

Baptist efforts continued to focus on evangelical activities throughout the postwar period, even when they challenged segregation. In Tifton, Georgia, those educational efforts directly challenged racial prejudices. There, blacks and whites got to know each other on a more equal basis. Tifton Baptist Church assisted in a Bible School that was so successful it ran out of space. According to Sam Olive McGinnis, wife of Tifton Baptist's pastor, young people involved in the school gained their first experience as missionaries. She said, "These boys and girls have been impressed with the cleanliness and good manners of the [black] children they teach, and have found Christian love in the hearts for them that was new to some." Most important, the instructors were an integrated group. The Tifton youth were not merely doing something for blacks, they were doing something *with* blacks and interacting with blacks on a more equal footing. That experience helped undercut the legitimacy of segregation in the minds and hearts of the white youths who participated. McGinnis continued: "too often we white and colored people see each other only on an employer-servant level, and neither really gets to know the other. In this effort we have all come to respect each other more, and genuinely to love one another."[39]

Claude Broach, the pastor at St. John's Baptist Church in Charlotte, North Carolina, wrote the column "If You Ask Me" for the *Baptist Student*. A student identified as W. I. V. from Georgia wrote to Broach asking if segregation was Christian, regardless of its legality. Broach responded, "I must confess that I am a bit afraid of this question—afraid, at least of putting answers in print in such a limited space." He did, however, put his answer in print. He wrote: "in the sense that segregation, in any form, imposes arbitrary limitations upon a man's freedom to earn and enjoy the spiritual, material, political, and cultural values of life, we cannot reconcile it with the teachings of Jesus." Broach believed that his short answer to the question opened him up for attack, and he invited Baptist students to "fire away."[40]

One student wrote to Broach asking his advice but hardly "firing away." Broach answered that Christian students had the unique opportunity of serving the nation in the early, difficult days of integration. Christian students, he said, should be "natural, courteous, and helpful." Moreover, he wrote, "if occasion demands it, we should be ready to defend the rights of the minority group."[41]

By 1958 civil rights had come out of the courtroom and into the streets. In the aftermath of the Montgomery bus boycott and the Little Rock High School integration episode, the Home Mission Board determined to redouble its efforts among blacks. John Caylor, managing editor of *Home Missions*, wrote, "In this period of tension and misunderstanding, the Home Mission Board has the opportunity of rendering its services unhampered by clashes of organized groups meeting in conflict." Caylor believed that Baptists, black and white, could come together as Christians, put aside racial animosity, and solve the race problem. Baptists, therefore, had a particular responsibility for solving that problem.[42]

Toward that end, the Home Mission Board increased its cooperative efforts with the black Baptists. Victor T. Glass, head of the board's Department of Work with National Baptists, explained that the biblical principles guiding the work were oneness and togetherness. Glass emphasized working together with black Baptists, not the more paternalistic effort of doing something for them, reflecting a subtle change in the board's approach after World War II and more reminiscent of what the Tifton youth had actually done. Pointing to the Acts of the Apostles, where Paul reminded early Christians that God "hath made of one blood all the nations of men," Glass noted, "We share a oneness not only with the National Baptists but with all men." Glass added, "We also share with National Baptists a oneness that is different: we are one with them in that we are members 'of the household of faith,'" a reference to Paul's letter to the Galatians.[43]

Glendon McCullough, personnel secretary for the Home Mission Board, believed that changing attitudes about race made cooperative work with National Baptists one of the most challenging tasks the Home Mission Board undertook. He asked Southern Baptists, "Could it be that our prejudices and our short sightedness are the basic reasons that our witness is lacking in power in this country and abroad?" He chastised Baptists, saying, "We are too often last in realms where our Christian faith should have helped us lead the way." Charlie S. Mills, a Southern Baptist military chaplain, questioned the very idea of cooperation. Progressive Baptists had long expounded on the essential unity of the human race, and Mills argued that cooperation was only possible between two different groups. He claimed that once Baptists began "to treat all people as the creations of God, then we as Southern Baptists will have begun to assume the stature which I am certain that our Christ would have us assume."[44]

Some Baptists moved in the direction Mills urged. In Corpus Christi, Texas, ministers voted to accept messengers from St. John's Baptist and Friendship Baptist, two National Baptist churches. The situation in Texas was certainly unique. Only a few other Southern Baptist associations, all in the Southwest, had extended messenger status to black ministers. Such decisions rested entirely with the local association. Mission leaders could point to the Corpus Christi Association's decision as an example to be followed, but they could do nothing to force other associations to follow that example.[45]

The mission leaders tried to push churches toward increased involvement in the racial situation, and with some success. By the end of 1958, over forty-four hundred churches had sponsored Vacation Bible Schools for blacks, often in conjunction with black churches. While that was not insignificant, there was a lot of work yet to be done in a Convention with nearly thirty thousand member churches. The Home Mission Board surveyed the churches and found that once a church began cooperating with black Baptists on one project, it was likely to undertake more cooperative projects. The board also discovered that rural and town churches were slightly more active than city churches, suggesting that urban Christians were not always more progressive on race relations than their rural counterparts. Only a few, but still a few, churches responded to the poll by saying that they did not "believe in cooperation between two races." Church members that did not even believe in the cooperation of the races could hardly be expected to accept racial integration.[46]

While agency and church efforts were important, progressive Baptists believed that, ultimately, race relations were the responsibility of each individual Christian. With that in mind, John Caylor reminded readers that "every Baptist is a home missionary." He believed Baptists had an obligation to minorities in their own communities. Baptists in places like Tifton, Georgia, had accepted that responsibility. In addition to sponsoring Bible Schools and other community efforts, however, Baptists needed a deeper understanding of the overall race problem. R. Elmer Dunham, the superintendent of city and rural missions in Texas, recommended that Baptists conduct study courses on race relations. Reflecting the leadership's emphasis on education and the international dimensions of the American race situation, Dunham also suggested Baptists correspond with foreign missionaries, a suggestion not unlike the pen pal programs for Baptist youth. His suggestions reflected the Baptists' belief that racial problems stemmed from ignorance, and that ignorance bred fear and hatred.[47]

Ignorance included being unaware of one's own feelings. In her article "Are You an All-American Citizen," which appeared in the *Window* in 1959, Marjorie Moore Armstrong asked young women to take stock of their prejudices. Armstrong asked young women, "Do you tell racial jokes?" "Do you use racial and national nicknames? . . . Do you go in for blanket condemnations?" She demanded that young women recognize that generalizations were slanderous. Typical of progressive Baptists, Armstrong also believed that American racism had worldwide implications. She reminded readers that "the whole white race is a minority in the world" and suggested they "consider the relationship of our attitude toward minority races in America to the attitude of the colored peoples throughout the world toward us."[48]

Just as American racism had a damaging effect on Baptist missions around the world, a deeper understanding of the world race question could lead to a better understanding of the domestic issues. After an extended study program on Africa, leaders at the Woman's Missionary Union asked Baptist women if they had "felt the heavy heart beat of a people in bondage, seeking freedom?" They reminded Baptist women that "freedom from ignorance, freedom from superstition, freedom from oppression are desired by Africans whether in Africa or in the United States of America." They hoped that studying Africa would encourage Baptist women to have a "greater appreciation for the Negro people." Progressive leaders also hoped that a greater appreciation of the black struggle would lead whites to abandon racist ideas and discriminatory practices. One of the most obvious opportunities for learning about the problems of local blacks involved working with black churches, through Vacation Bible Schools and other church-related activities.[49]

Black and white Baptists shared their basic beliefs. Still, few Baptists worshipped in integrated congregations, and only slightly better than one in ten held a cooperative Vacation Bible School with a black church. As a result, student summer missionaries often had their first experiences with black Baptists on the mission fields. The program provided students with experiences that could permanently change the student's view of blacks and of race relations. One student, Patricia Milton, wrote, "I had never really worshipped with another racial group. I expected a different experience, but I soon came to realize in my own heart that people are essentially the same when they worship the true, living God." Margaret Arnold had a similar experience when she found herself "holding closely a little colored girl who was frightened." Arnold's experiences undermined the prejudices she had learned living in the South. She told readers: "I did not consider her color when she came to me for comfort and love, even though [I was] reared with bitter prejudice all about me." The experience transformed Arnold. She said, "I could see the barriers of prejudice secretly harbored in my own life slowly crumble . . . and I was glad."[50]

Progressive Baptists believed that positive interracial experiences could undercut racism, as Arnold had demonstrated. Such experiences were particularly important for future missionaries. S. Kathryn Bigham, the director of field work at the Woman's Missionary Union's Training School, wrote about an unnamed student's experience. The student taught roughly thirty adolescents in Sunday School and then dined with them before helping with the recreation program. The student's report read: "for the first time in my life I ate with Negroes; for the first time in my life I shook hands with Negroes. We were the first white people these boys and girls had ever accepted as brothers and sisters. . . . If I haven't given them anything, they have given me everything for they have made me a better Christian."[51]

In many white churches, however, blacks were unwelcome, so most Southern Baptists continued to worship in all-white congregations. As the 1960s opened, the civil rights movement became more confrontational. The sit-in movement, spawned by the lunch-counter action of four black students in North Carolina, also led to the "kneel-ins," which challenged segregation in the churches. In September 1960, black students sought seats in white Atlanta churches, and several Atlanta churches, including First Baptist Church and Second Ponce de Leon Baptist, seated the students. Students were also welcomed at First Presbyterian, St. Luke's Episcopal, St. Philip's Episcopal, and the Lutheran Church of the Redeemer. However, Druid Hills Baptist, the Baptist Tabernacle, and Druid Hills Methodist either turned the students away or offered them segregated seating, which they refused. Blacks were also turned away from Grace Methodist, where they had previously been welcomed. Indeed, as historian Joel L. Alvis noted, some churches adopted restrictive access policies only after blacks began attending services.[52]

Atlanta offered an important target for testing segregation in churches. It was the headquarters city for the Home Mission Board. Further, several Atlanta ministers, including Louis D. Newton of Druid Hills Baptist Church, signed the "Atlanta Manifesto" before the kneel-ins. Newton, in many ways a progressive, had been president of the Southern Baptist Convention, vice president of the World Baptist Alliance, and continued to author the weekly newspaper column "This

Changing World." The manifesto declared that the ministers admitted, "Our own example has been all too imperfect." The ministers believed that Christians had a special responsibility in the race crisis. They declared that "if, as Christians we sincerely seek to understand and apply the teachings of our Lord we shall find the answer" to the race problem and that "we do believe that all Americans whether black or white have a right to the full privileges of first class citizenship." Yet Newton's church, like many other churches in Atlanta, was unable to accommodate black worshippers on an equal basis with white worshippers.[53]

The resistance to church integration prompted Walker L. Knight, editor of *Home Missions*, to announce that churches had lost sight of their original missionary purposes. He argued, "Instead of sharing our faith, we are seeking only what personal benefits can be derived from it. The selfish closing of the membership of a church underscores such trends." Acknowledging the changing ethnic composition of many southern neighborhoods and tying local ministries to world missions, Knight asked, "If the church can be closed to those around it, why should it be concerned with those beyond it?"[54]

Continued segregation created practical problems for missionaries and was a symptom of the "sickness" and sin of racism. Edward A. McDowell of Southeastern Baptist Theological Seminary noted, "The tragedy of our situation in the South is that for the most part our people do not realize that they are the victims of spiritual sickness in accepting and perpetuating unchristian racial patterns." That was especially frustrating in light of the board's efforts to promote progressive views of race throughout the postwar years. In particular, McDowell argued, "It is difficult to see how the minister can escape accepting some responsibility for the racial situation in his community." While many southern Christians did not realize that segregation was unchristian, McDowell believed that whites had to recognize their prejudices for what they were, sins, before much progress could be made. The onus was on whites—they had to overcome racism before southern society could be truly Christian.[55]

Some Southern Baptists who resisted church integration noted that the black churches were the most powerful institutions in the black community and, therefore, those blacks who tried to enter white churches were merely "testing" them. Few of the blacks who attempted to worship in white churches sought to gain permanent membership in those churches. Rather, they were challenging whites to practice the Christian doctrines of equality and unity in their churches. The question was less whether blacks would join white churches than it was whether whites would close their churches to blacks. McDowell recognized that many whites viewed the kneel-ins as tests and responded, "Even when Negroes come to a church to worship as a test, the white congregation should receive them in Christian love and seat them with the congregation." To do otherwise would be to fail the test.[56]

Walker Knight agreed with McDowell. He chastised Baptists for taking inadequate steps toward solving the race problem, saying, "Too often we have been part of the problem, instead of being involved in the solution." Knight urged Baptists to learn about the "status of the Negro and other races in the United States." He noted that many pastors deplored violence in race relations but did not take steps toward recognizing either blacks' civil rights or the barriers to their exercising those rights. From a practical point of view, he proposed that churches "should announce they are open to all people, regardless of race, for worship."[57]

As he expected, Knight received several letters from readers regarding his proposals. Some readers canceled their subscriptions while others threatened to discontinue their financial support of the Home Mission Board. Other writers indicated their support. One had considered affiliating with another denomination, but after reading Knight's editorial "decided there was some hope." Only the letters that said his proposals were fine but "too little, too late" or "weak" surprised Knight.[58]

While Knight had the luxury of speaking theoretically, church pastors had to face a variety of challenges in their changing neighborhoods. Their congregations were moving to the suburbs, and several churches opted to follow them. Courts Redford of the Home Mission Board noted that many blacks had moved into previously white neighborhoods. He worried less about the Southern Baptists' ability to maintain their churches than their ability to "give guidance and help to our colored brethren."[59]

By the early 1960s, Capital Avenue Baptist Church was the only white church remaining in its Atlanta district. Fred Propst felt challenged by the situation facing the church, left retirement, and took over the pulpit. With the help of his wife, he began "weekday ministries," including nurseries, Bible classes, guided activities for children, women's groups, teenage groups, and adult literacy classes. Programs grew. Within a year of Propst's arrival, 360 people, including both whites and blacks, enrolled in church activities. For the Baptist leadership, the case of Capital Avenue Baptist proved that "the relevance of Christianity can become a reality on the crowded bustling streets around downtown churches." Propst was clearly in the vanguard of progressive Baptists. Not until 1966 did the Home Mission Board sponsor a study of problems that churches faced in transitional communities—problems that Propst had been facing at Capital Avenue for three years.[60]

Propst's leadership represented quite a different response to neighborhood change than Lynn T. Richardson of St. Louis had demonstrated a few years earlier. Richardson was pastor of Bethel Baptist Church, a church of roughly nine hundred members that found itself in "a very serious situation, one which we have no control over." In a private letter to Porter Routh at the Executive Committee, Richardson indicated that real estate companies in St. Louis were promoting "our community for the Negro population[,] and the majority of our members have had to move out of the neighborhood because the colored people have bought their homes." While it seems unlikely that anyone, black or white, could have purchased the homes if their owners had not sold them, Richardson came to conclusions quite different from the ones that Baptist mission leaders hoped for from pastors in his situation. "We find we have only one alternative," Richardson concluded, "and that is to sell our building to a Negro congregation." Richardson was looking for another pulpit, presumably at a lily-white church.[61]

Since the churches themselves determined their membership, Baptist leaders could only cajole them toward inclusive membership policies. They could not directly influence those decisions. The state conventions did, however, have some influence on the Baptist colleges. By 1952, the Southern Baptist Convention had desegregated all of its seminaries. Institutions affiliated with state conventions were slower to integrate, especially in the Southeast. In 1951 Wayland Baptist in Plainview, Texas, had become the first white Baptist college to accept black students. Oklahoma Baptist University and Georgetown College, in Kentucky, had both integrated by 1956. By 1960 Grand Canyon in Arizona and California Baptist, Southern Illinois Baptist, and Hannibal La Grange in Missouri had followed suit. Notably, to that point, none of the integrated Baptist colleges were in the Deep South. By 1960, 150 blacks— Americans and Africans—were registered at Southern Baptist colleges and seminaries. While many decisions regarding racial integration involved concern about world missions, two Baptist educational institutions integrated in direct reaction to the mission issue: Wake Forest in North Carolina and Mercer in Georgia.[62]

In 1960, Edward Reynolds, a recent convert from Ghana, applied to Wake Forest College. The college took more than a year to act on Reynolds's application. Meanwhile, editors at *The Commission* speculated that the questions raised by a mission convert's applying to the school prompted Wake Forest to integrate its graduate-level programs. A year later, the college admitted Reynolds and removed all racial barriers from undergraduate admission. After the decision, the college administration wrote the Ghana Baptist Mission stating Wake Forest's willingness to accept students of any race. The mission responded, sending a letter of appreciation to the college trustees.[63]

While Wake Forest was grappling with integration, *Who's Who Among Students in American Universities and Colleges* recognized Vincent Armachree, a Nigerian student at Oklahoma Baptist University. James R. Scales, president of the university, said Armachree was "the embodiment of a Christian gentleman." Additionally, in the fall of 1962, as Mercer University was considering integration, the state Baptist Student Union in Georgia announced that "race should not be a factor influencing relations among men" and noted the damage that racial prejudice did to foreign missions. The spring semester of 1963 brought the integration question of Georgia Baptists' flagship educational institution, Mercer University, to the forefront.[64]

Harris Mobley, a missionary in Ghana, and Sam Jerri Oni, a convert, decided to challenge segregation at Mercer in 1962. Mobley had graduated from Mercer and Southeastern Seminary in North Carolina. He had already helped secure scholarships for two Ghanaian Baptists, Stephen Akinleye and Alfred Oteng, to attend Southeastern Seminary. Once there, the two men had joined Wake Forest Baptist Church. But Southeastern, unlike Mercer, had been integrated for a decade.[65]

Mobley and Oni intended to use Oni's application to Mercer to challenge their "Southern Baptist brothers and sisters in America to confront the gross contradictions in their Christian witnesses at home and abroad." They believed that Oni, as an African convert, offered the "most compelling and unassailable argument against the continuation of racial segregation as practiced in Southern Baptist churches, schools, hospitals and other establishments across the Southern United States."[66]

In the fall of 1962, Mercer's president, Rufus C. Harris, urged the university to consider integration. He believed that "as a Christian there is a matter of conscience involved . . . in the seemingly unchristian act of drawing a color line in education." The Trustee Committee charged by Harris with investigating integration opposed the move. In January 1963, it reported that Mercer should not integrate and hoped for the "influence of time" and further study. Time, however, was one thing Mercer did not have—Oni had already applied to the university. He was, according to the director of admission, John Mitchell, "the ablest international student to apply for admission to Mercer in recent years." Mitchell told Harris, on December 20, 1962, that "were it not for his color, he would already have been accepted without question."[67]

The situation at Mercer was not particularly different from that at Wake Forest, but the question of Mercer's integration became a matter of public debate in a way that Wake Forest's integration never did. Russell Hillard, a Southern Baptist missionary serving in Spain, wrote to John Hurt, editor of the *Christian Index* (the weekly publication of the Georgia Baptist Convention) about Oni's application. In response, Hurt wrote an editorial, quoting Hillard as saying Oni's acceptance would "not signify a change in our tradition, but it will mean a slight change in our hearts!"[68]

Hurt recommended separating the issue of integration from Oni's admission, a suggestion that was contrary to the missionary leadership's persistent view that racism in America and racism in Africa were intertwined. Hurt believed that separating the two issues was the only possible way that the acceptance of an African student at a segregated university would not be "a change in our tradition." The idea had precedent. In 1962, Ouachita Baptist College in Arkansas had established a policy of accepting converts from the mission fields but not accepting American blacks. Two black students from Rhodesia, a husband and wife, attended Ouachita.[69]

Most Georgia Baptists writing to the *Christian Index* argued that Oni's application was inextricably tied to integration. Rowena Almand of Doraville asked, "What would Christ think about the hair-splitting legalistic distinctions made by the recent editorial advising that the admission of the Ghana student be separated from the broader issue of our own American Negroes[?]" In doing so, she reflected the international perspective missionaries had been expounding for well over a decade. Almand also believed that "the time is long past for Mercer, if it is really a Christ-centered college, to accept all students on the basis of character and ability, rather than the color of their skin." Baptists who opposed integration also saw the issues as intertwined. K. H. Hines of Leslie said that admitting Oni would be "a way of letting the gap down for all Negroes as one Rufus Harris would have it."[70]

Even for Hurt, Oni's application was inextricably tied to the mission program. He announced, "We either admit him [Oni] or we should have the courage to call home all of our missionaries and go out of the business." He believed that if Mercer did not admit Oni, it would prove that "we are in greater need of missionary preaching than Ghana." Only a few correspondents were willing to close the missions. One, W. J. Thurmond, believed that if the success of mission activity was "contingent upon the admission of this Negro student to Mercer, then I also say let's call all our missionaries home." That would not happen. As Romeo J. Martin of Atlanta realized, calling home the missionaries would make the Georgia Baptists the "ultimate hypocrites."[71]

As Mobley and Oni had intended, the Mercer case caused some Baptists to reconsider their stand on integration. Jack Carpenter of Dahlonega believed that "my good friends and brethren will understand and forgive me if I say that, in spite of my middle-age conservatism, I cannot help but gag at the idea of excluding a young African convert from our beloved Mercer simply because God gave him dark skin." The trustees came to the same conclusion. They met on April 18, barely four months after the committee had recommended against integration. By a vote of thirteen to five, with three abstentions, Mercer dropped all racial barriers in admissions to the university. Hurt wrote that missionaries could "point to Mercer University, in Georgia and in the Deep South, as having sacrificed comfort to show Christian concern for young men and women 'without regard to race, color of skin, creed, or origin.'"[72]

Clearly, some Baptists disagreed with integrating Baptist universities, but more and more of those universities *were* integrating. Furman University in South Carolina was considering dropping racial barriers to admission in 1963, and members of Cameron Baptist Church, in Cameron, South Carolina, declared their objections, announcing, "We feel that segregation of the races is a plan set up by God for the ultimate good of all men." Two votes were cast against the resolution, the minister's and his wife's. The minister wrote to Porter Routh, "I sadly regret such impulsive action based on such tragically unsound biblical exegesis and interpretation, and I prayerfully support the Board of Trustees of Furman University in the action taken." Once again, the congregations and the leadership held differing views, and both believed their own view was the one supported by the Bible.[73]

At the University of Florida the decision to integrate the institution for the 1962–63 academic year was beyond the influence of the state's Baptists, but members of the university's Baptist Student Union took a stand for racial equality. Johncyna Williams entered the University of Florida as one of the school's first seven black students and joined the Baptist Student Union. The students had planned a progressive dinner at local churches, but the possibility of hosting an integrated group disturbed some of those congregations. The union adopted a policy stating, "In order to maintain the integrity of our Christian witness . . . we feel that we cannot participate, as a group, in any activity where all our members or guests are not received with equal dignity." Baptist students took a stand for racial equality that went beyond merely accepting the blacks' civil rights. They insisted that blacks and whites be treated with equal dignity in an entirely social setting, a progressive dinner. The churches ultimately accepted the group.[74]

Johncyna Williams attended Westside Baptist in Gainesville, raising the question of church integration. Her presence caused those members who opposed integration to demand that the church's planning committee do something. The debate reflected several themes that the progressive Baptist leadership had stressed over the years: the promise of youth, the belief that racism was learned, and the international dimensions of the race question. Members believed that rejecting Williams would disillusion the young people of the church. One noted, "I grew up with prejudice because my parents taught it to me. I don't want to teach my children prejudice." Another asked, "How can we send missionaries to Africa and then discriminate against the American Negro[?]" Some members still made distinctions in the type of "equality" they were willing to allow blacks to achieve. They opposed integration, but believed that they could not bar someone from a church based on race. The committee determined to accept any Christian regardless of race. The congregation accepted the recommendation, with about one-fourth dissenting.[75]

Events in Winston-Salem, Macon, and Gainesville demonstrated the divisions within the Southern Baptist Convention in the 1960s, but each seemed to indicate progress. Baptist foreign missionaries home on furlough met in May of 1963 and expressed their gratitude for the efforts to improve race relations that they saw being made across the South. Still, progressive Baptist leaders continued to face several problems in bringing their denomination to accept more progressive attitudes about race. According to Samuel Southard, a professor at the Southern Baptist Theological Seminary, "congregational self-government . . . helped to isolate Southern Baptists from national awareness," and historians since have agreed. Southard informally polled churches and pastors and found that "the peripheral member, the member who is spiritually dormant, and the social climber . . . tended to be mentioned most often as those opposed to desegregation in the churches." Peripheral members, who were only minimally involved, were also the members least affected by the leadership's views and writings. The chasm between the leadership and membership continued, and Baptist churches presented "at best, a split image" on the race issue.[76]

Baptist leaders continually tried to repair that "split image" and to present a unified, progressive front on the racial issue. Yet the Convention remained deeply divided by the race issue. The "split image" Baptists presented was a fair reflection of the Convention. Still, Baptist efforts were not just about image. Progressive leaders worked to repair the fissures in the Convention by bringing Southern Baptists to a Christian view of race relations. In North Carolina, C. R. Grigg, who headed cooperative work with National Baptists in that state, announced, "Baptists have found ways of keeping lines of communication open and have discovered methods of cooperation in spite of racial prejudice and other kindred barriers." Black and white Baptists met in joint fellowship at their annual sessions, and churches held schools of missions without regard to race. Four North Carolina Baptist colleges officially accepted blacks, although only two, Mars Hill and Wake Forest, had blacks attending. Grigg understood, as did his progressive colleagues, that racial harmony demanded more than merely a good image.[77]

Grigg called on Baptists to take a stand for peace and justice. Noting that blacks who demanded their civil rights were arrested for disturbing the peace, he argued, "Indeed, they have disturbed the peace and complacency of white people." Grigg called on Baptists to be "renewed by the spirit of Christ." Baptists should "be transformed and thus show forth in our lives and in the life of our communities what is the acceptable word of God." Christianity, in his view, should transform society rather than validate it.[78]

While the Southern Baptist leaders called for a Christian transformation of American society, the federal government took increasingly stronger measures. In 1964, the Johnson administration pushed through the Civil Rights Act, outlawing segregation in public accommodations. President Lyndon Johnson addressed a gathering of Southern Baptists, urging them to continue to value the separation of church and state but not to let that "mean the divorce of spiritual values from secular affairs." Johnson's speech urging Southern Baptists to support the Civil Rights Bill had been written by Bill D. Moyers, a Baptist minister who had graduated from Southwestern Seminary. Involvement in secular affairs, however, was a point of contention among Southern Baptists. The leadership had tried, since World War II, to get Baptists more involved in social issues, while conservative Baptists continued to fear that that would lead to the Social Gospel, which they believed was unbiblical.[79]

Specifically regarding the Civil Rights Act of 1964 and the Voting Rights Act of 1965, Norman Bowman of the Sunday School Board wrote that the passing of the laws "bore testimony to the fact that love had fallen short of the ideal. Love had seemingly done less than justice demanded." The laws were needed because calls for voluntary action in the name of Christian love had not solved the race problem. Still, the law could not solve the problem by itself. Bowman believed that before the race crisis could be solved, "man must first learn that God's will is His will and not man's."[80]

Southern attitudes stifled blacks' attempts to exercise the rights laid out in the Civil Rights Act and frustrated progressive Baptists. The civil rights movement became increasingly confrontational. In 1964 the nation turned its attention to the voter registration efforts in Mississippi. Freedom Summer laid bare the contradictions in American society. Summer's end brought even more problems. After the Democratic National Convention seated the all-white delegation from Mississippi over the integrated Mississippi Freedom Democratic Party delegation, many blacks lost what faith they had left in white liberals to pursue true racial equality.[81]

That year, Foy Valentine, who had assumed leadership of the

Christian Life Commission from A. C. Miller, noted that a decade after *Brown* "the racial revolution at our doorsteps is not abating. It is accelerating in the current racial crisis." Valentine continued, "We urge that Christians dedicate themselves to the challenging task of gaining the initiative in racial reconciliation in the current crisis." Finally, Valentine admitted that Christians had done far too little to end racism: "our thunderous silence in the face of oppressive injustice for American Negroes has amounted to a serious complicity in the problem. We have been part of a culture which has crippled the Negro and then blamed him for limping. Our failure to create a climate of Christian good will, based on the weightier matters of justice, mercy, and love has resulted in the racial protest movements which have been used for the redress of legitimate grievances. Indeed we have contributed to the belief of many Negroes that these movements offer their only avenue of recourse." In 1964 the annual convention passed a resolution calling on Baptists to "rededicate ourselves in the spirit of Christ to a ministry of reconciliation among all men." The resolution urged Baptists to remember that "all men stand as equals at the foot of the cross without distinction of color."[82]

Mary Allred, a North Carolina Baptist, realized that "there must be something wrong with me." Allred lost no sleep worrying about losing her rights in the face of civil rights legislation. She did not fear sending her four children to school with black children or worry about sitting next to blacks on the bus or at a lunch counter. Finally, Allred admitted there was something wrong with her. She wrote, "I suppose I must be 'color blind' and I pray God that I will stay that way." While many southerners disagreed with her, she believed that "God's voice has thundered through the centuries, reminding us that he made of all nations, one blood." She concluded, "I must also remember that even when in the minority, I must always look at all men with God's eyes—eyes of love. This is his commandment and I must obey. He does not give a choice."[83]

After her article appeared in *Royal Service* in the spring of 1964, Allred reported, "I have had a good many telephone calls from friends and neighbors and people in nearby churches who have read 'Using God's Eyes' . . . almost without exception they have all said 'thank you.'" Allred said that many of the people she spoke to had never taken a position on the race issue. They called to say "I admire you for the position you are taking," even though some could not agree with her. The article, however, was a topic of discussion in *Royal Service* for several months after its publication, mostly focusing on the response from Dorothy Robinson.[84]

Dorothy Robinson found Allred's article disturbing. She believed that *Royal Service* and other Baptist publications constantly told readers to examine the "other side" of the race question but refused to see the segregationist side. Indeed, Baptist mission leaders, and especially those at the Woman's Missionary Union, persistently promoted the progressive view of race relations. While some had suggested equality and segregation were compatible before 1954, even that line of argument had disappeared from missionary literature since the *Brown* decision. Segregationists were increasingly on the defensive and had their say only in letters to the editors. As a result, Dorothy Robinson got the impression that Baptist leaders believed that "either I believe in integration or I am unchristian." Robinson, like other Southern Baptists who continued to resist integration, believed that she was a Christian. Baptist leaders challenged a central part of her identity by suggesting that she was, in fact, unchristian because she believed in segregation. Such an attack on her identity necessarily aroused resistance. Further, Robinson believed that supporting segregation did not make her prejudiced. While Baptist leaders had argued personal friendships would help people overcome racism, Robinson's letter suggested a shortcoming in that view. Robinson noted that she considered several blacks among her dearest friends and, therefore, could not be a racist. She wrote, "There are many thousands of us in America who believe absolutely in racial separation but have no hate or ill will toward any Negro."[85]

Other Baptists took exception to Robinson's views. Mrs. S. A. Williams of Arkansas asked Robinson, "You say you have not 'pre-judged' the Negro. Haven't you? Haven't you already judged him as not being eligible to be a citizen in the country in which he was born?" Williams wrote, "I am not young. I was born the year the Yankee soldiers were called back home." She also directly addressed the issue of federal legislation, saying, "The new Civil Rights Bill only forces us to do that which the Constitution has always guaranteed should be done to all citizens." She noted that the act did "not require that we accept them socially or intermarry with them." She pointed out that integrated schooling did not necessarily lead to intermarriage, rejecting a consistent claim of racial conservatives. The act did not require blacks and whites to interact socially, but "it does not forbid it to those who wish to do so. Here in America we have always been free to choose our own friends. We still are." Her views were reflected by other writers, including Gladys M. McClain.[86]

Gladys McClain, a black woman, had recently moved to Hawaii, where she was active in her Southern Baptist church. When Robinson objected to "forced mixing," McClain agreed. She would not go where she was unwelcome, but she believed that she ought to be welcome, especially in a church. She stressed that "if people are concerned about lost souls, color makes no difference." Color, however, made a difference in many churches. Even in North Carolina, with one of the more progressive state conventions, the Christian Life Commission admitted that "in virtually none of our churches are Negroes welcome."[87]

In 1965 the Convention added Race Relations Sunday to the official calendar, though it had encouraged churches to observe the day in previous years. Even so, Southern Baptists were latecomers to the observance. It had been initiated in the 1920s by the Department of Racial and Cultural Relations of the National Council of Churches. Arthur Rutledge and Foy Valentine wrote to pastors announcing that the purpose of the observation was "to call attention to the role we all can play as persons in resolving conflict, building fellowship, and developing the ministry of reconciliation which God has committed to his people." In 1966, Marguerite Babb of Edifield Baptist Church in Nashville, Tennessee, wrote that she had checked through the bulletins of many churches and found that most had held "simple, dignified, and educational" observances. An unnamed Louisiana layman announced that members of his church "saw the huge stake Southern Baptists have in the solution of racial problems." One pastor in Alabama temporarily lost his church for "committing the crime . . . of observing Race Relations Sunday." The pastor reclaimed his pulpit after vacationing members returned and the voting majority swung in his favor. Some pastors were not so lucky.[88]

Race relations remained a divisive issue among Southern Baptists. Some Baptists believed that the Convention leadership had resorted to "high-handed" tactics. R. F. Hallford of New Ellenton, South Carolina, worried that Baptist leaders were using the same tactics "used and encouraged by what I honestly believe to be a Communist controlled government and society." Although Hallford did not actually accuse

Convention leaders of being communists, his view of the government reflected a wider and persistent belief that integration was a communist plot. Like most Southern Baptists, however, Hallford could not bring himself to believe that the Convention, a solidly southern institution, was communist. Its leaders were just, for now, misguided.[89]

Likewise, T. B. Gillooly of Pelican, Louisiana, believed that the Convention's leadership had no intention of damaging its own mission work but that it was misguided on the issue of race. He believed that "surely they are just unaware of the feelings of our people in regard to this [integration] issue." Gillooly obviously disagreed with the leadership's view that segregation, not integration, damaged the Convention's mission work. He also resisted the idea that the Christian message should transform society. Instead, he suggested that the leadership should conform to the will of the membership and the traditions of society, a view quite at odds with the leadership's vision of a Christian transformation of society.[90]

Virginia Molett of Orriville, Alabama, wrote to *Home Missions* in early 1967, saying that Jesus "was not a member of any group for the advancement of social, economic or racial groups while he was on this earth." Molett believed the leadership was tending toward a liberal interpretation of the Gospel. Likewise, Virginia Barker of North English, Iowa, feared that the Southern Baptists were adopting the Social Gospel and abandoning their fundamentalist roots. She said that a missionary magazine like *Home Missions* should not tell the churches how to conduct their business and canceled her subscription.[91]

Barker also addressed one of the more difficult issues facing the Convention: church integration. She wrote, "I can't understand what our leaders mean to want to integrate the churches. The Negroes has [*sic*] been free 100 years and many, many are doing well. The white people have civilized and educated them. They should encourage them to take pride in their own race and in their own schools and churches." Barker not only believed that segregation was fair—a view the leadership had clearly abandoned by 1967—but she also sounded one of the most persistent fears of segregationists: interracial marriage. She believed that blacks wanted to "overrule" whites and that when that happened, black men would begin marrying white women.[92]

The issues of church segregation often demonstrated the chasm between the leadership and the congregations. In Virginia, Richmond pastor Theodore F. Adams found himself at odds with the board of deacons of First Baptist Church, which had narrowly voted against his recommendation to accept two Nigerian students studying at Virginia Union University into fellowship at the church. The situation was particularly problematic, as Rogers M. Smith noted when he wrote T. B. Maston, because "there are several members of the Foreign Mission Board staff who are in First Baptist Church." Smith was one of those members. Along with the others, he was "trying to give Dr. Adams all the encouragement" possible. The situation at First Baptist captured few headlines in the denominational press; the Convention's attention was, once again, drawn to Macon, Georgia, where Sam Jerri Oni was turned away by Tattnall Square Baptist Church.[93]

In 1966, three years after Oni arrived at Mercer University in Macon, he twice attempted to worship at Tattnall Square, on September 25 and October 2. He was rebuffed both times. Tattnall Square, which was contiguous with the Mercer campus, made it clear that it would remain segregated. Oni felt obligated to tell the church that "their segregationist policy is torpedoing their own mission program in Africa." But he was not surprised that he was refused a seat. Indeed, he said he would have been surprised "if they had run up to me and said, 'Ah! Lost brother, welcome, come on in.'"[94]

Following Oni's attempt to attend, Tattnall Square ousted its interim pastor, Thomas Holmes, who favored integrating the church. Several deacons were bitter and believed that Oni was responsible for the torrent of criticism that was launched at the church. Condemnation came from East Africa, the Netherlands, and missionaries around the world. Holmes had received over four hundred letters, the vast majority supporting his position favoring church integration. Enough members supported Holmes that the church split and his supporters formed a new congregation. Progressive Baptist leaders like James O. Duncan publicly supported Holmes's position. Duncan, editor of Washington's *Capital Baptist*, suggested that since Tattnall Square's actions were damaging foreign mission work, Baptists should divorce the church from those missions. He suggested, "Southern Baptists ought, in a dramatic way, say we disapprove of such actions by giving back to the church all that they have given to foreign missions."[95]

After Tattnall Square's decision made headlines around the Convention, other churches tackled the question of integration. Holmes reported that several churches integrated as a result of the incident. First

Baptist of Macon, under the leadership of Pastor Albert Cardwell, admitted blacks into membership. In Atlanta, one deacon said his congregation had "firm convictions for segregation but feel [that] barring someone from worship conflicts with their Christian beliefs." The impact of the Tattnall Square incident was felt beyond the Baptist churches, however, for Centenary Methodist Church announced it would adhere to the Methodist General Conference directive of 1964 ordering integration in the church.[96]

Into the later 1960s, then, Southern Baptists continued to be a divided people. Contrary to the mission leaders' views, many Baptists held that integration was unchristian, communist inspired, and encouraged mainly, if not only, by "outside agitators" hoping for political and financial gains. Such persistent resistance to their message frustrated the progressive Baptist leadership. It demonstrated the depths of prejudices that southerners had long defended as divinely sanctioned. In the process, southerners often denied that those prejudices were even prejudices at all.

Perhaps most problematic for the Baptist leadership, state Convention leaders like Leon Macon, editor of the *Alabama Baptist*, promoted those segregationist themes throughout the postwar years. Historian Edward Queen writes of Macon, "He may not have been a virulent racist, but he was definitely a segregationist." Queen notes that Macon feared that integrated schools would lead to intermarriage and resented the intrusion of outsiders in the South's racial problems. Macon was, according to Queen, "active among those Deep South clergymen who worked to weaken the Convention's pronouncements on race." Macon had written Porter Routh at the Executive Committee, noting that some denominational literature promoted racial integration. He told Routh, "My personal conviction in the matter is that no Southern Baptist agency should promote integration. Policies as vital as this should not come from the top but should be originated within our individual churches." Macon thereby demonstrated not only resistance to integration but a continued belief that the Convention should follow its membership rather than offer a prophetic vision. Baptists shared these problems with other denominations. Methodist and Presbyterian ministers also defended segregation. Indeed, a former Presbyterian missionary to China, L. Nelson Bell, began the *Southern Presbyterian Journal*, which advocated fundamentalism and endorsed segregation on theological grounds. Such southern clergymen significantly contributed to the leadership's difficulties in moving southern Christians to a more progressive view of race.[97]

In the deeply divided Convention of the later 1960s, Southern Baptists who agreed with the progressive leadership thanked them for expounding Christian views of race. One, William L. Turner of Louisville, Kentucky, thanked the editors of *Home Missions* for "consistently calling upon Southern Baptists to be a church, Christ's Church!" He argued that racial segregation in the churches could not be in harmony with the spirit of Christ. Turner did not promote the Social Gospel or theological liberalism. Instead, like the Baptist leadership, he insisted that the Convention be a New Testament church. Turner explained, "The only pattern for a truly New Testament church is openness, acceptance, and fellowship with men of all races for whom God is Lord. A church which denies this cannot be a Christian Church."[98]

Turner was not alone. Pastor Raymond Parker of Meridian, Mississippi, wrote that he was grateful to the board leaders for making Southern Baptists examine their prejudices: "this is painful but so necessary if we are to become the kind of churches Christ can use in this needy world." Parker believed that the racial climate was slowly changing and credited the continuing attention given to the race issue by Baptist journals for promoting that change. Similarly, R. D. Fillpot, a pastor in Fort Worth, Texas, wrote that "your many articles on our responsibility to Negro people have given me great encouragement to lead Eastland Baptist Church into an integrated ministry." Like Capital Avenue Baptist Church in Atlanta, Eastland integrated both its services and membership. To those who said religion should not be involved in social movements, Henry B. Shirley responded that "neither Jesus nor the early church defended the status quo."[99]

Such encouraging letters led Victor T. Glass to believe that Southern Baptists were changing their attitudes about race. He cited an increasing integration among colleges and churches, and joint meetings and worship with National Baptists at associational and state levels. The most serious problem in race relations, Glass believed, was the "great and fundamental lack of knowledge concerning each other as persons and as Baptists." After twenty years of efforts to educate Baptists about the race problem and about minority groups, ignorance still fueled racism and discrimination. Still, Glass believed that in 1966 and 1967 more cooperation and understanding between the races existed than ever before, though much more was still clearly needed.[100]

Mission leaders attributed some of the changes in attitudes to their short-term missionary programs. Between 1944 and 1968, approximately ten thousand college students served as summer missionaries. Mission leaders argued that "one inevitable by-product is the changes brought about in the lives of the students who serve." In the 1960s, the mission boards increased the number of opportunities for youth to participate in programs. They introduced the US-2 program, which offered two years of home mission work, as well as the Christian Service Corps and the Journeyman Missionary program, for short-term foreign mission experience.[101]

For women who wanted to participate in missionary activity without leaving home, the Woman's Missionary Union initiated the Mission Action program. When Marie Mathis and Elaine Dickson announced the program, they asked Southern Baptist women, "Is it possible that there are geographic, racial, social, and cultural barriers within the local community which are just as real as those on the foreign mission field?" The authors explained that the Mission Action program was for "dedicated Christians who are able to break out of their narrow circle of concern to become involved in meeting the needs of mankind." They added, "Meeting the needs of people in the name of Jesus Christ and witnessing for him are daily responsibilities of every Christian." Christians had to do more than learn about racial problems; they had to live their faith.[102]

Time also aided the change in attitudes. Baptists had long put their hopes in the denomination's youth. College students in the late sixties had grown up in the postwar world with the progressive leadership's view dominating the denomination's literature for youth. Even youths who had missed, or avoided, denominational literature could hardly have missed the dramatic events of the civil rights movement. By 1965, integration had ceased to be merely a topic for debate; it had become a reality to be faced. John Jeffers Jr., a "recent graduate" of Auburn University, wrote, "Our attitude toward a desegregation order is very important, for our attitude must be the one God wants us to have." Jeffers pointed to the problem of peer pressure, admitting that "in matters as deeply rooted and all encompassing as race relations, it is easy to be swayed by the crowd and by prejudices." Nevertheless, Jeffers felt that it was his responsibility as a Christian to keep his "mind and heart in tune with God and to look to Him for guidance rather than follow the leadership of the crowd."[103]

One student, Jerry Riddle, a senior at the University of Mississippi, offered insight into why so many Baptists resisted that message: "the placid surface of our detached indifference has been ruffled. . . . Our first reaction is natural bitterness and resentment. But it *is* a reaction, and as such marks the first necessary and essential step—a confrontation of the problem." Riddle further explained, "We have ignored, closed our minds automatically at the mention of the words 'integration' and 'race relations.'" Those words, however, were no longer merely words. They were "facts in our social system." Riddle believed that Christians had to approach those facts with "open, unprejudiced, honest, clear thinking."[104]

In 1967, a survey of Baptist college students found them disgruntled with the lack of social action on the part of Southern Baptists, particularly in the field of race relations. In a moderated discussion among Baptist students that same year, Nita Boyd of the Mississippi State College for Women emphasized the impact of time and changing generations. She argued that "generally college students don't have the attitudes their parents do." She worried, however, that students pushed their parents' generation too hard at times, especially on issues like church integration. Roger Brunner of Frostburg State College in Maryland believed that students could still do something. He said students should accept people of all races into the Baptist Student Unions, as had happened at the University of Florida. Students would thereby "make them feel so welcome that perhaps eventually the adults in the church will see that we aren't just being radical. We are just living our Christianity."[105]

By the end of the 1960s many denominational institutions, apart from churches, had integrated, and the mission program continued to grow. In 1968, Baker James Cauthen welcomed Sue Thompson as the first black appointed as a career missionary by the Foreign Mission Board. Cauthen indicated that the board would have appointed a black missionary earlier if one had applied for appointment. He told Thompson, "We have waited for you a long time." Yet the problems were far from solved. Some Baptist institutions remained segregated well into the 1960s. Indeed, as late as 1969, the Southern Baptist Convention urged the Baptist hospital in New Orleans to practice its stated policy of accepting patients regardless of "race, creed, color, national origin, or ability to pay." As the hospital situation showed, even when Baptists adopted a policy of racial desegregation, prejudice made it difficult for them to put those policies into action. That made the Baptists seem hypocritical and their policies and promises appear hollow.[106]

In 1967, as Baptists sought ways to implement their beliefs, the state convention in Kentucky debated merging with the black convention. The moderator of the National Baptist General Association in Kentucky urged merging and noted that the youth night, "which was well integrated," demonstrated "the oneness of Christ and Christianity in action." Henry A. Buchanan and Bob W. Brown, pastors from Lexington, told Southern Baptists that the "merger would also involve Southern Baptists in the Negroes' struggle for Civil Rights and racial equality. We would no longer be able to pass resolutions calling for justice and Christian brotherhood, then go home again to our churches and forget the whole unpleasant affair for another year." They realized that the proposal and its implications could be divisive, and the two conventions never merged. Race was clearly one reason. Southern Baptists, Buchanan and Brown lamented, had not even accepted Martin Luther King Jr. "as one of the primary spiritual leaders of our day."[107]

While Kentucky Baptists were struggling with the merger question, Baptist college students were taking the initiative for improving race relations at the local level. Believing that they could make a difference as individuals if they lived according to their Christian beliefs, students at Wake Forest revived the settlement house idea. In the 1967–68 academic year, three students lived at Patterson Avenue House in a poor, black neighborhood. There, local children got help with their homework and borrowed books. While the Baptist Student Union's "listen team" lived in the house, several organizations met there, including the local Girls' Club. One participant, "LA," wrote to the *Baptist Student* about an evening at Patterson Avenue House, saying the experience "exposed me to a group of students who felt that witnessing for Christ meant not a weekly visit but a living example — living where the hurt and need can be shared." When the school year ended, however, America was in disarray.[108]

The year 1968 was a traumatic one in the United States. The assassination of Martin Luther King Jr. shocked the Baptist leadership, as it shocked the nation. Baker James Cauthen of the Foreign Mission Board called on Baptists to take the matter personally. He said, "There must be a confession of our own shortcomings and a recommitment to our Lord for the full dimensions of discipleship." He warned Baptists that "it never helps to defend our errors. Peace only comes when we confess our sins, blunders, shortcomings, and failures." Cauthen believed that a better future was possible, but that necessitated a "fresh commitment to our worldwide task." He instructed Baptists to examine the New Testament and "pray for such infilling of our hearts by the Holy Spirit that the love of God may flow from us to others." Cauthen added that "this outflow must be communicated in attitude and deed as well as in words." Other Baptists agreed.[109]

John Nichol, pastor of Oakhurst Baptist Church in Decatur, Georgia, spoke to his congregation about the King assassination the Sunday after it happened. *Home Missions* reprinted the sermon. Nichol assailed Christians for continuing to see religion as "part of the hereafter, not the here and now." He believed that "it is this very irrelevance, this insulation of religion from life, that has served as a seedbed wherein have flourished the coarse weeds of prejudice and hate, injustice and oppression— producing a harvest of social ferment, fear, hostility, and irrationality in our land." Nichol told his congregation that what blacks were fighting for was not in the hands of whites to deny, a clear shift from the latter 1940s, when even progressive Baptists couched their ideas in ways that implied that whites had the right to grant or deny blacks their civil rights. Nichol added, "We would be less than honest, we white members of this congregation, if we did not confess that Martin Luther King's life and work were a constant source of irritation to us . . . this man with a dream of a better day for the disenfranchised peoples of our world kept pushing us, goading us, disturbing us, irritating and provoking us."[110]

Nichol also attended a pastors' conference following King's assassination where "the question of sending a message of condolence to the King family was debated rather hotly." At issue was the suggestion that "we should confess our own complicity in his death because of the thunderous silence of our pulpits in the South on the question of racial justice." After the conference, at which he favored the confession, Nichol came to the realization that "we have selected with great care the sins we have opposed." He said, "The same man who trusts God alone to cure the racist undertakes to help Him with the alcoholic! I would suggest that God expects us to accept a full measure of Christian responsibility for both men."[111]

Nichol had led his church toward taking that responsibility. Oakhurst Baptist Church had been, for most of the 1960s, a white, middle-class church. That changed dramatically toward the end of the decade. In the process, Nichol and the congregation discovered that "the hardest map to follow in the atlas of missionary responsibility was the map that marked the streets surrounding our sanctuary." Nevertheless, "God enabled us to see that if we did not have a valid witness at home . . . our witness anywhere else we went would be invalid." Oakhurst developed an integrated program for children and a full program for Spanish speakers. Nichol believed that "retreat from the community is no longer a viable alternative. We have to be the church there, or we cannot be the church anywhere."[112]

Bill Sherman agreed with John Nichol. He awoke to the Christian message regarding race when he took the pulpit at University Heights Baptist Church in Stillwater, Oklahoma. There, whites, blacks, Indians, and Asians all gathered for worship and held membership in the church. Sherman wrote, "This church had taken to heart the New Testament teachings concerning human equality," adding that "to see people who had outgrown the conspiracy of silence was refreshing. The membership of the church spoke out against racial superiority."[113]

On the other hand, Martin Luther King's ministry and the events of the 1960s had provoked some Southern Baptists without transforming them. One, William M. Watts of Huntsville, Alabama, wrote that while King had called for nonviolence, his marches consisted of "nothing but" sexual immorality, destruction of property, and defiance of the law. Some, like Charles T. Heltman, a Baptist pastor in Tuscaloosa, Alabama, objected to the portrait of King that appeared on the back of *Home Missions*, saying it "will only serve to divide Southern Baptists." Heltman believed it celebrated a man who had brought only violence and discord. Further, he noted that King was a known sympathizer with Stokely Carmichael and H. Rap Brown, who were "openly disloyal to America and its aim for peace and freedom throughout the world." Mrs. Walter C. Dean of Birmingham added, "It is bad enough that the leaders of our nation have bowed down to this Communistic leader . . . but to have our Southern Baptist colleges and leaders promote and allow it [his movement] to infiltrate our literature is unforgivable." She was willing to go further than even most of the segregationists of the era and accuse the Convention itself of being infiltrated by communists. Her accusation showed the deep fissures within the Convention, especially between the leadership and the laity.[114]

Despite King's being a Baptist preacher, Jack L. Hamilton challenged *Home Missions* to search his writings and "give me some indication that he was a Christian. Give some word of testimony of how he came to Jesus as a sinner and trusted him as Lord and Saviour of his life." Hamilton wanted the Home Mission Board to know that "here is one Southern Baptist pastor that did not approve of the Ministry of Martin Luther King." Baptist ministers like Hamilton and Heltmen and state editors like Macon posed a serious problem to the mission leadership as it tried to move Baptists to a more progressive stand on race. They could hardly be expected to preach the progressive view on Sundays. But they were also increasingly on the defensive within the Convention.[115]

Home Missions printed "We Eulogized Martin Luther King," by C. Norman Bennette Jr., on the same pages as the letters denouncing King. Bennette was the pastor at Azalea Baptist in Norfolk, Virginia. There, two events coincided to bring the church face to face with racial issues in the church. Bennette presented a sermon eulogizing King, and three black families unexpectedly attended the service. He recalled that church members feared that Sunday School teachers would quit and contributions would decline if the church integrated. The church integrated anyway. Bennette noted, "Sunday School teachers are teaching the Negro children and not one person has resigned from any church office or position. No one has left the membership for another church because of the presence of these three families." Indeed, the Sunday School meetings, which included two black women, continued to meet in homes rather than move to meeting rooms at the church.[116]

Progressive Baptists throughout the South rejected the characterization of King that appeared in the hostile letters after his death. They saw King's ministry as pointing toward a more Christian America and hoped to impress that view upon their children. Leslie Whiteley of Louisville, Kentucky, explained that King had not caused any violence but rather laid bare the hatred prevalent in American society. He pointed out that it was not King who loosed police dogs on women and children. He wrote, "I, my wife, and my three small sons just thank God for Dr. King's ministry here and for the fact that many true Christians are finally recognizing that there can be no racial distinctions among us."[117]

Jane Gill Tombes of Clemson, South Carolina, wrote that *Home Missions'* stand allowed her to avoid despair on the race issue. Like Whiteley, she wrote that "all of us—even our young children—read [and] discuss the articles, use them in our Sunday School class and are helped by them." Mrs. J. T. Hammett of Lone Grove, Oklahoma, enjoyed *Home Missions* so much that she sent it to her friends. She explained "my face got red when I read how some Baptists feel about our colored people. How a Christian could feel like that I will never understand." Her embarrassment, or anger, was real, though her language was reminiscent of a fading paternalism. Mrs. Sam McGinnis of Knoxville, Tennessee, who read the letters with her daughter, agreed. She wrote that too many Baptists had forgotten Jesus' command to "love thy neighbor as thyself." In a gesture of support for the board's position, Norman D. Stephenson, an army chaplain, wrote, "As a fellow Christian I was disappointed to read the many negative expressions to the picturing of the late Dr. Martin Luther King Jr. In an effort to offset loss of readers, I would be pleased to receive any one of the half dozen canceled subscriptions!"[118]

Changes in the Southern Baptist Convention encouraged Ottis Denny of Barberton, Ohio, who had been ashamed of his denomination during most of the 1950s and 1960s. While blacks were struggling for their rights, Denny complained, "Southern Baptists kept their backs turned or buried their heads in the sand all the while." By 1968, however, he could see "a great awakening" throughout the Convention, and he was again proud to be a Southern Baptist. Likewise, Felix V. Greer of Jackson, Mississippi, wished to "thank God for such men" as John Nichol and Dave Fillpot, pastors of integrated churches. True, not all agreed. Mrs. Chester P. Jones canceled her subscription in response to the stories on integrated churches. But others, like Mrs. William Lee Jones, a Southern Baptist writing from San Diego, California, noted that "it is encouraging to see progress being made toward integration in our churches." She believed that church integration would improve race relations in other areas of life. When that happened, she said, "God will smile on us."[119]

When the Southern Baptists gathered in Houston, Texas, for their annual Convention in the summer of 1968, King was dead and cities were burning. By a vote of 5,687 to 2,119, they adopted the Houston Statement. Baptists admitted, "We are a nation that declares the equality and rights of persons irrespective of race. Yet, as a nation, we have allowed cultural patterns to persist that have deprived missions of black Americans, and other racial groups as well, of equality of recognition and opportunity in the areas of education, employment, citizenship, housing, and worship. Worse still, as a nation, we have condoned prejudices that have damaged the personhood of blacks and whites alike. We have seen a climate of racism and reactionism develop resulting in hostility, injustice, suspicion, faction, strife, and alarming potential for bitterness, division, destruction, and death."[120]

The Baptists rededicated themselves to improving race relations. Following the themes progressive Baptists had long sounded, they announced, "We will personally accept every Christian as a brother beloved in the Lord and welcome to the fellowship of faith and worship every person irrespective of race or class." They would exercise their "civic responsibility as Christians" to defend people against prejudice and injustice. They agreed to "strive to become well informed about public issues, social ills, and divisive movements that are damaging to human relations." The Convention determined to "resist prejudice and combat forces that breed distrust and hostility." It called on "individuals, the churches, the associations, and the state conventions to join the Southern Baptist Convention in a renewal of Christian effort to meet the national crisis."[121]

The Convention asked the Home Mission Board to lead in implementing the statement, and Arthur Rutledge, who considered the statement "extremely significant," immediately called a meeting to examine possible strategies for action. The board continued to place its faith in educating Southern Baptists about the racial situation and determined that "Southern Baptists need to hear from leaders in government, education, poverty, and civil rights areas." The board demonstrated its commitment by dedicating $498,000 to the task, more than double what the board had budgeted for it ten years earlier. Henlee Barnette, a professor at the Southern Baptist Seminary, recommended that Baptist seminaries, with integrated student bodies since 1952, move toward having integrated faculty. C. E. Autrey, director of the Department of Evangelism at the Home Mission Board, noted that Baptists had to work with other denominations to establish justice, human dignity, and eliminate poverty. Finally, Alma Hunt, head of the Woman's Missionary

Alma Hunt led the Woman's
Missionary Union as it rededicated
itself to education about race relations
after the Houston convention. Photo
courtesy of the Southern Baptist
Historical Library and Archives,
Nashville, Tennessee.

Union, said that her organization would produce a study series on race, a continuation of its long-established program.[122]

Rutledge presented his own views on the Houston Statement a month after the leadership meeting. Nearly thirty years after Das Kelly Barnett identified the social implications of the Gospel as a "new theological frontier for Southern Baptists," Rutledge urged Baptists to realize that "our strongly individualistic heritage has made it difficult for many Baptists to understand that Christianity is concerned also about society." Rutledge believed that the Houston Statement rested on a "background of strong theological heritage." He argued that, "with clear biblical insights into sin, repentance, faith, and new life in Christ, we are well equipped for a continuing, effective proclamation of the gospel to both individuals and society, and for increasing expressions of love for the least and lowest among us."[123]

With that rededication, leaders again looked to the integration of church programs and the establishment of open-door policies for worship. Walker L. Knight urged pastors to take a leadership role and to divorce the question of integration from congregational control. He noted that well-meaning pastors often called for a vote on dropping racial bars from church membership, but Knight argued that Christians had no right to vote on the question. He said, "To vote on whether to accept a person because of race is actually to be taking a vote on whether or not the organization is a church, since by its nature the church must be open to all people." The church, he argued, was Christ's bride, but as bride it was "always bossing Christ around, trying to reshape his message." Barring Christians from church because of race clearly altered Christ's message.[124]

Baptist missionaries and mission board leaders strove to bring Southern Baptists to an understanding of the Christian message and its application to civil rights. They realized that civil rights required more than platitudes and articles. Rather, "justice is something you do." Sam W. Williams, black pastor of Friendship Baptist Church in Atlanta and professor of philosophy at Morehouse College, told Baptists that "listening sincerely is not enough." Baptists had to work to alleviate injustice. Baptists needed to open their churches "in spirit as well as in fact." Some churches continued to practice segregation in both spirit and fact and changed their weekly bulletins, no longer announcing that all were welcome.[125]

The social and theological meanings of the Bible were intertwined. M. Thomas Starkes of the Home Mission Board believed that because whites failed to act in accord with their belief that "God made all men in His image," blacks became more militant, and the result was the Black Power movement of the late 1960s. Starkes said that any time someone treated another person as inferior, it was "a refutation of the place in creation God already has granted him." Baptist leaders realized that perennial excuses like "it takes time" and "you can't legislate morality" were stalling tactics, but the time to stall was over. Braxton Bryant, director of the Tennessee Council on Human Relations, wrote that Black Power activists essentially demanded that attention be given to the "mountain of unfinished need for freedom and opportunity" rather than the "molehill of accomplishments." Bill Junker, editor of the *Baptist Student*, commented that Black Power demonstrated that white America, particularly Christian white America, had failed to realize the biblical demands for brotherhood. He said, "It is a sad commentary on U.S. society if a large portion of its Negro members have to withdraw from it to gain dignity and self esteem. Can't those of us who feel 'in' do better?"[126]

Young Baptists continued to act on the social message of the Gospel and to "do better." Members of the Young Woman's Auxiliary in Caycee, South Carolina, found the experience transformative. Margaret Ann Niceley reported to the *Window* that her auxiliary had donated money to Wilkinson Home, an orphanage for black girls. The young women found, however, that "to do something easy is almost less than doing nothing at all." The next year, 1968, in the midst of one of America's worst summers, the Holland Avenue Baptist Church Auxiliary organized a variety of activities with the girls from the Wilkinson Home, including an outing to an amusement park. At the park, Niceley sat on a bench next to an older woman who had brought her grandchildren to the park. The woman reportedly said, "Look at that white girl and that nigger sitting together! That's integration for you. I think it's disgusting." Niceley responded, "I don't think it's disgusting at all," and added, "That's my sister." She reminded Baptist young women of the generation gap: "looking from the viewpoint of the region in which she had lived so long, the older woman had not known that the girls she had pointed out were friends, and friends like to do things together." In a year, the young women's world was changed. They had tried to take the easy path but found that the more difficult path led to a truer understanding of Christian race relations. They had broken down barriers, economic and racial, and had become friends with people quite unlike themselves. Like the Wake Forest students who lived at the Patterson Avenue House and the Baptist Student Union at the University of Florida before them, the young women from Holland Avenue were trying to do their part to foster better race relations—they were trying to live their Christianity.[127]

Even in the late 1960s, the basic ideas underlying the Baptist missionaries' and mission leadership's approach to the race question remained essentially the same as they had been in the late 1940s. Subtle changes showed the maturing of Southern Baptists' ideas regarding race. Mission leaders had long abandoned any belief that racial equality could be achieved in a segregated society, and paternalism diminished considerably, though it never quite disappeared. Yet at the heart of the missionary program for better race relations remained education, especially of the rising generation, and personal contact and friendship across racial lines. The leadership continued to remind Baptists that each Christian was responsible for working to improve race relations. Mission leaders focused on the biblical principles of equality and unity and continued to stress the need for a spiritual awakening both to the reality of the oneness of humanity and equality before God and to the impact of American race relations on missionary efforts around the world. At the end of the 1960s, the Baptist leadership held fast to its vision of a

Christianized America complete with true racial harmony, but not all Baptists were willing to be transformed by the Christian message in the way the leadership hoped. Leaders and missionaries had tried to pass that vision on to Southern Baptists and especially to the youth of their denomination. The youth at the University of Florida, Wake Forest, and in the Holland Avenue Baptist Church Auxiliary had worked toward that vision. They worked to "live" their Christian faith.

CONCLUSION

In one of his books, Baptist and former president Jimmy Carter looked back at the civil rights movement and the changes that had taken place around his southwest Georgia home. He wrote, "Even during these times, however, there was an evolutionary, unpublicized conversion of most white Southerners by the civil rights leaders concerning the compatibility of their cause with the teachings of Jesus. But this was a slow process." The Southern Baptist missionaries and the progressive leaders helped make that conversion possible. They saw racial equality as not only compatible with the teachings of Jesus but mandated by those teachings. On that basis, they challenged the reigning social systems in the South. Progressive Baptists could not be dismissed as either outsiders or communists. They led the denomination to which most white southerners belonged. Thus, by arguing that segregation was not sacred, that in fact it was unchristian, they undermined its legitimacy and contributed to its unraveling. The federal government demanded and instituted the demise of formal segregation. The decline of racist attitudes, however, was a far slower and more subtle, if less complete, process.[1]

From the end of World War II to the end of the 1960s, Southern Baptist missionaries and mission leaders called on Baptists to practice Christian principles in race relations. Some mission leaders had held progressive ideas long before World War II, but only after the war did the Convention make disseminating those ideas an overt part of its program. Progressive leaders and missionaries pointed to the biblical basis for racial equality, the international dimensions of the race question, and each individual Christian's personal responsibility to improve race relations. Baptist mission leaders stressed the need for education because they believed that ignorance bred misunderstanding and lay at the heart of racism.[2]

Changing attitudes are difficult to assess. Actions speak louder than words. Southern Baptists integrated their seminaries, their universities and colleges, and their hospitals without government mandates. They were often slow to do so, but when they integrated their institutions, they did so voluntarily and in an effort to act according to their religious beliefs. Church integration progressed slowly, but churches did integrate. In 1989, Ellen Rosenberg pointed out the fact that blacks held state-level and convention-wide leadership positions. She also noted that the Foreign Mission Board estimated that 10 percent of Southern Baptist churches in the South had black members, a fact she believed demonstrated entrenched racism. While race and religion continue to have a problematic relationship, church integration is not an entirely valid way of judging changing attitudes. Many churches may be open to minority members but simply never have anyone present themselves for membership. The African American churches in the United States remain powerful institutions. There is little incentive for blacks to leave a black denomination in order to join predominantly white churches. The larger questions revolve around shifting beliefs regarding race, and, clearly, Baptist youth were increasingly involved in interracial religious activities and were increasingly accepting—sometimes even demanding— of integrated religious activities.[3]

The Baptist mission leadership consistently called for better race relations throughout the postwar period. Indeed, that consistency is one of the most remarkable aspects of this study. While the world around them was changing dramatically, Baptist missionaries and leaders continued to call for a progressive view of race based on their religious beliefs. Paternalism declined. Baptist leaders abandoned the idea that segregation and racial equality were compatible. Baptist institutions integrated. Yet not all Baptists were paternalistic in the early postwar years, nor had all overcome paternalism by 1970. Not even in 1945 had all Southern Baptists thought that Christian race relations could be achieved in a segregated society. Many, however, still grappled with the issue into the late 1960s. Some institutions, like the Southern Baptist Seminary in Louisville, integrated early in the era, while others, like the hospital in New Orleans, still struggled with integration at the end of the 1960s.[4]

The Southern Baptist Convention's reputation for being racially conservative is not altogether deserved. Congregations tended to remain considerably more conservative than the denominational leadership and especially the missionary leadership. Some of this can be explained by pointing to the commitment missionaries and denominational leaders had to the Christian ideal, and some can be explained by pointing to higher levels of education among the leadership. The leadership clearly held a more global view of events and ideologies than many in the congregations. These factors and others led to significant differences between the missionary leadership and the congregations. Missionaries and their leaders focused on the international dimensions of the American racial situation. The congregations rarely did. Furthermore, missionaries and mission leaders tended to view Christianity as transformative and believed that it had an active role to play in solving social issues. Yet in the South, as Mark Newman, John Lee Eighmy, Martin Marty, Ed Queen, Sam Hill, and other scholars note, "Baptist culture" dominated the society. For many, the church reinforced and supported the society and its structures. Other Baptists believed that the churches should not become active in social issues, as that would lead to the Social Gospel, which they believed was unbiblical. The leadership, on the other hand, embraced social Christianity, if not the theological liberalism of the Social Gospel.[5]

Several historians have demonstrated that Baptists at the state and congregational levels held firm to their segregationist views. Some pastors went so far as to join the White Citizens' Councils to maintain segregation. Other Baptists even joined the Klan and actively engaged in violence to maintain the southern racial caste system. Demonstrating that the Baptist leadership actively engaged in promoting a progressive view on race in the postwar period only adds condemnation to such actions. The persistent efforts of the Baptist leadership suggest that no pastor, and certainly no Baptist state leader, could have been unaware of an alternative Christian view of southern society. Baptist mission leaders had clearly and consistently shown that racism was unchristian and that it damaged the Christian cause around the world. Defending segregation and traditional race relations on religious grounds distorted the Christian message and showed that the churches had, indeed, become captives of the culture, not beacons of the Kingdom of God.[6]

The Southern Baptist Convention survived the race question, but it was not easy. As historian David Edwin Harrell notes, the most significant independent church movement of the twentieth century involved congregations leaving the Southern Baptist Convention because of the leadership's stand on race and civil rights. The basically conservative, free-church nature of the Southern Baptist Convention prevented the progressive leadership from moving the denomination to a more liberal position. The conservatives, labeled "fundamentalists" in recent battles, eclipsed the progressive leadership almost entirely. On race, however, there are clear indications that the progressive view still holds sway.[7]

As conservatives increasingly filled leadership positions within the Convention, the progressive ideas faded on most issues but not on race. According to Barry Hankins, "for the conservatives, race is the one topic where the progressives were right." He notes that conservatives give high marks to progressives like Foy Valentine on the racial issue. The conservative leadership even apologized for the Convention's legacy of racism. In 1995, the Southern Baptist Convention adopted a resolution admitting that "Southern Baptists failed, in many cases, to support, and in some cases opposed, legitimate initiative to secure the civil rights of African-Americans." The resolution reflected the progressive Baptists' view of the unity of humanity, saying "racism has divided the body of Christ and Southern Baptists in particular, and separated us from our African-American brothers and sisters." Interestingly, at that point the resolution abandoned the past tense and admitted that, even in 1995, "many of our congregations have intentionally and/or unintentionally excluded African-Americans from worship, membership, and leadership. . . . Racism profoundly distorts our understanding of Christian morality, leading some Southern Baptists to believe that racial prejudice and discrimination are compatible with the Gospel." The Convention resolved to "commit ourselves to be doers of the Word (James 1:22) by pursuing racial reconciliation in all our relationships." The resolution reflected, also, the continuing importance of mission work, stating, "Be it finally RESOLVED that we pledge our commitment to the Great Commission task of making disciples of all peoples (Matthew 28:19), confessing that in the church God is calling together one people from every tribe and nation (Revelations 5:9) and proclaiming that the Gospel of our Lord Jesus Christ is the only certain and sufficient ground upon which redeemed persons will stand together in restored family union as joint-heirs with Christ (Romans 8:17)."[8]

On race, then, the conservative leaders who rose to power in the 1980s seem to have adopted several of the views expounded by the progressives in the 1940s, 1950s, and 1960s. However, they tended to shy away from involvement in social issues and to focus primarily on evangelism. They stressed the biblical mandate to evangelize all people, as progressives had done in earlier decades, but some African Americans found it incongruous that the Convention would call for racial reconciliation while opposing nearly all government programs designed to end racial injustice. In a sense, even here they built on the progressive view. Progressives believed that law and government action were insufficient. Only by creating a truly Christian America could racial justice be achieved. While progressives accepted a role for government action, conservatives argued that the government is essentially limited to the task of eliminating barriers.[9]

Still, there can be little doubt that the progressive view of race contributed to a substantial alteration in the racial views among Southern Baptists. No longer was segregation sanctified as Christian, as it had been for over half a century. That was quite a shift from the 1950s, when G. W. Simmons wrote that over 90 percent objected to the pro-*Brown* resolutions passed by the Convention, and the DeSota Parish Baptist Association went on record as "standing aggressively and steadfastly for continued segregation in our churches and schools" and condemned the Christian Life Commission for "its promotion of integration."[10]

In his article on the Fellowship of Southern Churchmen for *Church History*, Robert F. Martin notes that "the Churchmen never expected immediate social transformation; they were prophets in the wilderness, not commanders of the heavenly host." Scholars generally agree that any attempt to assess the significance of the fellowship "in terms of discernible impact" would determine it was of little consequence. Yet, Martin says, "prophets must be judged by the degree of their commitment and the quality of their vision." Baptist leaders deserve the same consideration.[11]

The Baptist mission leadership spoke against cultural norms, norms that were enforced through intimidation, economic sanction, and violence. Segregation was, from the end of the nineteenth century, the southern way of life. Many southern leaders defended it as divinely sanctioned. The leadership's challenge to that claim undermined the legitimacy upon which social systems rest. The Baptist leadership never became silent. The ways in which other challengers were silenced simply had little effect on missionaries or mission leaders. As segregation crumbled under the weight of the civil rights movement and federal power, its support system was also slowly undermined by progressive Baptists. Baptist leaders offered a vision of a different South that younger generations could more easily adapt to the new, desegregated South.

From 1945 to 1970, progressives held the leadership positions at the mission boards. Those leaders, along with the missionaries, progressive leaders at other denominational agencies, and progressive seminary professors, expounded a vision of America, the world, and, especially, race relations that collided with cultural norms. Baptist missionaries and their leaders called for an end to racism as the only way to promote the Christian message around the world and ensure world peace. They denounced colonialism because it was inherently racist. They decried materialism because it accentuated economic differences, reinforced racial animosity, and led America away from God. They stressed the unity of the human family and the biblical mandates of racial equality. They understood the deep roots of racism in southern society and, therefore, spent considerable energy on educating the future generation of leaders to abandon the racist legacy of the South.

Most important, the Southern Baptist missionaries and leadership showed to a society that endowed segregation with divine approval that segregation was a sin in the eyes of God. They understood the world as it was but declared that it did not have to be that way. It could be transformed through the power of Christianity. And only through the power of Christianity.

NOTES

Abbreviations

AIB	*All-Indian Baptist*
AL	*Ambassador Life*
BHF	Baptist History File
BHH	*Baptist History and Heritage*
BJC	Baker James Cauthen Papers
BR	Biblical Recorder
BS	*The Baptist Student*
CABM	Central African Baptist Mission Book of Reports
CI	*The Christian Index*
CJA	Clifton J. Allen Collection
ECR	Executive Committee Records
FMB	Foreign Mission Board
GBC	Minutes and Book of Reports of the Georgia Baptist Convention
HM	*Southern Baptist Home Missions/Home Missions*
HMP	Harris Mobley Papers
HRLP	Homer R. Littleton Papers
JCMP	Joanna C. Maiden Papers
KJV	King James Version
MFMB	Minutes of the Foreign Mission Board
MGBC	Minutes of the Ghana Baptist Conference
MHMB	Minutes of the Home Mission Board
MNBM	Minutes of the Nigerian Baptist Mission
RE	*Review and Expositor*
RS	*Royal Service*

RLSWT	Archives and Special Collections, Roberts Library, Southwestern Baptist Theological Seminary, Fort Worth, TX
SBC	Minutes and Book of Reports of the Southern Baptist Convention
SBBQ	*Southern Baptist Brotherhood Quarterly*
SBHLA	Southern Baptist Historical Library and Archives, Nashville, TN
TBMP	T. B. Maston Papers
URL	Una Roberts Lawrence Collection

Introduction

1. George M. Fredrickson, *The Comparative Imagination: On the History of Racism, Nationalism, and Social Movements* (Berkeley: University of California Press, 1997), 85.

2. E. P. Sanders, *The Historical Figure of Jesus* (New York: Penguin Books, 1993), 6.

3. Melton McLaurin, *Separate Pasts: Growing Up White in the Segregated South* (Athens: University of Georgia Press, 1987), 31.

4. Robert W. Wuthnow, *The Restructuring of American Religion: Society and Faith since World War II* (Princeton, NJ: Princeton University Press, 1988), 17–25, 183; Mrs. Lamar Jackson, "Trends in Home Missions," *RS* 60, no. 8 (February 1966): 35–40; Karl Flemming, "SBC Goes Nationwide," *HM* 32, no. 2 (November 1961): 5–7, 15; J. C. Bradley, "Profiles of Home Mission Board Executives," *BHH* 30, no. 2 (1995): 31; "Rural Church Conference," *CI*, May 20, 1954, 6; Samuel S. Hill Jr., *Southern Churches in Crisis* (New York: Holt, Rinehart, and Winston, 1967), passim, esp. 10–11; Barry A. Kosmin and Seymour P. Lachman, *One Nation Under God: Religion in Contemporary American Society* (New York: Harmony Books, 1993), 51–55; W. Seward Salisbury, *Religion in American Culture: A Sociological Interpretation* (Homewood, IL: Doresey Press, 1964), 80–82; Bill J. Leonard, *God's Last and Only Hope: The Fragmentation of the Southern Baptist Convention* (Grand Rapids, MI: William B. Eerdmans, 1990), 2.

5. Das Kelly Barnett, "The New Theological Frontier for Southern Baptists," *RE* 38 (July 1941): 274–75; Hill, *Southern Churches in Crisis*, 172; David Edwin Harrell, *White Sects and Black Men* (Nashville, TN: Vanderbilt University Press, 1971), 26–27.

6. John Lee Eighmy, *Churches in Cultural Captivity: A History of the Social Attitudes of the Southern Baptists*, Introduction and Epilogue by Samuel S. Hill Jr. (Knoxville, TN: University of Tennessee Press, 1972), 147–48; J. B. Weatherspoon, "Committee on Race Relations," SBC, 1945, 47–48, 340–43.

7. Eighmy, *Churches in Cultural Captivity*, 147–48; H. Cornell Goerner, *America Must Be Christian* (Atlanta, GA: Home Mission Board, 1947), 97; John F. Havlik, "A 'Social Gospel' or a Gospel That Is Social?" *HM* 38, no. 3 (March 1967): 30–32; Martin E. Marty, *Modern American Religion*, vol. 3, *Under God, Indivisible, 1941–1960* (Chicago: University of Chicago Press, 1996), 277–330.

8. T. B. Maston, *"Of One": A Study of Christian Principles and Race Relations* (Atlanta, GA: Home Mission Board, 1946); T. B. Maston, *The Bible and Race* (Nashville, TN: Broadman Press, 1959); Ellen M. Rosenberg, *The Southern Baptists: A Subculture in Transition* (Knoxville, TN: University of Tennessee Press, 1989), 56; Humphrey K. Ezell, *The Christian Problem of Racial Segregation* (Newark: Greenwich Book Publishers, 1959), 13; Vetress Bonn Edwards, *Go South with Christ* (New York: Exposition Press, 1959), 60.

9. Rosenberg, *Southern Baptists*; Eighmy, *Churches in Cultural Captivity*; Edward L. Queen, *In the South the Baptists Are the Center of Gravity*, Preface by Martin E. Marty (Brooklyn, NY: Carlson, 1991); Baker James Cauthen et al., *Advance: A History of Southern Baptist Foreign Missions* (Nashville, TN: Broadman Press, 1970); Larry L. McSwain, "Swinging Pendulums: Reforms, Resistance, and Institutional Change," in *Southern Baptists Observed: Multiple Perspectives on a Changing Denomination*, ed. Nancy Tatom Ammerman (Knoxville, TN: University of Tennessee Press, 1993), 256–75.

10. Maston, *"Of One"*; Maston, *Bible and Race*; George D. Kelsey, *Social Ethics among Southern Baptists, 1917–1969* (Metuchen, NJ: Scarecrow Press, 1973), 6–7, 207–67; Eighmy, *Churches in Cultural Captivity*; Queen, *Center of Gravity*, 75–79.

11. Maston, *"Of One"*; Maston, *Bible and Race*; Weatherspoon, "Committee on Race Relations," 32; Peter L. Berger, *The Sacred Canopy: Elements of a Sociological Theory of Religion* (Garden City, NY: Doubleday, 1967).

12. Goerner, *America Must Be Christian*, 46; Eighmy, *Churches in Cultural Captivity*; Kelsey, *Social Ethics*, 6–16, 206–67; John E. Barnhart, "What's All the Fighting About? Southern Baptists and the Bible," in *Southern Baptists Observed: Multiple Perspectives on a Changing Denomination*, ed. Nancy Tatom Ammerman (Knoxville, TN: University of Tennessee Press, 1993), 73.

13. Andrew M. Manis, *Southern Civil Religions in Conflict: Black and White Baptists and Civil Rights, 1947–1957* (Athens, GA: University of Georgia Press, 1987); Mark Newman, "Getting Right with God: Southern Baptists and Race Relations, 1945–1980" (PhD diss., University of Mississippi, 1993). Mark Newman's dissertation has been published as *Getting Right with God: Southern Baptists and Desegregation, 1945–1995* (Tuscaloosa: University of Alabama Press, 2001), but most citations in this text are to the more extensive dissertation.

14. Mrs. F. W. Armstrong, "Missionary Education of Young People," *SBBQ* 14, no. 3 (July, August, September 1945): 172–74; Albert McClellan, "Work and Ministry of our Denominational Press," *SBBQ* 24, no. 3 (July, August, September 1954): 25; Fred Forester, "What About the Boys?" *SBBQ* 26, no. 2 (April, May, June 1956): 13.

15. McClellan, "Work and Ministry," 25; Leonard, *God's Last and Only Hope*, 1.

16. Beth Barton Schweiger, "Forum: Southern Religion," *Religion and American Culture* 8, no. 2 (Summer 1998): 165.

17. Leon Macon to Porter Routh, January 31, 1958, ECR, SBHLA; Andrew M. Manis, "'Dying from the Neck Up': Southern Baptist Resistance to the Civil Rights Movement," *BHH* 34, no. 1 (1999): 33–48; Newman, "Getting Right with God," passim.

18. Newman, "Getting Right with God," 186.

19. Berger, *Sacred Canopy*, 23–52; Marty, *Modern American Religion*, 134–35, 231–47; Larry Eskridge, "'One Way': Billy Graham, the Jesus Generation, and the Idea of an Evangelical Youth Culture," *Church History* 67, no. 1 (March 1998): 83–106; Shari Goldin, "Unlearning Black and White: Race, Media, and the Classroom," in *The Children's Culture Reader*, ed. Henry Jenkins (New York: New York University Press, 1998), 136–58.

20. Manis, "'Dying from the Neck Up,'" 33–34; Barry Hankins, *Uneasy in Babylon: Southern Baptist Conservatives and American Culture* (Tuscaloosa, AL: University of Alabama Press, 2002), passim, esp. chapter 8; David T. Morgan, *The New Crusades, the New Holy Land: Conflict in the Southern Baptist Convention, 1969–1991* (Tuscaloosa, AL: University of Alabama Press, 1996), passim.

21. Bill J. Leonard, "Southern Baptists and Southern Culture," *American Baptist Quarterly* 6, no. 2 (June 1985): 200–212; Dale Moody, "The Shaping of the Southern Baptist Polity," *BHH* 14, no. 3 (1979): 2–11; Kelsey, *Social Ethics*, 6–16; Hill, *Southern Churches in Crisis*; Kenneth K. Bailey, *Southern White Protestantism in the Twentieth Century* (Gloucester, MA: P. Smith, 1964); Manis, "'Dying from the Neck Up.'"

22. Eighmy, *Churches in Cultural Captivity*; Cauthen et al., *Advance*; Arthur Rutledge, "Annual Report of the Executive Secretary-Treasurer," MHMB, November 30, 1965, Home Mission Board Library, Atlanta, Georgia; Salisbury, *Religion in American Culture*, 49–50.

23. Stephen Neill, *A History of Christian Missions*, rev. ed. (1964; repr., New York: Penguin Books, 1986), 421 n. 8; William R. Estep Jr., "Course-Changing Events in the History of the Foreign Mission Board, SBC, 1845–1944," *BHH* 29, no. 4 (1994): 10; Cauthen et al., *Advance*; Wayne Flynt, *Alabama Baptists: Southern Baptists in the Heart of Dixie* (Tuscaloosa, AL: University of Alabama Press, 1998), passim, esp. 259.

24. Kelsey, *Social Ethics*; Cauthen et al., *Advance*; Wuthnow, *Restructuring of American Religion*; Morgan, *New Crusades*; Flynt, *Alabama Baptists*, 517–624; Hankins, *Uneasy in Babylon*, 240–71; Manis, "'Dying from the Neck Up,'" 33–34.

25. Newman, "Getting Right with God," vi, 150–65; Berger, *Sacred Canopy*; Eighmy, *Churches in Cultural Captivity*; Donald G. Mathews, "'We have left undone those things which we ought to have done': Southern Religious History in Retrospect and Prospect," *Church History* 67, no. 2 (June 1998): 305–25; T. J. Jackson Lears, "The Concept of Cultural Hegemony: Problems and Possibilities," *American Historical Review* 90, no. 3 (1985): 567–93.

Chapter One

1. T. B. Maston, *Segregation and Desegregation: A Christian Approach* (New York: Macmillan, 1959); Queen, *Center of Gravity*; Hill, *Southern Churches in Crisis*; Bailey, *Southern White Protestantism*; Kelsey, *Social Ethics*, 7–15. See also Alfred T. Davies, ed., *The Pulpit Speaks on Race* (New York: Abingdon Press, 1965).

2. Havlik, "'Social Gospel,'" 30–32; Kelsey, *Social Ethics*, 7–15. Eighmy,

Churches in Cultural Captivity, 145–48; Leonard, "Southern Baptists and Southern Culture," 200–212; Moody, "Southern Baptist Polity," 2–11.

3. H. Richard Niebuhr, *Christ and Culture*, Harper Torchbook edition (New York: Harper and Row, 1975); Marty, *Modern American Religion*, vol. 3, *Under God, Indivisible*, 348–49; Manis, "'Dying from the Neck Up,'" 34.

4. Maston, *Bible and Race*, about the author, 100; T. B. Maston to Dr. Henri J. M. Nouwne, September 22, 1983, "Yale Divinity School," Box 22, and "Niebuhr, H. Richard," Box 17, TBMP, RLSWT.

5. Maston, *"Of One,"*; Maston to Catherine B. Allen, March 11, 1986, Box 22, TBMP, RLSWT; Maston, *Segregation and Desegregation*; Maston, *Bible and Race*; Maston, "Southern Baptists and the Negro," *HM* 37, no. 7 (July 1966): 18–19; Maston, "The SBC Acts through Resolutions and Statements," *HM* 37, no. 8 (August 1966): 23–24; Maston, "Southern Baptists and the Negro," *HM* 37, no. 9 (September 1966): 38–42; Maston to Dr. Henri J. M. Nouwen, September 22, 1983, "Yale Divinity School," Box 22, TBMP, RLSWT; Katharine Parker Freeman, "Christ the Answer to Racial Tension," *RS* 43, no. 9 (March 1949): 25; Jacqueline Durham, "Program for Circle or Second WMS Meeting: Being Christian in Human Relations," *RS* 56, no. 12 (June 1962): 30; William M. Pinson Jr., "Texas Baptist Contributions to Ethics," *BHH* 33, no. 3 (Fall 1998): 7.

6. Maston, "Southern Baptists and the Negro," *HM* 37, no. 7 (July 1966): 18; Maston, "SBC Acts through Resolutions, Statements," 23; Davis C. Woolley, "Uniquely Baptist," *RS* 55, no. 3 (September 1960); Mrs. R. H., "We Get Letters: One Single Guide For Her," *RS* 43, no. 8 (May 1964): 9; Eighmy, *Churches in Cultural Captivity*.

7. Claude T. Ammerman, "Home Missions Foundations," *HM* 23, no. 1 (January 1952): 10; R. L. O'Brien, "Report on Home Missions," GBC, 1952, 44; Matthew 28:19–20, KJV.

8. Mrs. Fred Neiger, "Program: The World at Our Doorstep," *RS* 48, no. 7 (January 1954): 32; Acts 1:8, KJV; J. I. Bishop, "Our Young People: Every Boy a Missionary," *RS* 43, no. 5 (November 1948): 24.

9. Clifton E. Fite, "Report on State Missions," GBC, 1948, 37; Lawson H. Cooke, "Jurisdictional Disputes," *SBBQ* 15, no. 3 (July, August, September 1946): 135; Bob Banks, "Junior Royal Ambassador Meetings, Third Junior Meeting: Advance," *AL* 11, no. 4 (September 1956): 21–22.

10. J. B. Lawrence, "Appeal from Dr. J. B. Lawrence," *RS* 40, no. 8 (February 1946): 5; Rogers M. Smith, "Why Do Baptists Conduct Foreign Missions?" Papers of Administrative Associate Rogers M. Smith, 1954–65, 1968–70, Executive Correspondence, BJC, FMB Archives; Queen, *Center of Gravity*, 5; Paul Tillich, *What Is Religion?* trans. James Luther Adams (New York: Harper and Row, 1969), 118.

11. Andy Blane, "World Evangelism: The Christian's Responsibility," *BS* 34, no. 4 (January 1955): 11, 38; Foy Valentine, "Whetting Your Social Conscience," *BS* 33, no. 9 (June 1954): 14.

12. Frank Stagg, "The Church in the World," *BS* 43, no. 8 (May 1964): 56; W. T. Moore, "Southern Baptists and Race Relations," *HM* 36, no. 1 (January 1965): 14; Ralph A. Phelps Jr., "Be Not Conformed," *BS* 34, no. 6 (March 1955): 8.

13. Maston, "*Of One*," 108–9. See also John H. Marion Jr., "Iron Curtain around the Campus," *BS* 27, no. 8 (May 1948): 12–14.

14. James C. Barry, "Radical Christianity," *BS* 34, no. 8 (March 1955): 21.

15. Maston, *Bible and Race*, 93; Lillian Smith, *Killers of the Dream*, rev. ed. (1949; repr., New York: W. W. Norton, 1961), 214–15.

16. Fite, "Report," 37; Maston, *Bible and Race*, 87; T. B. Maston, *Biblical Ethics: A Guide to the Ethical Message of Scriptures from Genesis through Revelation* (1967; repr., Macon, GA: Mercer University Press, 1982), 243, 251–52. See also Adolf van Harnack, *What Is Christianity?* trans. Thomas Bailey Saunders (New York: Torchbook of Harper and Row, 1957), 176–89.

17. Ken E. Edwards, "Debate," *CI*, March 21, 1963, 7; Eighmy, *Churches in Cultural Captivity*; Queen, *Center of Gravity*; Ezell, *Christian Problem*, 9; William D. Workman, *The Case for the South* (New York: Devin-Adair, 1960), 95–101.

18. T. B. Maston, "Biblical Concepts and Race Relations," *BS* 39, no. 6 (March 1960): 18; Maston, "Bible and Racial Distinctions," 6; Ralph A. Phelps Jr., "The Inescapable Fact," *BS* 34, no. 5 (February 1955): 10–12, 25. See also Joel L. Alvis Jr., *Religion and Race: Southern Presbyterians, 1946–1983* (Tuscaloosa: University of Alabama Press, 1994), 46–76.

19. T. J. Preston, "Baptists and Segregation," *CI*, January 6, 1955, 8.

20. Ezell, *Christian Problem*, 14–15.

21. Maston, *Segregation and Desegregation*, 99–100, 106; Maston, *Bible and Race*, 111–14; Maston, "Bible and Racial Distinctions," 6; Phelps Jr., "Inescapable Fact," 10–12, 25; R. Lofton Hudson, "Sons of Ham," *CI*, August 30, 1956, 7.

22. Freeman, "Christ the Answer to Racial Tension," 24; McLaurin, *Separate Pasts*, 65; James J. Kilpatrick, *The Southern Case for School Segregation* (New York: Crowell-Collier Press, 1962), 59–64; Ezell, *Christian Problem*, 9–10; Herman Talmadge, *You and Segregation* (Birmingham: Vulcan Press, 1955), 15, 42–45; Harold D. Workman, *Case for the South*, 99, 214–16; Gunnar Myrdal, *An American Dilemma* (New York: Harper and Brothers, 1944), 60, 603; Foy Valentine to T. B. Maston, October 4, 1962, "Dr. Foy Valentine Correspondence Christian Life Commission, 1958–1962," Box 31, TBMP, RLSWT; Maston, *Segregation and Desegregation*, 73–75.

23. Maston, "*Of One*," 91; Maston, *Segregation and Desegregation*, 51, 86–90; Maston, "Biblical Concepts and Race Relations," 18; Rogers M. Smith, "Meeting for Intermediate Royal Ambassadors, First Intermediate Meeting: The Bible and World Missions," *AL* 11, no. 5 (October 1956): 14; Alvis Jr., *Religion and Race*, 72–73.

24. Maston, "*Of One*," 65–72; Maston, *Bible and Race*, 33–47.

25. James J. Kilpatrick, *Southern Case*, 58–65; Calvin Trillin, *An Education in Georgia: The Integration of Charlayne Hunter and Hamilton Holmes* (New York: Viking Press, 1963), 68, 174–78. See also Charlayne Hunter-Gault, *In My Place* (New York: Farrar, Straus and Giroux, 1992).

26. Charles Marsh, *God's Long Summer: Stories of Faith and Civil Rights* (Princeton, NJ: Princeton University Press, 1997), chapter 2.

27. Maston, *Segregation and Desegregation*, 79; T. B. Maston to Ninabelle Nichols, November 19, 1959, "N. Miscellaneous," Box 17, and T. B. Maston to

Louis R. Cobbs, March 18, 1969, "Cobbs, Louis R.," Box 3, TBMP, RLSWT; Deuteronomy 7:3–4, KJV; Ezell, *Christian Problem*, passim, esp. 18–20.

28. Maston, *Segregation and Desegregation*, 73–74; Leonie Chong Siler, "A Story To Ponder," *RS* 58, no. 4 (November 1963): 27–28; "We Get Letters, A Comment to Ponder," *RS* 58, no. 10 (April 1964): 28.

29. Talmadge, *You and Segregation*, 44–45; Workman, *Case for the South*, 99; Acts 17:26, KJV; Freeman, "Christ the Answer to Racial Tension," 23; Maston, *Segregation and Desegregation*, 87.

30. Hugh Brimm, "A Christian Anthropologist's View of Man," *BS* 40, no. 2 (November 1960): 15.

31. Maston, *Bible and Race*, 17, 22–24; Maston, *Biblical Ethics*, 252; Maston, "Bible and Racial Distinctions," 5; Maston, "Biblical Concepts and Race Relations," 18; Ezell, *Christian Problem*, 14–15.

32. Maston, *Segregation and Desegregation*, 51, 86–90, 98; Maston, "Biblical Concepts and Race Relations," 18.

33. Leonard A. Duce, "Christ and Culture," *BS* 30, no. 2 (November 1950): 5.

34. Moore, "Southern Baptists and Race Relations," 15; Phelps Jr., "Inescapable Fact," 10–12, 25.

35. Maston, *Bible and Race*, 27; Maston, *Biblical Ethics*, 50; Doris DeVault, "Viewpoint," *Window* 33, no. 11 (June 1962): 3; Matthew 22:39–40, KJV.

36. Mary-Ellen Garrett, "Who Is My Neighbor," *BS* 34, no. 2 (November 1955): 18–21, 31; Maston, "Biblical Concepts and Race Relations," 18–20; Maston, *Bible and Race*, 58, 74; Luke 10:25–37, KJV.

37. Vivian Hackney, "And I Love You, Too," *RS* 59, no. 3 (September 1964): 11–12; Jean Russell, *God's Lost Cause: A Study of the Church and the Racial Problem* (London: SCM Press, 1968), 7–13, 100; Robert McAfee Brown, "Residential Segregation," *Christianity and Crisis* 16, no. 12 (July 9, 1956): 90; T. B. Maston, "Christian Men and Race Relations," *SBBQ* 32, no. 4 (October, November, December 1961): 33.

38. Reinhold Niebuhr, "The Race Problem in America," *Christianity and Crisis* 15, no. 22 (December 26, 1955): 169; Chevis Horne, "The Gospel of Reconciliation," *HM* 40, no. 6 (June 1969): 20; Russell, *God's Lost Cause*, 7–13, 100.

39. Maston, *Segregation and Desegregation*, 102; Moody, "Southern Baptist Polity," 2–11; Leonard, "Southern Baptists and Southern Culture," 207.

40. Walker L. Knight, "Toward a Free Pulpit," *HM* 39, no. 1 (January 1968): 4; Donald E. Collins, *When the Church Bell Rang Racist: The Methodist Church and the Civil Rights Movement in Alabama* (Macon, GA: Mercer University Press, 1998), passim.

41. "Ramsey Gets Vote of Confidence," *CI*, September 6, 1962, 5; "Accept Resignation," *CI*, September 29, 1960, 3; David Stricklin, *A Genealogy of Dissent: Southern Baptist Protest in the Twentieth Century* (Lexington, KY: University Press of Kentucky, 1999), 53.

42. Knight, "Toward a Free Pulpit," 4.

43. Maston, "Of One," 62; Maston, *Segregation and Desegregation*, 117; Maston, *Bible and Race*, 33–47; Maston, *Biblical Ethics*, 243; Frank Stagg, "He Who Was Colorblind," *BS* 30, no. 7 (April 1951): 10–11.

44. Freeman, "Christ the Answer to Racial Tension," 21–22.

45. Maston, "*Of One*," 29; Maston, *Segregation and Desegregation*, 86; Maston, *Bible and Race*, 10; Harnack, *What Is Christianity?* 176–89; F. D. Maurice, *Lectures on Social Morality* (London: Macmillan, 1852), 355–65.

46. Mrs. William McMurry, "Mission Study for *The Long Bridge* for Your Circle Program," *RS* 52, no. 7 (January 1958): 21; Maston, *Bible and Race*, 78–74; Maston, *Biblical Ethics*, 186; Maston, "What Is Man?" *Window* 33, no. 1 (February 1961): 1; Paul Tillich, quoted in Maston, *Bible and Race*, 81.

47. Maston, "*Of One*," 9, 17, 77; Maston, "Southern Baptists and the Negro," *HM* 37, no. 7 (July 1966): 18.

48. Ross Coggins, "The Christian and Social Conflict," *BS* 45, no. 5 (February 1966): 3; Flynt, *Alabama Baptists*, passim; Preston, "Baptists and Segregation," 8; Duce, "Christ and Culture," 4.

49. Marion Jr., "Iron Curtain around the Campus," 12–14.

50. Maston, "*Of One*," 77, 84; Phelps Jr., "Be Not Conformed," 7; Valentine, "Whetting Your Social Conscience," 12–14; "Graduate Students," Box 7, TBMP, RLSWT.

51. Valentine, "Whetting Your Social Conscience," 12–14; Stricklin, *Genealogy of Dissent*, 39–40.

52. Josef Nordenhaug, "Are You Looking for a Convenient Religion," *BS* 28, no. 9 (June 1949): 2.

53. Paul M. Stevens, "Blindspots in the Current Spiritual Renewal," *BS* 36, no. 6 (March 1957): 22; John C. Bennett, "Graham and Segregation," *Christianity and Crisis* 16, no. 18 (October 29, 1956): 142–43.

54. Phelps Jr., "Be Not Conformed," 20; Jacqueline Durham, "Program for Circle of Second WMS Meeting: The Bible Instructs Us—Thoroughly," *RS* 56, no. 10 (April 1962): 15.

55. Maston, "What Is Man?" 1. Maston cites several passages, including Acts 10:14, James 2:1, Corinthians 19:7, Job 34:19, Romans 2:11, Ephesians 6:9, and Colossians 3:25; Matthew 5:41, KJV.

56. Billie Pate, "Viewpoint," *Window* 33, no. 2 (October 1961): 7; Theron D. Price, "What Is the Church?" *BS* 36, no. 6 (March 1957): 8.

57. Foy Valentine, "Social Aspects of the Christian Gospel," *BS* 40, no. 7 (April 1961): 11–13.

58. Cyril E. Bryant, "From Washington: What Image Do Baptists Reflect?" *RS* 58, no. 2 (August 1963): 9; Havlik, "'Social Gospel,'" 30, 32; C. C. Goen, "Passing on the Other Side," *BS* 37, no. 3 (December 1957): 12; Phelps Jr., "Be Not Conformed," 6–7; Flynt, *Alabama Baptists*, passim.

59. Maston, "*Of One*," 77, 115; Maston, *Segregation and Desegregation*, 64.

60. "Resolution of First Baptist Church, Farmerville, Louisiana," November 6, 1957, Box 82, Folder 1, ECR, SBHLA; "Dear People" from William L. Bush, May 31, 1959, Box 82, Folder 2, ECR, SBHLA.

61. Ross Coggins, "Moral and Social Action Essential," *HM* 38, no. 11 (November 1966): 8.

62. Maston, "*Of One*," 89–90; Maston, "Bible and Racial Distinctions," 7; "Southern Baptists and the Negro," *HM* 37, no. 9 (September 1966): 42.

63. Maston, *Segregation and Desegregation*, 127; Maston, "The Bible and Racial Distinctions," *BS* 41, no. 4 (January 1962): 7.

64. Maston, *Segregation and Desegregation*, 127–32; Moore, "Southern Baptists and Race Relations," 14. See also Marty, *Modern American Religion*, 376–82.

65. Maston, *Segregation and Desegregation*, 135–36; Maston, *Biblical Ethics*, 262; Maston, "Southern Baptists and the Negro," *HM* 37, no. 9 (September 1966): 42; Mrs. RBH, "We Get Letters, Comments on December 'We Get Letters,'" *RS* 58, no. 10 (April 1964): 28.

66. Maston, *Segregation and Desegregation*, 140–41; Maston, *Bible and Segregation*, 84.

67. "The Long Hot August," *AL* 20, no. 12 (May 1966): 5–7.

68. Maston, *Segregation and Desegregation*, 140–41; Maston, *Bible and Segregation*, 84; Leonard, *God's Last and Only Hope*, 8.

69. Maston, "Southern Baptists and the Negro," *HM* 37, no. 7 (July 1966): 19; Charles Wellbron, "Baptist Student Forum," *BS* 31, no. 9 (June 1952): 22.

70. Goen, "Passing on the Other Side," 10; Daniel R. Grant, "Civic Righteousness," *BS* 35, no. 9 (June 1956): 7–8.

71. Charles Chaney, "Pride of the Old South," *HM* 39, no. 10 (October 1968): 20–22.

72. H. Guy Moore, "What Is a Christian," *BS* 39, no. 2 (November 1959): 11; Frank Stagg, "The Church in the World," *BS* 43, no. 8 (May 1964): 56.

73. Samuel S. Hill Jr., "Depth of Citizenship and the Christian Student," *BS* 38, no. 9 (June 1959): 5–7; Hill, "The Southern Baptists: Need for Reformulation, Redirection," *Christian Century* 80, no. 2 (January 9, 1963): 39–42. See also Hill, *Southern Churches in Crisis*, passim.

74. Hill, "Depth of Citizenship," 5–7; Hill, "Southern Baptists," 39–42; Hill, *Southern Churches in Crisis*.

75. William L. Self, "The Emerging Church," *BS* 45, no. 7 (April 1966): 2–3.

76. David K. Alexander, "Another Side of 'The Southern Baptists,'" *BS* 42, no. 8 (May 1963): 3; Ronnie Stutes, "Students Speak Out: Changing of Culture," *BS* 48, no. 9 (June 1969): 2.

77. Harrell, *White Sects and Black Men*, 26–27; "News in the Christian World," *BS* 43, no. 5 (February 1964): 38; Moody, "Southern Baptist Polity," 2–11; Leonard, "Southern Baptists and Southern Culture," 200–212; Eighmy, *Churches in Cultural Captivity*.

78. Howard G. McClain, "You Are Involved in a Changing World," *BS* 38, no. 8 (May 1960): 13–16; "News in the Christian World," *BS* 43, no. 5 (February 1964): 37.

Chapter Two

1. Mrs. C. D. (Myrtle Robinson) Creasman, "Program Material: The World Significance of Justice and Cooperation among the Races of the South," *RS* 40, no.

11 (May 1946): 22; J. B. Lawrence, "Spiritual Preparation for Peace," *HM* 16, no. 10 (October 1945): 3; John Morton Blum, *V Was for Victory: Politics and American Culture during World War II* (New York: Harcourt, Brace, Jovanovich, 1976), 312–15; A. C. Miller, "Report of the Christian Life Commission" SBC, 1959, 394.

2. W. R. White, "Post War Missions," *HM* 17, no. 6 (June 1946): 15; E. C. Routh, "Editorial," *Commission* 9, no. 4 (April 1946): 18; Routh, "Editorial," *Commission* 10, no. 8 (September 1947): 9.

3. W. O. Carver, "Civilization's Supreme Need," *Commission* 7, no. 6 (June 1945): 5.

4. Mary L. Dudziak, *Cold War Civil Rights: Race and the Image of American Democracy* (Princeton, NJ: Princeton University Press, 2000), 11; Penny M. Von Eschen, *Race against Empire: Black American and Anticolonialism, 1937–1957* (Ithaca, NY: Cornell University Press, 1997), 112–21; Eric Foner, *Who Owns History: Rethinking the Past in a Changing World* (New York: Hill and Wang, 2002), 67.

5. Creasman, "World Significance," 20; Charles D. Johnson, "Organizing for World Peace, Part 2" *SBBQ* 15, no. 1 (January, February, March 1946): 32.

6. Theodore F. Adams, "Peace is for Men of Good Will," *Commission* 8, no. 1 (January 1945): 1; Hermione Dannelly Jackson, "Programs, Choosing the More Excellent Way," *Window* 24, no. 2 (October 1952): 29.

7. W. O. Carver, "What Sort of New World," *Commission* 8, no. 10 (November 1945): 5; W. O. Carver, "Important Changes of Direction," *Commission* 10, no. 3 (March 1947): 5; Robert Kinloch Massie, *Loosing the Bonds: The United States and South Africa in the Apartheid Years* (London: Doubleday, 1997); Lewis H. Gann, *Central Africa: The Former British States* (Englewood Cliffs, NJ: Prentice Hall, 1971), 139.

8. George W. Sadler, "Report of the Secretary for Africa, Europe and the Near East," MFMB, April 8, 1947; Sadler, "Report," MFMB, April 11, 1951.

9. Harry S. Truman, "Ours Should Be a Continuous Thanksgiving," repr., *BS* 26, no. 2 (November 1946): 2–3; Porter Routh, "Peace on Earth is a Battle," *BS* 31, no. 3 (December 1951): 33.

10. J. B. Lawrence, "Report of the Home Mission Board," SBC, 1948, 168; Una Roberts Lawrence, "New Urgency in the Study of Missions," *HM* 17, no. 4 (April 1946): 11.

11. H. Cornell Goerner, "Meetings for Intermediate Royal Ambassadors, Second Intermediate Meeting: All Nations in God's Plan," *AL* 3, no. 7 (December 1948): 15; Goerner, *America Must Be Christian*, passim, esp. 21, 105; Alvis Jr., *Religion and Race*, 72–73.

12. H. Cornell Goerner, "Race Relations: A Factor in World Missions," BJC, FMB Archives. See also Goerner, *Race Relations: A Factor in World Missions* (Nashville, TN: Christian Life Commission, [1957?]).

13. Goerner, "Race Relations."

14. Daniel R. White, "Race Prejudice: A Factor in Christian Missions," *Commission* 26, no. 8 (September 1963): 6–9, back cover; Dudziak, *Cold War Civil Rights*, 237–40.

15. Victor Glass, "Missionary Implications of Racial Tensions," *HM* 37, no. 7 (July 1966): 16–17.

16. Ibid.

17. Marjorie Moore Armstrong, "It's Happening Now," *RS* 47, no. 7 (January 1953): 17; E. W. Thornton, "The Christian Student and World Peace," *BS* 31, no. 2 (November 1951): 11–12; Charles R. Gage, "Wanted: Student Ambassadors," *BS* 31, no. 2 (November 1951): 19.

18. W. O. Carver, "Kingdom Facts and Factors: Minorities," *Commission* 8, no. 12 (December 1945): 9; "Report on World Peace," SBC, 1946, 65.

19. A. E. Lacy Jr., "The U.N. in Action," *BS* 33, no. 2 (November 1953): 8.

20. E. C. Routh, "Editorial: The World Charter and Christian Missions," *Commission* 8, no. 8 (September 1945): 14; J. W. Marshall, "Report of the Secretary for Missionary Personnel," MFMB, April 9, 1946; William Flemming, "Men and the Christian World Mission: World Missions for Peace," *Commission* 9, no. 4 (April 1946): 8; W. O. Carver, "Kingdom Facts and Factors: Minorities," 9.

21. H. Cornell Goerner, "Meetings for Intermediate Royal Ambassadors, Fourth Intermediate Meeting: Peace and Good Will," *AL* 2, no. 7 (December 1947): 19.

22. Rosalee Mills Appleby, "America's Supreme Need Today . . . A Revival," *HM* 20, no. 12 (December 1949): 9; "Evangelism the Hope of the World," *HM* 22, no. 7 (July 1951): 6; Marty, *Modern American Religion*, 126–29.

23. M. Theron Rankin, "Report of the Executive Secretary," MFMB, October 9, 1945; J. W. Marshall, "Report," MFMB, April 9, 1946; Courts Redford, "For Such a Time," *HM* 25, no. 5 (May 1954): 3; E. C. Routh, "Editorials," *Commission* 10, no. 2 (February 1947): 18; Estep, "Course-Changing Events," 10; Lewis R. Cobbs, "The Missionaries' Call and Training for Foreign Missions," *BHH* 29, no. 4 (1994): 32.

24. J. B. Weatherspoon and Hugh A. Brimm, "Report of the Social Service Commission," SBC, 1952, 408; J. W. Marshall, "Report," MFMB, April 9, 1946; Baker James Cauthen to all missionaries, undated letter from mid-1950s (letters are in chronological order; it is probably from 1956), Papers of Administrative Associate Rogers M. Smith, 1954–65, 1968–70, Executive Correspondence, 1954–1970, BJC, FMB Archives; Harry S. Truman quoted in Marshall, "Report," MFMB (April 9, 1946); Mrs. W. C. James, "Current Missionary Events," *RS* 41, no. 1 (July 1946): 30.

25. George W. Sadler, "Report," MFMB, October 11, 1949; Mrs. Edgar L. Bates, "Program: Baptist Women around the World," *RS* 47, no. 7 (January 1953): 25. See also Margaret Ballinger, *From Union to Apartheid: A Trek to Isolation* (New York: Preager, 1969).

26. Mrs. J. Walsh Watts, "It's Happening Now," *RS* 43, no. 1 (July 1948): 10; Matthew Frye Jacobson, *Whiteness of a Different Color: European Immigrants and the Alchemy of Race* (Cambridge, MA: Harvard University Press, 1998), 8, 246–73.

27. Freeman, "Christ the Answer to Racial Tension," 24–25.

28. Mrs. C. D. (Myrtle Robinson) Creasman, "Program Material: Peace for Tomorrow," *RS* 39, no. 9 (March 1945): 24; Creasman, "Program Material: Patriotism," *RS* 40, no. 1 (July 1945): 19–26.

29. J. B. Lawrence, "Home Mission Report," SBC, 1950, 186–90; Earl Hester Trutza, "Program: Christ is the Answer for the World," *RS* 44, no. 6 (December 1949): 24; Jameson Jones, "A Young Christian and World Peace Today," *Window* 21, no. 4 (December 1949): 4.

30. Hugh Brimm, "Race Relations—What Can I as a Christian Do?" *BS* 31, no. 4 (January 1952): 27.

31. Frank K. Means, "Editorials: Making the World Right," *Commission* 14, no. 11 (December 1951): 18–19; William Henry Kellar, *Make Haste Slowly: Moderates, Conservatives, and School Desegregation in Houston* (College Station, TX: Texas A&M University Press, 1999), 69.

32. Mrs. L. E. M. (Katharine Parker) Freeman, "An Experiment in Race Relations in Raleigh," in Mrs. Edgar Godbold, "Community Missions," *RS* 41, no. 9 (March 1947): 9.

33. W. O. Carver, "Pressing Issues," *Commission* 12, no. 2 (February 1949): 9; E. C. Routh, "Editorial," *Commission* 11, no. 4 (April 1948): 19; Eighmy, *Churches in Cultural Captivity*, 147–48; George D. Kelsey, *Social Ethics*, 206–67.

34. Romans 10:12–13, KJV; Ed M. Arendall, "Under the Skin," 8; Leila Lequire, "From Missionaries: Evangelizing among the Pueblos," *RS* 41, no. 8 (February 1947): 6.

35. Mrs. J. M. Dawson, "Imagine the United Nations without Women," *RS* 43, no. 1 (July 1948): 9; Thelma Brown, "Give Attention to Reading: Christians Building Interracial Good-Will," *RS* 40, no. 9 (March 1946): 9.

36. Itsuko Saito, "We Are Sisters," *RS* 45, no. 3 (October 1950): 9.

37. T. G. Dunning, "The Youth Conference at Copenhagen," *BS* 27, no. 3 (December 1947): 10; Fraser J. Harbutt, *The Iron Curtain: Churchill, America, and the Origins of the Cold War* (New York: Oxford University Press, 1986).

38. Frank K. Means, "Editorial," *Commission* 21, no. 8 (September 1958): 14; Walter LaFeber, *America, Russia, and the Cold War, 1945–1992*, 7th ed. (1967; repr., New York: McGraw Hill, 1993), 193–202.

39. "Editorially," *BS* 27, no. 7 (April 1948): 31; Bill Cody, "Window to the World," *BS* 33, no. 1 (October 1953): 49.

40. Jane Ray Bean, "Third-Dimensional Friendships," *BS* 38, no. 1 (October 1958); 32–34.

41. Dwight Wilhelm, "Meeting for Intermediate Royal Ambassadors, Second Intermediate Meeting: Revealing the Saviour through the Baptist International Center," *AL* 8, no. 8 (January 1954): 14.

42. W. O. Carver, "Today's World Calls for Christianity in Terms of Jesus' Ideals," *Commission* 15, no. 1 (January 1952): 4–5; George W. Sadler, "We Ought," *Commission* 17, no. 1 (January 1954): 9.

43. Adams, "Peace is for Men of Good Will," 1; W. O. Carver, "Light from Christ on Life Today," *Commission* 8, no. 2 (February 1945): 5; Carver, "Kingdom Facts and Factors: Minorities," 9; J. B. Lawrence, "Appeal," 5–7.

44. Mrs. Taul B. White, "Program: Christ, the Answer for the Individual," *RS* 43, no. 7 (January 1949): 21.

45. Loyd Corder, "Meetings for Intermediate Royal Ambassadors, First Intermediate Meeting: United States' Part in World Missions," *AL* 10, no. 9 (February 1956): 13.

46. J. B. Lawrence, "Missions and the March of Events," *HM* 17, no. 12 (December 1946): 2; "Report of the Social Service Commission," SBC, 1947, 301; Dr. and Mrs. William R. Norman, "Mangled Missions," *BS* 38, no. 9 (June 1959): 28.

47. H. Cornell Goerner, "Meetings for Intermediate Royal Ambassadors, Fourth Intermediate Meeting: Communism and World Missions," *AL* 4, no. 3 (September 1949): 18.

48. Charles A. Wells, "Road Building Vs. Wall Building," *AL* 5, no. 10 (March 1951): 24.

49. Billy Graham quoted in Marty, *Modern American Religion*, 152; John C. Bennett, *Christianity and Communism* (New York: Association Press, 1948).

50. White, "Post War Missions," 15; J. B. Lawrence, "Missions and the March of Events: The Answer to Communism," *HM* 19, no. 12 (December 1948).

51. Maston, *Segregation and Desegregation*, 15, 60, 152–53.

52. Clyde Dotson quoted in M. Theron Rankin, "Report of the Foreign Mission Board," SBC, 1952, 108–9; Gann, *Central Africa*, 135–40.

53. Baker James Cauthen to Miss Annie Mae Smith, November 1, 1961: Administration: Africa/Europe/Near East—Secretary: Cornell Goerner, 1957–1961, Executive Correspondence, 1954–1979, BJC, FMB Archives.

54. Charles A. Wells, "Trends: Get Tough Pays?" *BS* 27, no. 6 (March 1948): inside cover; W. O. Carver, "Some Major Concerns," *Commission* 9, no. 6 (June 1946): 4; J. B. Lawrence, "Spiritual Preparation for Peace," 10; Adams, "Peace is for Men of Good Will," 1.

55. E. C. Routh, "Editorial: Russia and the U.S.A.," *Commission* 8, no. 8 (September 1945): 14–15; "Fellow Believers of the U.S.S.R.," *Commission* 8, no. 11 (December 1945): 8; George W. Sadler, "We Went to Russia," *Commission* 22, no. 9 (October 1959): 12; Walker L. Knight, "The War Against Religion," *HM* 31, no. 2 (February 1960): 6; Claudia Tyrtova, "Going Forth . . . with the Youth of Russia," *BS* 34, no. 4 (January 1956): 38.

56. Harold G. Sanders, "World Peace . . . Beginning in Christian America," *HM* 18, no. 8 (August 1947): 12; "Report of the Social Service Commission," SBC, 1951, 412; Jenny Lind Gatlin, "From *Baptist Student* Editor's Desk," *BS* 25, no. 4 (January 1946): 23. See also Fred Kaplan, *The Wizards of Armageddon* (New York: Simon and Schuster, 1983).

57. "Report of the Social Service Commission," SBC, 1951, 412; Weatherspoon and Brimm, "Report of the Social Service Commission," 409; J. B. Lawrence, "This is God's World," *HM*, 23, no. 5 (May 1952): 4; James T. Patterson, *Grand Expectations: The United States 1945–1974* (New York: Oxford University Press, 1996), 58, 122, 289–90, 440–41.

58. "Missions and the March of Events," *HM* 20, no. 11 (November 1949): 4; Cyril E. Bryant, "Today," *RS* 52, no. 8 (November 1957): 10; Frederick W. Marks III, *Power and Peace: The Diplomacy of John Foster Dulles* (Westport, CT: Preager, 1993); Marty, *Modern American Religion*, 97–129.

59. Marjorie Moore Armstrong, "It's Happening Now," *RS* 46, no. 11 (May 1952): 18; Weatherspoon and Brimm, "Report of the Social Service Commission," 412.

60. A. C. Miller, "Report of the Christian Life Commission," SBC, 1955, 330; Joe W. Burton, "Military Training and Our Families," RS 50, no. 1 (July 1955): 4–6.

61. Richard E. Welch Jr., *Response to Revolution: The United States and the Cuban Revolution, 1959–1961* (Chapel Hill, NC: University of North Carolina Press, 1985), 3–26; Frank K. Means, "Editorial," *Commission* 19, no. 4 (April 1955): 18.

62. Arthur B. Rutledge and William G. Tanner, *Mission to America: A History of Southern Baptist Home Missions*, 2nd ed. (Nashville, TN: Broadman Press, 1983), 162–63; Aaron F. Webber, "What About the New Cuba," RS 54, no. 7 (January 1960): 1–2; Welch, *Response to Revolution*, 6, 10, 29.

63. "Language Group Ministries: Cuba," MHMB, May 5, 1961; Courts Redford, "Report," MHMB, August 3, 1961; Redford, "Report," MHMB, December 3–4, 1963.

64. Mrs. William McMurry, "Did You Read It?: Dialogue between Two Cultures," RS 57, no. 1 (July 1962): 25.

65. Walker L. Knight, "Editorials: How Quickly Goes the Veneer," HM 34, no. 8 (August 1963): 6.

66. Courts Redford, "Report," MHMB, December 1–2, 1964.

67. Ione Gray and Dallas M. Lee, "Missions Here and There: Cubans in Miami," RS 62, no. 5 (December 1967): 6–7; Cyril E. Bryant, "From Washington," RS 63, no. 1 (July 1968): 13.

68. Martha Ann Clay, "Arley Arrives in America," *Window* 34, no. 1 (September 1962): 9–10.

69. "Resolution," MHMB, February 9, 1967; "Miscellaneous: Recommendation on Cuban Nationals Working in the United States," MHMB, March 15, 1967; Rutledge and Tanner, *Mission to America*, 164–65.

70. Ross Coggins, "You Could Tie Our Hands," BS 37, no. 2 (November 1957): 19.

Chapter Three

1. Gann, *Central Africa*, 135–39; Thomas Pakenham, *The Scramble for Africa: The White Man's Conquest of the Dark Continent from 1876 to 1912* (New York: Random House, 1991), 669–80; Roland Oliver, *The African Experience: Major Themes in African History from Earliest Times to the Present* (New York: Harper-Collins, 1991), 227–40; Martin Staniland, *American Intellectuals and African Nationalists, 1955–1970* (New Haven, CT: Yale University Press, 1991).

2. Harris Mobley, "Divine Involvement and the Christian World Mission," HMP, FMB Archives; Geoffrey Parrinder, *Religion in Africa* (New York: Preager, 1969); Noel Q. King, *Christian and Muslim in Africa* (New York: Harper and Row, 1971); Elizabeth Isichei, *A History of Christianity in Africa: From Antiquity to the Present* (Grand Rapids, MI: William B. Eerdmans, 1995).

3. "Postwar Program of Your Foreign Mission Board," *Commission* 8, no. 6 (June 1945): 2; M. Theron Rankin, "Tragedy and Glory," BS 33, no. 2 (November 1953): 25.

4. L. Howard Jenkins, "Foreign Missions in Spite of War," *Commission* 11,

no. 3 (March 1945): 1; "Africa's 'Remarkable Progress' Noted," *Commission* 24, no. 3 (March 1965): 36.

5. I. N. Patterson, "Meetings for Intermediate Royal Ambassadors, Second Intermediate Meeting: Awakening Nigeria Learns of Love," *AL* 7, no. 6 (November 1952): 12.

6. Marjorie Moore Armstrong, "It's Happening Now . . . in Africa," *RS* 52, no. 2 (August 1957): 22; Marjorie Moore Armstrong, "Are You an All-American Citizen," *Window* 30, no. 11 (July 1959): 18–19.

7. "YWA—Organization for the Up-to-Date," *Window* 29, no. 2 (October 1957): 20; Carroll Hubbard, "Mission Study Makes a Difference," *AL* 8, no. 11 (April 1954): 9.

8. "A Picture, the Call of God and a Missionary," *AL* 14, no. 12 (May 1960): 4.

9. "Pen Pals," *AL* 11, no. 1 (June 1956): 5; "Pen Pals," *AL* 12, no. 6 (November 1957): 6; "News and Views," *Window* 33, no. 1 (February 1961): 19.

10. J. I. Bishop, "There's No Difference Under the Skin," *AL* 7, no. 6 (November 1952): 6; "Royal Ambassador Activities in Nigeria and the Gold Coast," *AL* 6, no. 11 (April 1952): 4–5; J. I. Bishop, "Nigerian Boys Go To School, Too," *AL* 7, no. 5 (October 1952): 4–5.

11. Patsy Parker, "Why? Why? Why?" *Window* 30, no. 8 (April 1959): 14–16.

12. George W. Sadler, "Report," MFMB, 1949; Sadler, "Report of the Foreign Missions," SBC, 1950, 5; Jean Favell, "Epistles," *Commission* 24, no. 8 (September 1961): 23; Sadler, "Rising Expectations," *Commission* 20, no. 4 (April 1957): 2–3; Sadler, "Report," MFMB, November 10, 1955; Sadler, "Report," MFMB, October 9, 1956; "Foreign Mission News," *Commission* 23, no. 6 (June 1960): 13; "Foreign Mission News," *Commission* 27, no. 8 (September 1964): 8.

13. M. Theron Rankin, "The World Demands Proof," *Commission* 15, no. 1 (January 1952): 9; John R. Sampey Jr., "Equatorial Africa," *Commission* 9, no. 12 (December 1946): 17, 24; W. O. Carver, "What Sort of New World," 5; Marjorie Moore Armstrong, "Program: Choosing the Most Excellent Way (Christian Citizenship)," *RS* 47, no. 4 (October 1952): 30.

14. Armstrong, "Choosing the Most Excellent Way," 30.

15. H. Cornell Goerner, "Meetings for Intermediate Royal Ambassadors, Third Intermediate Meeting: Do You Have What it Takes?" *AL* 3, no. 8 (January 1949): 8.

16. W. E. Wyatt, "Epistles," *Commission* 26, no. 8 (September 1963): 16; Sydney Pearce, "Epistles," *Commission* 26, no. 8 (September 1963): 16.

17. Mrs. William McMurry, "Program: Fourth Week: Where You Are," *Window* 33, no. 8 (April 1962): 32; William M. Dyal Jr., "Aloof or Involved," *Window* 34, no. 4 (December 1962): 14; Betty Bock, "Follow through for *So Sure of Tomorrow*," *Window* 34, no. 3 (November 1962): 42; Dudziak, *Cold War Civil Rights*, 169–87.

18. Baker James Cauthen, "Comments on Race," *RS* 58, no. 6 (December 1963): 8–9.

19. M. Theron Rankin, "Report," MFMB, April 10, 1945; J. W. Marshall, "Report," MFMB, October 9, 1945.

20. Sadler, "Report," MFMB, October 8, 1954.

21. Sadler, "Report," MFMB, April 30, 1949; Sadler, "Report," MFMB, April 10–11, 1956; W. O. Carver, "What Hope," *Commission* 11, no. 3 (March 1948): 20.

22. M. Theron Rankin, "Report," MFMB, April 8, 1952; "Foreign Mission News," *Commission* 21, no. 1 (January 1959): 14; "Nationals are Stewards Too," *RS* 50, no. 7 (January 1956): 40; Julliet Mather, "For God So Loved . . . That He Called from All Races," *RS* 52, no. 6 (December 1957): 69; Marty, *Modern American Religion*, 277–92.

23. Barbara Epperson, "These Things Abide," *Commission* 19, no. 8 (September 1955): 8; "Africanization," MNBM, 1950, 2, FMB Archives.

24. John R. Sampey Jr., "Equatorial Africa," 17, 24; Dr. W. L. Jester, "Ten Decades in Nigeria," *AL* 5, no. 2 (July 1950): 8; "Foreign Mission News," *Commission* 27, no. 7 (July 1964): 27; Mrs. H. P. McCormick, "Your Program: What of Our First Hundred Years in Africa?" *RS* 45, no. 1 (July 1950): 22–30.

25. I. N. Patterson, "The Battle For Africa," *AL* 6, no. 5 (October 1951): 4–5; Patterson, "On The Threshold," *RS* 60, no. 1 (July 1965): 1; Johnni Johnson, "One Who Knows Honor," *Commission* 30, no. 11 (December 1967): 1; Sadler, "In Africa, Europe, and the Near East," *Commission* 14, no. 5 (May 1955): 12.

26. H. Cornell Goerner, "Meetings for Intermediate Royal Ambassadors, First Intermediate Meeting: An African Anniversary," *AL* 4, no. 4 (October 1949): 14–16; Elizabeth Isichei, *History of Christianity in Africa*, 324.

27. Sadler, "In Africa," 12; H. Cornell Goerner, "New Day for the Nigerian Seminary," *Commission* 11, no. 5 (May 1948): 10–11, 15; M. Theron Rankin, "Spreading Light over the Dark Continent," *Commission* 21, no. 7 (July 1958): 26.

28. Goerner, "New Day," 10–11, 15; Mrs. Pat Hill, "Letter-ettes," *RS* 47, no. 11 (May 1953): 20.

29. John E. Mills, "All Things to All Men," *Commission* 16, no. 5 (May 1953): 4–5; Frank K. Means, "God So Loved Nigeria," *Commission* 16, no. 10 (November 1953): 5; Quinn Morgan, "Epistles," *Commission* 13, no. 7 (July 1950): 21; Marilyn S. Wagnon, "Passing the Torch," *Window* 34, no. 10 (June 1963): 29.

30. E. L. Akisanya, "The Road to Becoming Headmaster," *AL* 3, no. 8 (January 1949): 6, 19; E. Milford Howell, "Epistles," *Commission* 14, no. 4 (April 1953): 21.

31. Mills, "All Things to All Men," 4–5; Emanuel O. Akingbala, "The Iron Curtain of Mohammedanism," *Commission* 12, no. 10 (November 1949): 14–15; Isichei, *A History of Christianity in Africa*, 324.

32. Mills, "All Things to All Men," 4–5; Elizabeth Ferguson, "Epistles," *Commission* 13, no. 6 (June 1950): 21; Cal Guy, "Meetings for Intermediate Royal Ambassadors, Third Intermediate Meeting: What of Our First Hundred Years in Africa?" *AL* 5, no. 2 (July 1950): 16; George W. Sadler, "Students in Nigeria," *BS* 29, no. 6 (March 1949): 4–5.

33. Edna Francis Dawkins, "Your Program: Yearning Youth," *RS* 45, no. 10 (April 1951): 24; McCormick, "What of Our First Hundred Years in Africa?" 22–30; Samuel A. Lawoyin, "Who Will Educate Nigeria?" *Commission* 12, no. 6 (June 1949): 6–7; I. N. Patterson, "On the Threshold," 2; Massie, *Loosing the Bonds*, 46–47, 166, 344.

34. Frank K. Means, "Editorial: Thirst for Education," *Commission* 16, no. 6 (June 1953): 19; M. Theron Rankin, "Advance Has Begun," *Commission* 8, no. 5 (May 1950): 5; Stella Austin, "New Day for Women of Nigeria," *Window* 26, no. 11 (July 1955): 23; "Agbor's First Honor Graduate Speaks," *Commission* 19, no. 4 (April 1956): 22.

35. Ruth Swann, "Woman's Place in a Moslem Home," *Window* 24, no. 4 (December 1952): 21; Mary H. Saunders, "Epistles: Gender Discrimination in Igede, Nigeria," *Commission* 16, no. 8 (September 1953): 23; Paul Ebhomlelien, "Because My People Do Not Know," *BS* 28, no. 8 (May 1949): 13; Dana L. Robert, *American Women in Missions: A Social History of Their Thought and Practice* (Macon, GA: Mercer University Press, 1996). On women's position in Africa generally, see Nancy J. Hafkin and Edna G. Bay, eds., *Women in Africa: Studies in Social and Economic Change* (Stanford, CA: Stanford University Press, 1976).

36. Means, "Thirst for Education," 19; Mildred Crabtree, "Unbeaten in Sports and Scholastically," *Window* 28, no. 9 (May 1957): 9–10. For a discussion of the missions and women's social status, see Robert, *American Women in Missions.*

37. Carl F. Eaglesfield, "White Woman's Medicine," *BS* 27, no. 1 (October 1947): 12–13; Page Smith, *Rediscovering Christianity: A History of Modern Democracy and the Christian Ethic* (New York: St. Martin's Press, 1994), 27–31, 167–68; JCMP, FMB Archives.

38. Sadler, "Report," MFMB, April 6–7, 1954; Sadler, "Report," MFMB, October 12–13, 1954; King, *Christian and Muslim in Africa*, 76–98; Isichei, *A History of Christianity in Africa*, 344–45.

39. Doris DeVault, "Program: Three Knocks in the Night," *Window* 29, no. 3 (November 1957): 27–28; Mrs. Howard Smith, "Program," *Window* 32, no. 9 (May 1962): 37–38; Kwame Nkrumah quoted in Smith, "Program."

40. "Foreign Mission News: Racial Policy is Affirmed," *Commission* 26, no. 9 (October 1963): 29.

41. "Report of the Committee on Race Relations," MNBM, 1955, 46, FMB Archives; E. A. Dahunsi, "On Race Relations in the U.S.A," MNBM, 1955, 20–23, FMB Archives.

42. L. Raymond Brothers, "Wind of Change," *Commission* 23, no. 7 (July 1960): 2–3; H. Cornell Goerner, "A Sense of Gratitude," *Commission* 24, no. 1 (January 1961): 8; Marjorie Moore Armstrong, "It's a Small World," *Window* 32, no. 1 (September 1960): 20.

43. H. Cornell Goerner, "Report," MFMB, April 11, 1961; Favell, "Epistles," 23.

44. Harris Mobley, "Divine Involvement"; Copy of *Mercer Cluster* article, "The New Missionary," April 12, 1963, HMP, FMB Archives.

45. Mobley, "Divine Involvement," HMP, FMB Archives.

46. Ibid.

47. H. Cornell Goerner to Harris Mobley, April 25, 1963; Goerner to Mobley, May 21, 1963; Goerner to Joe S. Holliday, June 25, 1963; Mobley to Goerner, August 20, 1963, HMP, FMB Archives; Homer R. Littleton to Mobley, April 26, 1963, HRLP, FMB Archives.

48. H. Cornell Goerner to James Baker Cauthen, October 3, 1963, Administration: Africa/Europe/Near East—Secretary: Cornell Goerner, Executive Correspondence 1954–79, BJC, FMB Archives; Joanna C. Maiden quoted in "Foreign Mission News," *Commission* 20, no. 6 (June 1961): 12.

49. Mrs. William McMurry, "Did You Read It?: The Role of the Missionary in Africa," *RS* 56, no. 7 (January 1963): 15; King, *Christian and Muslim in Africa*, 105–6.

50. Goerner, "Report," MFMB, September 13, 1962; Goerner to Cauthen, November 27, 1961, Administration: Africa/Europe/Near East—Secretary: Cornell Goerner, Executive Correspondence, BJC, FMB Archives.

51. I. N. Patterson, "The Future Broadening Way," *Commission* 29, no. 5 (April 1966): 18; H. Cornell Goerner, "Confidential Report on Nigeria," Administration: Africa—Secretary: Cornell Goerner, June 1966–1967, Executive Correspondence, 1954–79, BJC, FMB Archives; Raymond V. Lindholm, "Epistles," *Commission* 30, no. 2 (February 1967): 22; Roy H. Fanoni, "Epistles," *Commission* 30, no. 2 (February 1967): 22.

52. Joanna Maiden to friends, November 15, 1967, JCMP, FMB Archives; H. Cornell Goerner, "Confidential Report on Eastern Nigeria," October 2, 1967, Administration: Africa—Secretary: Cornell Goerner, June 1966–67, Executive Correspondence 1954–79, BJC, FMB Archives; Maiden to Goerner, July 7, 1969, JCMP, FMB Archives.

53. James W. Carty Jr., "The Struggle for the Soul of Tanganyika," *Commission* 20, no. 3 (March 1957): 6–7.

54. Maxine Law, "Epistles," *Commission* 25, no. 11 (December 1962): 11; "Foreign Mission News," *Commission* 27, no. 4 (April 1964): 29.

55. Roslin D. Harrell, "New Frontiers in Africa," *Commission* 29, no. 2 (February 1966): 10–13; Velma Darbo Brown, "This Month in Your YWA: Is the First Year the Hardest," *Window* 39, no. 9 (May 1968): 36–38.

56. Khrushchev quoted in "Foreign Mission News," *Commission* 27, no. 7 (July 1964): 28; Helen Bond, "Epistle," *Commission* 26, no. 6 (June 1963): 21.

57. Hermione Dannelly Jackson, "Program: Headaches in the Far East," *Window* 23, no. 3 (November 1951): 33.

58. J. A. Imosun, "President's Address," MGBC, 1963, FMB Archives.

59. Mrs. Howard Smith, "Program," 37–38; Goerner, "Report," MFMB, February 12, 1959; Goerner, "Report," MFMB, April 11, 1961.

60. Goerner, "Report," MFMB, February 12, 1959; Goerner, "Report," MFMB, April 11, 1961. See, generally, Dudziak, *Cold War Civil Rights*.

61. Clyde J. Dotson, "Epistles," *Commission* 14, no. 7 (July 1951): 23; Sadler, "Report from Africa, Europe, and the Near East," *Commission* 13, no. 1 (January 1950): 15; Sadler, "Report," Minutes, FMB Archives (April 8, 1952); J. D. Fage, *A History of Africa*, 3rd ed. (London: Routledge, 1995), 450.

62. Goerner, "Report," MFMB, April 7–8, 1959; Goerner, "Report," MFMB, March 10, 1960.

63. "Foreign Mission News," *Commission* 23, no. 6 (June 1961): 13; Massie, *Loosing the Bonds*.

64. James N. Westmoreland, "Epistles," *Commission* 26, no. 10 (November 1963): 19.

65. Goerner, "Report," MFMB, February 8, 1962.

66. W. David Lockard, "At Home in Africa," *Commission* 17, no. 2 (February 1954): 12; Clyde Dotson, "Epistle," *Commission* 25, no. 2 (February 1962): 19.

67. Goerner, "Report," MFMB, February 8, 1962.

68. Goerner, "Report," MFMB, February 14, 1963; Edna Francis Dawkins, "Qualifications for Missionary Personnel," *RS* 50, no. 12 (June 1956): 4–5, 11.

69. Goerner, "Report," MFMB, February 14, 1963; W. David Lockard, "Epistles," *Commission* 18, no. 9 (October 1954): 23–24; Ralph Bowlin, "Chairmen's Comments," CABM, April 22, 1964, FMB Archives.

70. Mrs. Lamar Jackson, "Study in August: Christian Missions and the Tide of Nationalism: Zambia and Malawi," *RS* 62, no. 6 (August 1967): 32–38.

71. Goerner, "Report," MFMB, October 8–10, 1963. See also Massie, *Loosing the Bonds.*

72. Goerner, "Report," MFMB, July 16, 1964; Goerner, "Report," MFMB, October 12, 1965.

73. Goerner, "Report," MFMB, December 9, 1965; "News: Report on Rhodesia," *Commission* 29, no. 1 (January 1966): 27.

74. Goerner, "Report," MFMB, December 9, 1965; Cauthen, "Report," MFMB, May 12, 1966; Goerner, "Report," MFMB, May 12, 1966; Goerner to Cauthen, May 9, 1966; Goerner to Cauthen, "RE: Manpower Registration in Rhodesia," May 10, 1966, Administration: Africa—Secretary: Cornell Goerner, 1964–May 1966, Executive Correspondence 1954–79, BJC, FMB Archives.

75. Goerner to Cauthen, May 9, 1966; Goerner to Cauthen, "RE: Manpower Registration in Rhodesia," May 10, 1966; Cauthen to Goerner, May 13, 1966, Administration: Africa—Secretary: Cornell Goerner, 1964–May 1966, Executive Correspondence 1954–79, BJC, FMB Archives.

Chapter Four

1. Robert S. Ellwood, *The Fifties Spiritual Marketplace: American Religion in a Decade of Conflict* (New Brunswick, NJ: Rutgers University Press, 1997), 5, 23–26; Wuthnow, *Restructuring of American Religion*; Eighmy, *Churches in Cultural Captivity*; Paul Conkin, *When All the Gods Trembled: Darwinism, Scopes, and American Intellectuals* (Lanham, MD: Rowman & Littlefield, 1998), 107–8,169–75; Bennett, *Christianity and Communism.*

2. Rosenberg, *Southern Baptists*, esp. chapter 1, "The Hyper-Americans"; Stricklin, *Genealogy of Dissent*, 1–5; W. O. Carver, "A Call for Faith in the Midst of Confusion," *Commission* 12, no. 8 (September 1949): 7; Charles A. Wells, "Trends," *BS* 27, no. 2 (November 1947): 30; Maston, *Biblical Ethics*, 52–70.

3. Courts Redford, "For Such a Time," *HM* 25, no. 5 (May 1954): 3; W. E. Denham Jr., "Christian Affirmations," *BS* 24, no. 5 (February 1945): 22; Maston, *Biblical Ethics*, 52–70.

4. J. B. Lawrence, "For March Week of Prayer: An Appeal to the Women and

Young People of the Woman's Missionary Union," *RS* 39, no. 7 (January 1945): 27; Lawrence, "Missions and the March of Events," *HM* 16, no. 5 (May 1945): 2; "Home Missions," *HM* 16, no. 12 (December 1945): 3; "Christ for A Distraught World," *HM* 16, no. 10 (October 1945): 8.

5. Cal Guy, "Meeting for Intermediate Royal Ambassadors, First Intermediate Meeting: How Christian Is America?" *AL* 4, no. 8 (February 1950): 14.

6. Sanders, "World Peace," 3.

7. Baker James Cauthen, "Program: I Am the Door," *Window* 29, no. 4 (December 1957): 39; Cauthen, "Prayer Potential," *Commission* 18, no. 11 (December 1954): 9.

8. Mrs. George R. Ferguson, "Prepare Now!" *HM* 26, no. 1 (January 1955): 18.

9. Courts Redford, "Missions: Home and World," *RS* 57, no. 7 (January 1963): 1.

10. J. W. Storer, "The SBC President Speaks," *RS* 48, no. 4 (October 1953): 6–7; Courts Redford, "Watch Where You Are Going," *HM* 31, no. 4 (April 1960): 5; Redford, "Looking Ahead," *HM* 18, no. 2 (February 1947): 10; Tillich, *What Is Religion?* passim, esp. 34, 126–27.

11. Carver, "Deluding Illusions," *Commission* 11, no. 11 (December 1948): 11–12; Patterson, *Grand Expectations*, passim, esp. 129–33.

12. Juliette Mather, "Our Young People: Hearty Plans for Our Daughters," *RS* 39, no. 8 (February 1945): 8; Alma Hunt, *History of Woman's Missionary Union* (Nashville, TN: Convention Press, 1964), 111–13; Frank H. Leavell, "The Editor's Outlook: The Dance," *BS* 28, no. 8 (March 1949): 20; Mrs. F. W. Armstrong, "Missionary Education," 172–73.

13. White, "Christ, the Answer for the Individual," 21; "On My Campus," *BS* 25, no. 1 (October 1945): 22.

14. White, "Christ, the Answer for the Individual," 21; Earl Hester Trutza, "Program: Christ the Answer for the World," *RS* 44, no. 6 (December 1949): 27.

15. Mrs. Joe E. Burton, "Your Program: The Continuing Price of Freedom," *RS* 46, no. 1 (July 1951): 29; Eugene L. Hill, "Editorial," *Commission* 19, no. 1 (January 1956): 18.

16. E. C. Routh, "Editorial," *Commission* 10, no. 2 (February 1947): 18.

17. Hill, "Editorial," 18; Edith Huckabay, "Let's Talk About You: All American," *Window* 21, no. 7 (March 1950): 10; Carolyn Turnage, "Youth Looks at Its God," *Window* 23, no. 6 (February 1952): 20; Charles A. Wells, untitled political cartoon, *AL* 3, no. 8 (January 1949): 23.

18. "How Christian Is America," *Commission* 13, no. 2 (February 1950): 1; Virginia Cannata, "Epistles," *Commission* 26, no. 6 (June 1963): 18.

19. T. B. Maston quoted in "News: U.S. Racial Problem," *HM* 36, no. 4 (April 1965): 4.

20. Cyril E. Bryant, "Today," *RS* 52, no. 8 (November 1957): 10; Robert H. Culpepper, "A Look at America after Five Years Abroad," *Commission* 20, no. 9 (October 1957): 6; Ellwood, *Fifties Spiritual Marketplace*, 5, 175–79.

21. Irene Curtis, "Program: Christ the Answer in the Cities," *RS* 43, no. 8 (February 1949): 28, 31.

22. Kate Bullock Helms, "Program: How Christian Is America," *RS* 44, no. 8 (February 1950): 23–25.

23. Mrs. Davis Woolley, "Program: God Save America," *Window* 27, no. 6 (February 1956): 33–34; Helms, "How Christian Is America," 23–25.

24. Durham, "Being Christian in Human Relations," 30; Mrs. R. L. Mathis, "Do More than Talk," *RS* 56, no. 8 (February 1962): inside cover.

25. Helms, "How Christian Is America," *RS*, 23–25; Hermione Dannelly Jackson, "Let's Discuss Missions: Everybody Has a Part," *Window* 21, no. 6 (February 1950): 22; Manis, *Southern Civil Religions*; Kelsey, *Social Ethics*, 250–63.

26. Jackson, "Discuss Missions," *Window* 22, no. 11 (July 1951): 13; "Quotable Good News: Educational Segregation Waning," *Window* 23, no. 6 (February 1952): 13; Henlee Barnette, "Negro Students in Southern Baptist Seminaries," *RE* 53 (April 1956): 207–11; Albert McClellen to Advisory Council on Work with Negroes, April 11, 1963, "Advisory Council," Box 22, TBMP, RLSWT.

27. Edith Huckabay, "Ask Edith," *Window* 25, no. 6 (February 1954): 22–23.

28. A. C. Miller, "A Roadblock on the Mission Highway," *RS* 49, no. 7 (January 1955): 12.

29. Eighmy, *Churches in Cultural Captivity*; Newman, "Getting Right with God"; Manis, *Southern Civil Religions*; Leonard, "Southern Baptists and Southern Culture," 200–212; Moody, "Southern Baptist Polity," 2–11.

30. J. B. Weatherspoon, "Report of the Committee on Race Relations," SBC, 1947, 47–48, 341–42; Thomas Powell, *The Persistence of Racism In America* (Lanham, MD: University Press of America, 1992).

31. Mrs. Chester F. Russell, "A Newly Given Freedom," *RS* 49, no. 2 (August 1954): 7; Donald G. Nieman, *Promises to Keep: African Americans and the Constitutional Order, 1776 to the Present* (New York: Oxford University Press, 1991), 191–200.

32. Charles Prewitt, "Prejudice: Its Birth and Death," *HM* 26, no. 10 (October 1955): 24; Collins, *When the Church Bell Rang Racist*, 23–24.

33. Abbie Louise Green, "The Way of the Sunbeam Band," *RS* 56, no. 2 (August 1961): 1–4.

34. Ruth LaTuille Matthews, "Racial Attitudes for Tiny Tots," *RS* 43, no. 2 (August 1948): 20; Una Roberts Lawrence to Dr. S. A. Newman, Feb. 25, 1948, Box 2, Folder 15, URL, SBHLA.

35. Matthews, "Racial Attitudes," 20; Acts 10:34–35, KJV.

36. Jane Winchester Martin quoted in "Grown-up Sunbeams Overseas," *RS* 56, no. 2 (August 1961): 13; Mrs. Steve Ditmore, "We Get Letters: Missionary Appointees Tell of God's Call," *RS* 59, no. 12 (June 1965): 8–9.

37. Lucy Grace, "Reflections," *RS* 43, no. 9 (March 1949): 1. See also Charles A. Wells, "Trends: Jim Crow Disappearing," *BS* 25, no. 7 (April 1946): 30; Manis, *Southern Civil Religions*, passim.

38. Martha Anne Oakley, "We Protested the Ku Klux Klan," *Window* 20, no. 7 (March 1949): 2–3.

39. Mrs. A. L. Aulick, "Your Program: On the Rock or on the Rocks?" *RS* 44,

no. 12 (June 1950): 24; J. Ivyloy Bishop, "Ambassador Life Lines," *AL* 3, no. 12 (May 1949): 24. The idea of the Christian home is explored in Colleen McDannell, *The Christian Home in Victorian America, 1840–1900* (Bloomington, IN: Indiana University Press, 1986). On the Christian home as a missionary enterprise, see Robert, *American Women in Missions*.

40. Mary Dobbins, "Program: The Hardest Place," *Window* 23, no. 9 (March 1952): 31; "Overseas Students," *BS* 28, no. 3 (December 1948): 21.

41. H. Cornell Goerner, "Meetings for Intermediate Royal Ambassadors, First Intermediate Meeting: Better Homes for America," *AL* 3, no. 12 (May 1949): 11; Mrs. Noble Y. Beall, "Program: Tarry . . . Tell; Monday: Tell the Milling Multitudes," *RS* 53, no. 9 (March 1958): 22; Helen Fling, "Spiritual Life Development," *RS* 57, no. 9 (March 1963): 4; Kyle M. Yates Jr., "Intermediate Royal Ambassador Meetings, Second Intermediate Meeting: Foundations for a Christian Home," *AL* 12, no. 12 (May 1958): 18.

42. Freeman, "Christ the Answer to Racial Tensions," 22.

43. Russell, "Newly Given Freedom," 7.

44. Mrs. Douglas Harris, "Why Mommy: As a Child Thinketh So Is He," *RS* 44, no. 8 (February 1950): 16.

45. George M. Faile Jr., "Epistles," *Commission* 18, no. 6 (June 1955): 22; James E. Hampton, "Epistles," *Commission* 20, no. 4 (April 1957): 23. See also "Little Missionary," *Commission* 18, no. 3 (April 1954): 29.

46. H. Cornell Goerner, "Meetings for Intermediate Royal Ambassadors, Third Intermediate Meeting: Ways to Fellowship," *AL* 4, no. 1 (June 1949): 17; Mrs. John J. Hamilton, "The World at Our Hearth," *RS* 59, no. 10 (April 1965): 9.

47. J. T. Gillespie, "Baptists Colleges Can Be Missionary Centers," *HM* 23, no. 2 (February 1952): 20; Beatrice Bland, "Unforgettable Experiences: In Summer Field Work," *Window* 20, no. 6 (February 1949): 5.

48. Fred B. Moseley, "Give with the Need in Mind," *RS* 63, no. 9 (March 1969): 16.

49. "Young Woman's Auxiliary at Work," *Window* 20, no. 7 (March 1949): 22; L. M. Huff Jr., "Now is the Hour," *AL* 3, no. 10 (March 1949): 3; Irene Thomas, "Rewards Unlimited," *Window* 24, no. 7 (March 1953): 22; W. Boyd Hunt, "Local Church Sees It's [*sic*] Mission Opportunity," *HM* 22, no. 3 (August 1952): 15.

50. Eugene L. Hill, "Editorial: Discipleship and Our Task," *Commission* 19, no. 9 (October 1956): 22–23; John Caylor, "From the Pen of John Caylor: It Happened on a Trolley," *HM* 27, no. 6 (July 1956): 5.

51. Mrs. William McMurry, "African Safari for Mission Study," *Forecaster* insert in *RS* 52, no. 4 (October 1957): 7–8.

52. Hugh Brimm, "What's Wrong with Racial Segregation?" *Window* 27, no. 1 (September 1955): 2–4.

53. Brimm, "What's Wrong with Racial Segregation?" 2. See also Mark Chapman, "'Of One Blood': Mays and the Theology of Race Relations," in *Walking Integrity: Benjamin Elijah Mays, Mentor to Martin Luther King, Jr.*, ed. Lawrence Edward Carter Sr. (Macon, GA: Mercer University Press, 1998), 233–61.

54. Newman, "Getting Right with God," 186; Berger, *Sacred Canopy*, 23–52; T. B. Maston to Catherine B. Allen, March 11, 1986, "Woman's Missionary Union," Box 22, TBMP, RLSWT; G. Frank Garrison, "Church Schools of Missions," *SBBQ* 15, no. 1 (January, February, March 1946): 61; T. B. Maston, "Christian Men and Race Relations," *SBBQ* 32, no. 4 (October, November, December 1961): 31.

55. Clifton J. Allen to T. B. Maston, April 17, 1956, "Advisory Council on Negro Work, Correspondence, A–L," Box 22, TBMP, RLSWT; John P. Davies to Rev. Allen, April 30, 1958, Box 59, Folder 21, CJA, SBHLA.

56. Noble Y. Beall, "Maintaining the Status Quo: Preserving Our Little Gods," Box 1, Folder 9, URL, SBHLA; Mrs. W. L. Mayfield to Porter Routh, November 15, 1957, Box 82, Folder 2, ECR, SBHLA. See also Jimmy Carter, *Living Faith* (New York: Times Books, 1996), 120.

57. Mrs. William (Mildred Dodson) McMurry, "Our Freedoms," *RS* 57, no. 12 (June 1963): 10–12; Taylor Branch, *Parting the Waters: America in the King Years, 1954–63* (New York: Simon and Schuster, 1988), 673–845; Philip A. Klinkner, *The Unsteady March: The Rise and Decline of Racial Equality in America*, with Rogers M. Smith (Chicago: University of Chicago Press, 1999), 264–72.

58. Mrs. O., "We Get Letters: 'Our Freedoms' commended," *RS* 58, no. 4 (October 1963): 4–5; LB, "We Get Letters: 'Our Freedoms,'" *RS* 58, no. 6 (December 1963): 11; REF, "We Get Letters: Different Opinions Regarding Race Relations," *RS* 58, no. 9 (February 1964): 13–14.

59. A Member of a Circle, "We Get Letters: 'Our Freedoms,'" *RS* 58, no. 6 (December 1963): 11; AS, "We Get Letters: 'Different Opinions Regarding Race Relations," *RS* 58, no. 9 (February 1964): 13–14.

60. Courts Redford, "This is America's Hour," *RS* 59, no. 8 (February 1965): 5.

61. Arthur B. Rutledge, "The Great and Godly Society," *HM* 36, no. 2 (February 1965): 2.

62. Mrs. James T. Higgins, "Letters from Our Readers: Amazed at Persistence," *HM* 37, no. 7 (July 1966): 2.

63. L. Dudly Wilson, "Courage or Conformity," *Window* 40, no. 11 (July 1969): 6–7; Hankins, *Uneasy in Babylon*, 242.

64. Ellwood, *Fifties Spiritual Marketplace*, 180; Braxton Bryant, "Where Are We in Civil Rights?" *BS* 47, no. 5 (February 1968); 22.

Chapter Five

1. Loyd Corder, "To Many Tongues," *HM* 32, no. 3 (March 1961): 14–15; J. B. Lawrence, "Home Missions," *HM* 16, no. 3 (March 1945): 3; Alma Hunt, "On Our Doorstep," *RS* 44, no. 8 (February 1950): inside cover; Rutledge and Tanner, *Mission to America*, 159; Courts Redford, "He Died For Me Too," *HM* 27, no. 5 (May 1956): 3; *AIB* 10, no. 5 (November 1955): 1–4.

2. W. O. Carver, "Light from Christ on Life Today," 5; Saxon Rowe Carver, "Program: With One Accord," *Window* 31, no. 1 (September 1959): 31.

3. Ed M. Arendall, "Under the Skin," 8; Maston, *Segregation and*

Desegregation, 87; Raul Solis, "A Social Problem," *HM* 54, no. 8 (August 1953): 22; Loyd Corder, "Winning Our Minority Groups," *HM* 23, no. 8 (August 1952): 14.

4. Arnoldo De León, *Mexican Americans in Texas: A Brief History*, 2nd ed. (1993; repr., Wheeling, IL: Harlan Davidson, 1999), 110–15; Howard G. McClain, "Meeting for Intermediate Royal Ambassadors, Second Intermediate Meeting: Lifting Morals with the Lever of Respect," *AL* 8, no. 10 (March 1954): 15.

5. Maston, "*Of One*," 69, 83–85; Maston, *Bible and Race*, 21; Genesis 11:1–9.

6. W. O. Carver, "Light from Christ on Life Today," 5; J. B. Lawrence, "A Man Without a Chance," *HM* 19, no. 10 (October 1948): 3.

7. Miguel A. Lopez, "We Haven't Begun," *AL* 3, no. 10 (March 1949): 2; Rutledge and Tanner, *Mission to America*, 147–70.

8. "Three Hundred Sixty Five Student Missionaries," *AIB* 6, no. 12 (June 1952): 1; Clara Lee, "Letters," *AIB* 5, no. 3 (September 1950): 4; "Harmony at Inlow," *AIB* 10, no. 1 (July 1955): 4; Lawrence, "A Man Without a Chance," 3.

9. Lawrence, "A Man Without a Chance," 3; Jacqueline Durham, "Ten Weeks a Missionary," *HM* 30, no. 11 (November 1959): 13.

10. S. R. Carver, "With One Accord," 31.

11. Ibid.; Dwight W. Hoover, *The Red and the Black* (Chicago: Rand McNally College Publishing, 1976), 282–301.

12. Pen Lile Pittard, "For Your Program: The Mexican in Our Midst," *Window* 19, no. 2 (October 1947): 22; O. K. Armstrong, "Intermediate Programs, Second Intermediate Meeting: Our Next Door Neighbors, the Mexicans," *AL* 13, no. 2 (July 1958): 19.

13. Helen Dale Armstrong, "Unforgettable Experiences—in Summer Field Work," *Window* 20, no. 6 (February 1949): 3; John D. Freeman, "Choctaw Indians pay Dividends," *HM* 18, no. 2 (February 1947): 8; Phileo Nash, "Indians East of the Mississippi," *RS* 56, no. 11 (May 1962): 1.

14. James P. Wesberry, Wiley Henton, and Harold G. Sanders, "Report of the Committee on Migrant Evangelism," MHMB, December 3–4, 1946; Mrs. Sam T. Mayo, "Program: Faith Working through Love, Tuesday: Sons of God through Faith," *RS* 52, no. 9 (March 1958): 37–63; Alene Harris, "Gifts that Multiply," *Window* 20, no. 7 (March 1949): 12; De León, *Mexican Americans in Texas*, 111; Mildred Dunn, "Program: Up and Down the City Streets," *RS* 49, no. 11 (May 1955): 26.

15. Mrs. Ralph Gwin, "Program: 'Teach . . . the Good and Right WAY' to Indians East of the Mississippi," *RS* 56, no. 11 (May 1962): 38; Mrs. Lee M. Roebuck, "Bernalillo," *AIB* 2, no. 10 (April 1948): 22; Jean Hightower, "Letters from Summer Workers," *AIB* 5, no. 3 (September 1950): 3; Russell Means, *Where White Men Fear to Tread*, with Marvin J. Wolf (New York: St. Martin's Griffin, 1995), 35. See also Josephy, "Modern America and the Indian," in *Indians in American History: An Introduction*, ed. Frederick E. Hoxie and Peter Iverson, 2nd ed. (Wheeling, IL: Harlan Davidson, 1998); Edward H. Spicer, *Cycles of Conquest: The Impact of Spain, Mexico, and the United States on the Indians of the Southwest, 1533–1960* (Tucson, AZ: University of Arizona Press, 1962), 15–16.

16. "Indian Study Outstanding Feature," *AIB* 9, no. 1 (July 1951): 2; "Letter

from Jack Park," *AIB* 9, no. 5 (September 1954): 4; Hightower, "Letters from Summer Workers," 3.

17. C. W. Stumph, "Liquor for Indians," *AIB* 6, no. 2 (August 1951): 1; Robert Bushyhead, "An Indian's Plea," *HM* 23, no. 7 (July 1952): 20; Cyril E. Bryant, "From Washington: A New Indian Trail," *RS* 56, no. 11 (May 1962): 9.

18. J. B. Rounds, "Should Indians Vote," *AIB* 1, no. 9 (March 1947): 1–2; "Facts About Indians in America," *RS* 60, no. 7 (January 1966): 6–8; C. W. Stumph, "Indians and the Vote," *AIB* 2, no. 8 (February 1948): 3; C. W. Stumph, "Isleta," *AIB* 1, no. 5 (November 1946): 4; Josephy, "Modern America and the Indian," 198–99, 205–6.

19. C. W. Stumph, "Freedom of Religion," *AIB* 2, no. 9 (March 1948): 1, 4; Stumph, "Prince and Peasant and Religious Persecution," *AIB* 3, no. 9 (March 1949): 1–2; Stumph, "Worship Rights Come High," *AIB* 5, no. 11 (May 1951): 1; Stumph, "They Want Freedom!" *AIB* 7, no. 3 (September 1952): 1; A. C. Miller, "This Is Freedom?" *RS* 49, no. 9 (March 1955): 16–17.

20. Jane Geiger, "I Spent My Summer '45: Pioneering with the Indians," *BS* 25, no. 7 (April 1946): 12; C. W. Stumph, "Persecuted for Christ's Sake: The Case of Viviano Hererra, Zia Pueblo Indian Banished from His Tribe," *AIB* 3, no. 7 (January 1949): 1–2. See also Spicer, *Cycles of Conquest*, 501–18.

21. Eva Inlow, "When the Heart is at Rest," *RS* 56, no. 10 (April 1962): 11–12.

22. Doris Roebuck, "Letters from Missionaries: Indian Way or White Way?" *RS* 44, no. 2 (August 1949): 12; Lewis Grant, "Indians in Need of Christ," *AIB* 1, no. 1 (July 1946): 4; Gilbert Sears, "'Fields White Unto the Harvest': Student Summer Mission Program Report—1957," *BS* 37, no. 6 (March 1958): 40–41.

23. C. W. Stumph, "That Indian Liquor Vote," *AIB* 8, no. 2 (August 1953): 1. See also Stumph, "This Wasn't Smart," *AIB* 8, no. 4 (October 1953): 1, 2.

24. Mrs. E. C. Branch, "Beauty and Misery in Apacheland," *RS* 50, no. 9 (March 1956): 4–6; "Liquor's Contribution to Youth Delinquency," *AIB* 10, no. 8 (February 1956): 2; A. L. Davis, "Winning the Montana Indians," *HM* 30, no. 10 (October 1959): 14–15.

25. Doris Christensen, "Santa Fe," *AIB* 2, no. 11 (May 1948): 3; Pauline Commack, "Preach the Word," *AIB* 4, no. 9 (March 1950): 1, 3; Sears, "'Fields White Unto the Harvest,'" 40–41.

26. Marjorie Moore Armstrong, "What's Happening Now!: On the Indian Reservations," *RS* 50, no. 10 (April 1956): 25; Means, *Where White Men Fear to Tread*, 68.

27. Armstrong, "What's Happening Now!" 25; Josephy, "Modern America and the Indian," 206–8.

28. Armstrong, "What's Happening Now!" 25.

29. Troy R. Johnson, "Roots of Contemporary Native American Activism," *American Indian Culture and Research Journal* 20, no. 2 (1996): 127–54; Peter Iverson, *"We Are Still Here": American Indians in the Twentieth Century* (Wheeling, IL: Harlan Davidson, 1998), 118–35; Terry H. Anderson, *The Movement and the Sixties: Protest in America from Greensboro to Wounded Knee* (New York: Oxford University Press, 1995), 333–36; Patterson, *Grand Expectations*, 376–77.

30. A. C. Miller, "Group Studies: The Modern American Indian," *HM* 25, no. 10 (October 1954): 10.

31. Mrs. Melvina Roberts and Bernice Miller, "God's Word in His Pocket," *RS* 46, no. 9 (March 1952): 4; Gerald B. Palmer, "Has Indian Missions Failed?" *HM* 36, no. 1 (January 1965): 11–12.

32. W. O. Carver, "Looking Ahead," *Commission* 9, no. 10 (November 1946): 5; Solis, "A Social Problem," 22; Maston, "*Of One*," 23–24.

33. Solis, "A Social Problem," 22; Maston, "*Of One*," 23–24.

34. Solis, "A Social Problem," 22; Helen E. Falls, "In the Language of Their Hearts," *Window* 40, no. 7 (March 1969): 31.

35. William Russell, "Training the Whole Child," *HM* 19, no. 5 (May 1958): 15; Jacqueline Durham, "Program Notes: Third Week, Trials of the Trail," *Window* 33, no. 4 (February 1962): 25.

36. C. W. Stumph, "Indian School Party," *AIB* 1, no. 10 (April 1947): 2; Mrs. Ned P. King, "Program: May Know Our Saviour's Love: Indians of the Southwest," *RS* 55, no. 7 (January 1961): 38–39; "My Pen Pals," *AIB* 8, no. 7 (December 1953): 4; Goldin, "Unlearning Black and White," 136–58.

37. Pittard, "Mexicans in Our Midst," 22. On the issue of assimilation of Mexican Americans, see Ignacio M. García, *Chicanismo: The Forging of a Militant Ethos among Mexican Americans* (Tucson: University of Arizona Press, 1998).

38. Edith Stokely, "Hints to Committee Chairmen: To Community Missions Chairmen," *RS* 47, no. 8 (February 1953): 14; Hunt, *History of Woman's Missionary Union*, 160.

39. Terrell Smith, "Salvation for the Mexicans," *AL* 8, no. 9 (February 1954): 9.

40. A. Maurice Norton, "A Personal Approach to Language Groups," *HM* 34, no. 3 (March 1963): 14–15; José Angel Gutiérrez, *The Making of a Chicano Militant: Lessons from Cristal* (Madison, WI: University of Wisconsin Press, 1998), 122–29; Means, *Where White Men Fear to Tread*, 62–63.

41. Margaret Bruce, "Language Missions," *Forecaster* insert in *RS* 58, no. 2 (August 1963): 3.

42. A Student, "Pepe," *Window* 32, no. 6 (February 1961): 41; Benjamin DeMott, *The Trouble with Friendship: Why Americans Can't Think Straight about Race* (New Haven, CT: Yale University Press, 1995).

43. Maston, "*Of One*," 20–21.

44. Solis, "A Social Problem," 22; De León, *Mexican Americans in Texas*, 114.

45. George Marshall Rix, "A Day with the Indians," *AL* 10, no.8 (January 1956): 5; "Indian TB Death Rate," *AIB* 6, no. 12 (June 1952): 4; Gerald Palmer, "Southern Baptists and American Indians," *RS* 63, no. 2 (August 1968): 14–15.

46. Miller, "Modern American Indian," 10; Tom Trent, "Rising to the Son," *HM* 33, no. 12 (December 1962): 12–13.

47. Mr. and Mrs. L. W. Crews, "Challenge of a Lifetime," *HM* 29, no. 9 (September 1958): 14; David Wallace Adams, *Education for Extinction: American Indians and the Boarding School Experience, 1875–1928* (Lawrence: University Press of Kansas, 1995).

48. Spicer, *Cycles of Conquest*, 173–75; Walker L. Knight and Dallas M. Lee, "The Incredibly Quiet War," *HM* 39, no. 9 (September 1968): 18.

49. Frank E. Skilton, "Indian Girl Wins Degree," *HM* 23, no. 8 (August 1952): 22.

50. Andrea Jojola, "Inspiration," *AIB* 10, no. 12 (June 1956): 3; "Santa Clara Indian Girl Attends Baptist College," *AIB* 6, no. 4 (October 1951): 3.

51. Durham, "Being Christian in Human Relations," 31; Juanita Moral Wilkinson, "Week of Prayer for *HM*: 'So Send I You,' Wednesday: 'So Send I You . . . to Witness to the World at Home,'" *RS* 60, no. 9 (March 1966): 55; "Indian Graduates," *AIB* 9, no. 12 (June 1955): 2; Spicer, *Cycles of Conquest*, 145, 226.

52. Crews, "Challenge of a Lifetime," 14; Lee Roebuck, "Bernalillo," *AIB* 3, no. 4 (October 1948), 2; "Mission Opportunity," *AIB* 11, no. 4 (October 1956): 3; Armstrong, "What's Happening Now," 25.

53. "Frank Belvin to Lead Indian Work," *HM* 22, no. 6 (June 1951): 11; Loyd Corder, "Guides to the 'Jesus Way,'" *HM* 24, no. 8 (August 1953): 6–7.

54. "Leadership Classes Taught at Navajo Training School," *HM* 36, no. 3 (March 1965): 18–19; "Description of Plan for Navajo Leadership Training," MHMB, September 10, 1964; J. G. Allen, "'Home Missions' Part in Indian Missions," *Leadership* insert in *HM* 36, no. 11 (November 1965): 16-E.

55. Pittard, "Mexicans in Our Midst," 22; Gutiérrez, *Making of a Chicano Militant*; García, *Chicanismo*; De León, *Mexican Americans in Texas*, 117–19.

56. Dallas M. Lee, "The Mexican-American in Texas: A Restless, Forgotten Man about to be Heard," *HM* 38, no. 7 (July 1967): 12–17; De León, *Mexican Americans in Texas*, 111–12.

57. Hermione Dannelly Jackson, "Programs: Meeting the Needs of the Migrants," *Window* 25, no. 6 (February 1954): 32. See Devra Weber, *Dark Sweat, White Gold: California Farm Workers, Cotton, and the New Deal* (Berkeley: University of California Press, 1994).

58. J. Ed Taylor, "Missionary to the Moving Multitudes," *RS* 52, no. 9 (March 1958): 10–14.

59. Walker L. Knight, "Who's to Blame," *HM* 38, no. 7 (July 1967): 4; De León, *Mexican Americans in Texas*, 126–30; Matt S. Meier and Feliciano Rivera, *Dictionary of Mexican American History* (Westport, CT: Greenwood Press, 1981), 182, 211.

60. Lee, "Mexican-American in Texas," 12–17; De León, *Mexican Americans in Texas*, 126–30.

61. Milton L. Rhodes, Larry D. Farrell, and Jimmy Allen, "Letters from Our Readers," *HM* 38, no. 9 (September 1967): 2–3.

62. Raul R. Solis, "Letters from Our Readers," *HM* 38, no. 9 (September 1967): 2–3.

63. R. L. Kurth, "Letters from Our Readers," *HM* 38, no. 9 (September 1967): 2–3; Romans 13:1–4, KJV; Gutiérrez, *Making of a Chicano Militant*, passim.

64. Knight and Lee, "Incredibly Quiet War," 17; Johnson, "Roots of Contemporary Native American Activism," 127–54.

65. Josephy, "Modern America and the Indian," 209–15; W. Richard West Jr.

and Kevin Gover, "The Struggle for Indian Civil Rights," in *Indians in American History: An Introduction*, ed. Frederick E. Hoxie and Peter Iverson, 2nd ed. (Wheeling, IL: Harlan Davidson, 1998), 218–34.

66. Durham, "Being Christian in Human Relations," 31; Juanita Morrill Wilkinson, "'So Send I You,'" 55.

67. Geiger, "Pioneering with the Indians," 12.

68. Elizabeth Ann Allen, "Pray and Give," *Window* 30, no. 7 (March 1959): 2–3; Barbara Sue Johnson, "Pray and Give," *Window* 30, no. 7 (March 1959): 3.

69. Anne Keelin, "Letteretts," *RS* 51, no. 8 (February 1957): 30; Hoover, *Red and the Black*, 350–51; Means, *Where White Men Fear to Tread*, passim, quotation on 78; Selma Crawford, "Windows, Closed, Clouded—Opened," *Window* 20, no. 6 (February 1949): 11.

70. Geiger, "Pioneering with the Indians," 12; Lee Roebuck, "Bernalillo," *AIB* 2, no. 4 (October 1947): 3; J. B. Rounds, "The All-Indian Camp," *AIB* 4, no. 11 (May 1950): 1; Walker L. Knight, "Missions and Modern Man," *HM* 36, no. 3 (March 1965): 3; Keelin, "Letteretts," 30; Jack U. Harwell, "Religious Life of American Indians," *AL* 16, no. 10 (March 1962): 9; Henry Warner Bowden, *American Indians and Christian Missions: Studies in Cultural Conflict* (Chicago: University of Chicago Press, 1981), 21.

71. Davis, "Winning the Montana Indians," 15.

72. Sue Edison Nollette, "Well Spent Dollars," *RS* 57, no. 9 (February 1963): 1–2; Nell T. Campell, "The Shiprock School," *AIB* 9, no. 5 (September 1954): 4; "Language Group Minorities," MHMB, April 5, 1962; Bailey Sewell, "Help Us Thank God," *RS* 54, no. 3 (September 1959): 10–12.

73. Sara Hines Martin, "Study in Circle or Second WMS Meeting: Home Missions Work in Baptist Centers," *RS* 61, no. 8 (February 1967): 34; Gerald B. Palmer, "How to Open Your Church to Language Groups," *HM* 34, no. 3 (March 1963): 18.

74. Rutledge and Tanner, *Mission to America*, 160; "Texas, Mexican Baptist Conventions May Unite," *Leadership* insert in *HM* 31, no. 6 (June 1960): 16-E; J. Woodrow Fuller, "Changing Patterns," *RS* 44, no. 8 (February 1961): 10; Loyd Corder, "One Convention for Texas," *HM* 31, no. 9 (September 1960): 6; "Missions Today: First Mexican Elected to Convention Office," *HM* 32, no. 1 (January 1961): 2.

Chapter Six

1. "Fields of Service: Negroes," MHMB, August 5–6, 1946; Guy Bellamy, "Report of the Home Mission Board," SBC, 1951, 215; Von Eschen, *Race against Empire*.

2. "Report of the Christian Life Commission," SBC, 1946, 124; Olin T. Binkly, "Moral Issues Confronting Christian Youth," *BS* 28, no. 1 (October 1948): 15; Weatherspoon, "Report of the Committee on Race Relations," 340–43.

3. J. B. Lawrence, "Report of the Home Mission Board," 168.

4. Ibid.

5. Mrs. C. D. Creasman, "Program Material," *RS* 15, no. 11 (May 1946): 23.

6. James P. Wesberry, "Report of the Committee on Cooperative Work with

Negroes," MHMB, August 2, 1945; Wesberry, "Report of the Committee on Cooperative Work with Negroes," MHMB, July 11, 1946; Roland Smith, "Working Together in a Great Enterprise," *HM* 18, no. 8 (August 1946): 8–9; Alvis Jr., *Religion and Race*, 19–22.

7. L. S. Sedberry, "We Need a Trained Negro Ministry," *RS* 46, no. 4 (October 1951): 4–5; Daniel W. Wynn, "Is the Teacher Missionary Worthwhile?" *RS* 46, no. 9 (May 1952): 8–9; Wynn, "The Value of Teacher-Missionaries for Negroes," *HM* 23, no. 4 (April 1952): 20–21; J. B. Lawrence, "The Mission Program with the Negroes," *HM* 18, no. 1 (January 1947): 3; Guy Bellamy, "Helping Our Negro Friends," *HM* 21, no. 5 (May 1950): 16; Victor T. Glass, "Working with National Baptists," *HM* 36, no. 1 (January 1965): 16-I; Lawrence Edward Carter Sr., "The Life of Benjamin Elijah Mays," in *Walking Integrity: Benjamin Elijah Mays, Mentor to Martin Luther King, Jr.*, ed. Lawrence Edward Carter Sr. (Macon, GA: Mercer University Press, 1998), 6; Edwin Johnson, "The Interracial Baptist Institute," *HM* 27, no. 12 (December 1956): 20–21; Rutledge and Tanner, *Mission to America*, 139–40.

8. J. B. Lawrence, "Home Missions," *HM* 16, no. 5 (May 1945): 3; Rutledge and Tanner, *Mission to America*, 143.

9. Carrie U. Littlejohn, "Training School: 'God Save America! Here May All Races Mingle Together as Children of God!'" *RS* 39, no. 11 (May 1945): 11; H. Cornell Goerner, "Meeting for Intermediate Royal Ambassadors, First Meeting: City Missions in Our Midst," *AL* 3, no. 9 (February 1949): 14; Theodore F. Adams, "High Standards of Speech and Conduct," *RS* 54, no. 8 (February 1960): 6–7.

10. Courts Redford, "Youth Has a Stake in Home Missions," *BS* 26, no. 9 (June 1947): 4–5, 31; William Hall Preston, "From *The Baptist Student* Editor's Desk: A Hearty Welcome," *BS* 25, no. 1 (October 1945): 19.

11. Edith Stokely, "Hints to Committee Chairmen: Community Missions," *RS* 45, no. 11 (May 1951): 14–15; Hunt, *History of Woman's Missionary Union*, 160; Mrs. John M. McGinnis, "Jack and Jill Go up the Hill," *RS* 45, no. 9 (March 1951): 9–11.

12. H. C. Goerner, "Meetings for Intermediate Royal Ambassadors, First Intermediate Meeting: Trouble Shooters for Christ," *AL* 4, no. 1 (June 1949): 14; W. O. Carver, "Light from Christ on Life Today," 5; Collins, *When the Church Bell Rang Racist*, passim, esp. 15–18; Manis, *Southern Civil Religions*, 23–25; Sara Hart Brown, "Congressional Anti-Communism and the Segregationist South: From New Orleans to Atlanta, 1954–1958," *Georgia Historical Quarterly* 80, no. 4 (Winter 1996): 785–816.

13. J. B. Lawrence, "Missions and the March of Events: Race Relations," *HM* 18, no. 4 (April 1947): 2; Lawrence, "Missions and the March of Events: What Negroes Want," *HM* 18, no. 8 (August 1947): 2.

14. "Report of the Social Service Commission," SBC, 1948, 336–37; Charles A. Wells, "Trends: Christians Fight Jim Crow," *BS* 25, no. 1 (October 1945): 31; Richard Kluger, *Simple Justice: The History of* Brown v. Board of Education *and Black America's Struggle for Equality* (New York: Random House, 1977); Hoover, *Red and the Black*, 309–28; Charles A. Wells, "Trends: Jim Crow Disappearing," 30; Wells, "Federal Law and Discrimination," *BS* 26, no. 1 (October 1946): inside cover.

15. J. B. Lawrence, "Missions and the March of Events: The Need of the Negro," *HM* 18, no. 12 (December 1947): 2; Sedberry, "We Need a Trained Negro Ministry," 4–5; "Program: Lifting America's Morals," *RS* 48, no. 9 (March 1954): 27; Mrs. Bill V. Carden, "Prepare Ye the Way—through Teaching," *RS* 54, no. 9 (March 1960): 44; Powell, *Persistence of Racism in America*, p 308.

16. Grace Elizabeth Hale, *Making Whiteness: The Culture of Segregation in the South, 1890–1940* (New York: Pantheon Books, 1998); Richard Dyer, *White* (London: Routledge, 1997), 255; Maston, *"Of One,"* passim.

17. Edward Hughes Pruden, "Up from Slavery," *BS* 25, no. 7 (April 1946): 15, 29; Bonita Cunningham, "George Washington Carver," *RS* 48, no. 7 (January 1954): 16–17; Marty, *Modern American Religion*, 449.

18. Hermione Dannelly Jackson, "Discuss Missions," *Window* 22, no. 11 (July 1951): 13; Daniel R. Grant, "Human Liberty the Highest Goal," *BS* 33, no. 1 (October 1953): 2–5.

19. R. Orin Cornett, "Who Cares?" *Window* 27, no. 8 (April 1956): 6–8.

20. Cornett, "Who Cares?" 6–8; Margaret Culpepper Clark, "Dixie is My Name," *BS* 27, no. 2 (November 1947): 17; Newman, "Getting Right with God"; Powell, *Persistence of Racism in America*.

21. Mrs. L. E. M. (Katharine Parker) Freeman, "An Experiment in Race Relations in Raleigh," in Mrs. Edgar Godbold, "Community Missions," *RS* 41, no. 9 (March 1947): 9; Mrs. Edgar Godbold, "Community Missions: What Can We Do?" *RS* 42, no. 3 (September 1948): 20.

22. Freeman, "An Experiment in Race Relations in Raleigh," 9; Newman, "Getting Right with God," 240–41.

23. Godbold, "What Can We Do?" 20; Godbold, "Interracial Institutes Help," *HM* 24, no. 9 (September 1953): 11.

24. J. Perry Carter, "Long Run Association in Cooperative Work with Negro Baptists," *RS* 41, no. 12 (June 1947): 6; Patricia Jordan, "International YWA Camp," *Window* 25, no. 11 (July 1954): 25; Mrs. C. O. Walker, "A Trip to the 'Quarters,'" *Window* 20, no. 1 (September 1948): 10; Callie Grant, "Reaching Up by Reaching Out," *Window* 29, no. 5 (January 1958): 12–14.

25. Leo Green, "The Christian Solution," *AL* 7, no. 2 (July 1952): 2.

26. Green, "Christian Solution," 2; A. C. Miller, "Community Citizenship," *BS* 33, no. 4 (January 1954): 8–9; "Report of the Social Service Commission," SBC, 1948, 336–37. Salisbury, *Religion in American Culture*, passim, esp. 43–50; Powell, *Persistence of Racism in America*; Queen, *Center of Gravity*, 74–95.

27. Hugh Brimm, "Baptists in Interracial Progress," *RS* 44, no. 8 (February 1950): 4–6; Margaret Gooch Kiser, "New from Washington D.C.: Forward Moves," *Window* 23, no. 12 (August 1952): 10.

28. Jackson, "Discuss Missions," 13; Brimm, "Baptists in Interracial Progress," 4–6; Brimm, "We Help America to Be Christian," *AL* 4, no. 8 (February 1950): 8; Brimm, "Race Relations—What Can I Do as a Christian?" *BS* 31, no. 4 (January 1952): 27.

29. Barnette, "Negro Students," 207–8; Duke K. McCall, "Report of the Southern Baptist Theological Seminary," SBC, 1952, 361; T. Laine Scales, *All That*

Fits a Woman: Training Southern Baptist Women for Charity and Mission, 1907–1926 (Macon, GA: Mercer University Press, 2000), 253; Charles Shelby Rooks, "The Quest for Students: Reshaping African-American Ministry," 397.

30. Charles Hamilton, "What Makes Southern Baptists Tick?" *BS* 31, no. 8 (May 1952): 31–32.

31. Thomas E. McCollough, "What Causes Heathenism in Hyde Park?" *BS* 34, no. 8 (May 1955): 18.

32. McCollough, "What Causes Heathenism?" 18; Hill, *Southern Churches in Crisis*; Bailey, *Southern White Protestantism*, 145; Wuthnow, *Restructuring of American Religion*, 138–72.

33. J. B. Weatherspoon, "Report of the Christian Life Commission," SBC, 1954, 56, 402–5; "Ruling on Segregation Endorsed," *CI*, June 10, 1954, 9; "J. B. Weatherspoon," BHF, SBHLA; Newman, "Getting Right with God," 308. See also Len G. Cleveland, "Georgia Baptists and the 1954 Supreme Court Desegregation Decision," *Georgia Historical Quarterly* 59, Supplemental Issue (1975): 107–17.

34. "Ruling on Segregation Endorsed," *CI*, June 10, 1954, 9; Preston, "Baptists and Segregation," 8; Eighmy, *Churches in Cultural Captivity*, 190–91.

35. Alvis Jr., *Religion and Race*, 57–58.

36. Maston, *Segregation and Desegregation*, 24–32; C. C. Warren, "President's Address," SBC, 1956, 71–72. See also Talmadge, *You and Segregation*; Numan V. Bartley, *The Rise of Massive Resistance: Race and Politics in the South during the 1950s* (Baton Rouge, LA: Louisiana State University Press, 1969).

37. To Honorable J. Lindsey Almond Jr., Gov. of Virginia, from Vernon I. Tillar, chairman, November 25, 1958, Box 82, Folder 1, ECR, SBHLA.

38. Russell, "Newly-Given Freedom," 7.

39. Sam Olive McGinnis, "The Harvest is Right at Hand," *RS* 49, no. 8 (February 1955): 4–6; Edith Stokely, "Hints to Committee Chairmen: To Community Missions Chairmen," *RS* 47, no. 12 (June 1953): 16–17; Marian Graham, "Summer Work with Home Missionaries by College Students: In Mississippi," *Window* 21, no. 7 (March 1950): 14.

40. Claude U. Broach, "If You Ask Me," *BS* 33, no. 8 (May 1954): 34.

41. Claude U. Broach, "If You Ask Me," *BS* 34, no. 2 (November 1954): 37.

42. John Caylor, "From the Pen of John Caylor," *HM* 29, no. 1 (January 1958): 5. See also Patterson, *Grand Expectations*, 400–416; Klinkner, *Unsteady March*, 242–51.

43. Victor T. Glass, "Principles and Goals in Working with National Baptists," *RS* 56, no. 3 (September 1961): 24–25; Acts 17:26; Galatians 6:10.

44. Glendon McCullough, "Imperfect Vision in Changing Nation," *HM* 32, no. 5 (May 1961): 17; Charlie S. Mills, "Letters: April Issue," *HM* 33, no. 7 (July 1962): 3.

45. "Corpus Christi Association Accepts Negro Messengers," *HM* 32, no. 12 (December 1961): 12; Corder, "One Convention for Texas," 6. See also Moody, "Southern Baptist Polity," 2–11.

46. "Churches Active in Negro VBS," *HM* 31, no. 7 (July 1960): 9.

47. John Caylor, "From the Pen of John Caylor," *HM* 27, no. 12 (December

1956): 5; R. Elmer Dunham, "Texas Rural Churches Try Town and Country Program," *HM* 28, no. 3 (March 1957): 11; Elaine Dickson, "Understanding Missions through Experience," *RS* 60, no. 9 (March 1966): 33–34.

48. Marjorie Moore Armstrong, "Are You an All-American Citizen?" *Window* 30, no. 11 (July 1959): 19.

49. "What Are Some Needs," *Forecaster* insert in *RS* 52, no. 6 (December 1957): 4.

50. Jacqueline Durham, "Ten Weeks a Missionary [excerpts from student missionaries]," *HM* 30, no. 11 (November 1959): 13; Glendon McCullough, "Don't Miss the Thrill," *RS* 61, no. 9 (March 1967): 11–12; Louise Berge, "What did YOU do Last Summer?" *BS* 36, no. 4 (January 1967): 55; William Hall Preston, "Ten Years and 800 Summer Missionaries," *BS* 34, no. 6 (March 1957): 42–45; David Griffin, "I Loved My Negro Congregation," *HM* 25, no. 4 (April 1954): 22–23.

51. S. Kathryn Bigham, "WMU Training School: 'Whatever Be Thy Task,'" *RS* 47, no. 1 (July 1952): 18.

52. "Missions Today: Atlanta Churches Face 'Kneel-In' Incidents," *HM* 31, no. 9 (September 1960): 4; Alvis Jr., *Religion and Race*, 96–98. On the sit-in, see Terry H. Anderson, *Movement and the Sixties*; David Halberstam, *The Children* (New York: Random House, 1998); Clayborne Carson, *In Struggle: SNCC and the Black Awakening of the 1960s* (Cambridge, MA: Harvard University Press, 1981).

53. "Atlanta Churches Face 'Kneel-In' Incidents," 4; Mrs. William McMurry, "Did You Read It?: The Atlanta Minister's Manifesto," *RS* 53, no. 9 (March 1959): 50; Jack U. Harwell, *Louie D.: A Photographic Essay on "Mr. Baptist" Louie Devotie Newton* (Atlanta, GA: The Christian Index, 1979), n.p.

54. Walker L. Knight, "Editorial: Can a Church Close Its Membership?" *HM* 32, no. 1 (January 1961): 11; Marty, *Modern American Religion*, 276–83.

55. "Race Prejudice Termed Sickness of the Soul," *HM* 34, no. 4 (April 1963): 44.

56. Ibid.; Rosenberg, *Southern Baptists*, 114.

57. Walker L. Knight, "Race Relations Proposal for Southern Baptists," *HM* 34, no. 7 (July 1963): 3; "Resolution #3: Christian Responsibility," SBC, 1963, 65.

58. Walker L. Knight, "Letters: Race Relations Reaction," *HM* 34, no. 9 (September 1963): 3.

59. "Report of the Committee on Negro Work," MHMB, January 1, 1948; "Report of the Committee on Evangelism and Negro Work," MHMB (February 8, 1951); Courts Redford, "Report of the Executive Secretary-Treasurer," MHMB, November 29–30, 1955.

60. Jacqueline Durham, "Needs Every Day Downtown," *RS* 58, no. 1 (July 1963): 4–6; "Racial Study to Help Churches in Transition," *HM* 36, no. 6 (June 1965): 38; Mrs. Alpha Melton, "The Christian and the Shack Down the Street," *BS* 42, no. 2 (November 1962): 18–20; Rutledge and Tanner, *Mission to America*, 144.

61. Lynn T. Richardson to Porter Routh, November 18, 1957, Box 82, Folder 1, ECR, SBHLA.

62. R. Orin Cornett, "Report of the Education Commission," SBC, 1956, 318–19; "SBC Gives Education Emphasis," *HM* 31, no. 7 (July 1960): 10; Newman,

"Getting Right with God," 249; "What Makes a College Missionary," *Commission* 9, no. 8 (September 1946): 13–14.

63. "Foreign Mission News," *Commission* 20, no. 6 (June 1961): 12; "Report of the Executive Committee" and "Matters Arising from Minutes," MGBC, July 1962, FMB Archives; "Alumni Ministers Group Backs African Student Admissions," *BR*, April 8, 1961, 17; "Wake Forest to Admit Negroes to Graduate Schools," *BR*, May 6, 1961, 7; "All Racial Bars Dropped at Undergraduate Levels," *BR*, May 5, 1962, 6.

64. James R. Scales quoted in "Foreign Mission News," *Commission* 24, no. 6 (June 1961): 13; "Foreign Mission News," *Commission* 25, no. 11 (December 1962): 19.

65. "Foreign Mission News," *Commission* 26, no. 3 (March 1963): 29; Vele Keyata Y. Redding, "Mercer Celebrates Anniversary of Integration," *Mercerian* 4 (Spring 1994): 1. The general story of Mercer's integration is covered in William D. Campbell, *The Stem of Jessie: The Costs of Community at a 1960s Southern School* (Macon, GA: Mercer University Press, 1995). See also Alan Scot Willis, "A Baptist Dilemma: Christianity, Discrimination, and the Desegregation of Mercer University," *Georgia Historical Quarterly* 80, no. 3 (Fall 1996): 595–615.

66. Redding, "Mercer Celebrates," 1.

67. "Loans Approved for $1,850,000; Harris Supports Desegregation," *Mercer Cluster*, November 16, 1962, 1; "Letter from Mr. John Mitchell: Report of the President to the Board of Trustees of the Corporation of Mercer University," "Minutes: Board of Trustees and President's Council of Mercer University," April 18, 1963, 31–33, and "Minutes: Meeting of the Special Committee of the Board of Trustees of the Corporation of Mercer University, January 4, 1963, 2," Main Library, Mercer University, Macon, Georgia.

68. John J. Hurt Jr., "Separate Ghana Student from Integration Issue," *CI*, February 21, 1963, 6.

69. Hurt Jr., "Separate Ghana Student"; "Baptist College in Arkansas Accepts Rhodesian Students," *BR*, January 27, 1962, 18; "Debate Continues Over Student," *CI*, March 21, 1963, 7.

70. "Majority of Letters Favor Admitting Ghanaian," *CI*, March 7, 1963, 3; "Pros & Cons on Ghana Student," *CI*, April 4, 1963, 8; "Letters," *CI*, April 18, 1963, 8.

71. "Majority of Letters Favor Admitting Ghanaian," *CI*, March 7, 1963, 3; "Missionary Agrees," *CI*, March 14, 1963, 7; Dr. and Mrs. William R. Norman, "Mangled Missions," 28.

72. "Missionary Agrees," *CI*, March 14, 1963, 7; "Differ on Ghanian," *CI*, April 11, 1963, 8; John J. Hurt Jr., "Mercer Took Christian Action, Let's Do the Same," *CI*, April 25, 1963, 6; "Minutes: Board of Trustees and Presidents Council of Mercer University," April 18, 1963, 12; "News in the Christian World," *BS* 42, no. 8 (May 1963): 32.

73. W. Ray Avant to Porter Routh, October 22, 1963, Box 82, Folder 3, ECR, SBHLA, Nashville, TN.

74. Robert D. Scarborough, "Changes at Gainesville," *BS* 43, no. 9 (June 1964): 26.

75. John W. Touchberry, "The Westside Story," *BS* 43, no. 9 (June 1964): 27–28. See also Trillin, *Education in Georgia*, 176–79.

76. "Basis For Race Attitudes Reported to Advisory Council," *Leadership* insert in *HM* 35, no. 5 (May 1964): 16-A, 16-H; Cyril E. Bryant, "From Washington: What Image Do Baptists Reflect," *RS* 58, no. 2 (August 1963): 9; "Resolution of Furloughing Missionaries" quoted in Rogers M. Smith to T. B. Maston, January 12, 1965, "Southern Baptists and the Negro Correspondence—Advisory Council," Box 22, TBMP, RLSWT; Salisbury, *Religion in American Culture*, 49–51; Eighmy, *Churches in Cultural Captivity*; Queen, *Center of Gravity*, 74–95.

77. Victor T. Glass, "Work with National Baptists in North Carolina," *HM* 34, no. 3 (March 1963): 20.

78. Victor T. Glass, "Working with National Baptists," *HM* 36, no. 1 (January 1965): 16-K; "N.C. Race Council Calls for Justice," *Leadership* insert in *HM* 35, no. 2 (February 1964): 16-C; Cyril E. Bryant, "From Washington: Trends and Significant Events," *RS* 58, no. 7 (January 1964): 7; Warner Ragsdale, "A Preacher Writes the President's Speeches," *SBBQ* 34, no. 4 (October, November, December 1964): 6; Glenda Shipp, "SSM [Student Summer Missionaries]," *HM* 35, no. 10 (October 1964): 7.

79. Lyndon B. Johnson quoted in Cyril Bryant, "From Washington: Christians and Politics," *RS* 59, no. 2 (August 1964): 13; Eighmy, *Churches in Cultural Captivity*, 147–48; Barnett, "New Theological Frontier," 264–76; Kelsey, *Social Ethics*.

80. Norman Bowman, "The Legislation of Morality," *BS* 45, no. 4 (January 1966): 24.

81. Anderson, *The Movement and the Sixties*; Marsh, *God's Long Summer*.

82. Foy Valentine, "Report of the Christian Life Commission," SBC, 1964, 229; "Resolution #4: On Human Relations," SBC, 1964, 88–89.

83. Mary Allred, "Using God's Eyes," *RS* 58, no. 9 (March 1964): 37–38.

84. Mary Allred, "We Get Letters: 'Using God's Eyes,'" *RS* 59, no. 1 (July 1964): 4.

85. Dorothy Robinson, "We Get Letters: Persistent Question," *RS* 59, no. 4 (October 1964): 15; Queen, *Center of Gravity*, 74–95; Fredrickson, *Comparative Imagination*, 77–97; DeMott, *Trouble with Friendship*.

86. Mrs. S. A. Williams, "We Get Letters," *RS* 59, no. 6 (December 1964): 34–35.

87. Gladys M. McClain, "We Get Letters: Another Response to Mrs. Robinson," *RS* 59, no. 8 (February 1965): 12–13; Newman, "Getting Right with God," 68–69.

88. Marguerite Babb, "'Heart' Sunday in Our Church," *RS* 60, no. 8 (February 1966): 28–29; Margaret Bruce, "Bulletin Board: The Christian Life Commission," *Forecaster* insert in *RS* 61, no. 8 (February 1967): 7; Findley B. Edge, "Where Are We in Fulfilling the Mission of the Church," *HM* 40, no. 7 (July 1969): 18; James F. Findlay Jr., *Church People in the Struggle: The National Council of Churches and the Black Freedom Movement, 1950–1970* (New York: Oxford University Press, 1993), 18–19.

89. R. F. Hallford, "Letters from Our Readers: Cramming Down Our Throats," *HM* 38, no. 5 (May 1967): 2.

90. T. B. Gillooly, "Letters from Our Readers: Race Relations," *HM* 36, no. 6 (June 1965): 2.

91. Virginia Molett, "Letters from Our Readers: Race and Religion," *HM* 38,

no. 3 (March 1967): 3; Virginia Barker, "Letters from Our Readers: Race and Religion," *HM* 38, no. 3 (March 1967): 3.

92. Barker, "Letters from Our Readers: Race and Religion," 3; Bob Leavell and Mrs. Alva Gatewood, "Letters from Our Readers: Pro and Con on Race," *HM* 38, no. 4 (April 1967): 2.

93. Rogers M. Smith to T. B. Maston, January 12, 1965.

94. "Ouster Gets World-Wide Attention," *CI*, October 6, 1966, 5; "Tattnall Square Church Votes to Fire Pastors: Close Door To Negroes," *Mercer Cluster*, September 30, 1966, 4; "In the Wake of Tattnall Square," *HM* 37, no. 12 (December 1966): 4, 36; Roddy Stinson, "Crisis at Tattnall Square," *SBBQ* 38, no. 2 (April, May, June 1967): 6; Thomas J. Holmes, *Ashes for Breakfast* (Valley Forge, PA: Judson Press, 1969). See also G. McLeod Bryan, *These Few Also Paid a Price: Southern Whites Who Fought for Civil Rights* (Macon, GA: Mercer University Press, 2001), 142–45.

95. Stinson, "Crisis at Tattnall Square," 1, 4, 5–7; "In the Wake of Tattnall Square," 4, 36; Holmes, *Ashes for Breakfast.*

96. "In the Wake of Tattnall Square," 4, 36.

97. Queen, *Center of Gravity*, 90–96; Leon Macon to Porter Routh, January 31, 1958, Box 82, Folder 2, ECR, SBHLA; Marsh, *God's Long Summer*; Humphrey K. Ezell, *Christian Problem*; Collins, *When the Church Bell Rang Racist*, 15–22; Alvis Jr., *Religion and Race*, 51–53.

98. William L. Turner, "Letters from Our Readers: Churches Are Clubs," *HM* 38, no. 6 (June 1967): 2.

99. Raymond Parker, "Letters from Our Readers: A Mississippi Pastor Writes," *HM* 38, no. 8 (August 1967): 2; Henry B. Shirley, "Letters from Our Readers: A Revolutionary Force," *HM* 39, no. 8 (August 1968): 4; R. D. Fillpot, "Letters from Our Readers: An Integrated Ministry," *HM* 38, no. 2 (February 1967): 2.

100. Victor T. Glass, "Report of the Department of Work with National Baptists," MHMB, November 30–December 1, 1966; "Objectives and Goals: Work with National Baptists," MHMB, March 15, 1967; Glass, "Department of Work with National Baptists," MHMB, November 29–30, 1967.

101. E. Warren Woolf, "The Long Look in Short Term Missionaries," *Window* 39, no. 5 (January 1968): 2–4; McCullough, "Don't Miss the Thrill," 11–12; Patricia Lemonds, "Missionary Journeymen in Rhodesia," *RS* 63, no. 3 (September 1968): 8–10; Louise Cobb and Nathan Porter, "New Opportunities for Service," *BS* 44, no. 9 (June 1965): 20–21.

102. Marie Mathis and Elaine Dickson, "Let's Call It Mission Action: New Frontiers in Mission Action," *RS* 61, no. 12 (June 1967): 2–4; Elian Dickson, "Understanding Missions through Experience," *RS* 60, no. 9 (March 1966): 33–34.

103. John Jeffers Jr., "Confronting Our On-Campus Responsibilities," *BS* 44, no. 3 (February 1965): 16.

104. Ibid.

105. John H. McClanahan, "What's Right/Wrong with Southern Baptists," *SBBQ* 38, no. 2 (April, May, June 1967): 10–11; "What I'm Doing and What it Means," *BS* 46, no. 4 (March 1967): 14–16; O. C. Dawkins, "Outgrowing Segregation," *Window* 22, no. 9 (May 1951): 4–5.

106. Mary Anne Forehand, "Identity: Missionary," *Window* 40, no. 1 (September 1968): 7; "Resolution #5: New Orleans Hospital Integration," SBC, 1969, 74.

107. Henry A. Buchanan and Bob W. Brown, "Shall the Twain Become One?" *HM* 39, no. 1 (January 1968): 22–23.

108. I. A., "On Campus," *BS* 47, no. 6 (March 1968): 34; Kathy Crawford, "Girls' Club," *BS* 48, no. 8 (May 1969): 43–44. Earlier settlement houses often failed to overcome racial barriers. See Elisabeth Lasch-Quinn, *Black Neighbors: Race and the Limits of Reform in the American Settlement House Movement, 1890–1945* (Chapel Hill: University of North Carolina Press, 1993).

109. Baker James Cauthen, "Toward a Better Tomorrow," *Commission* 31, no. 6 (June 1968): 15.

110. John Nichol, "A Dream to Be Shared," *HM* 39, no. 5 (May 1968): 34–36.

111. "Crisis—Our Challenge: Rural-Urban Missions Colloquium," February 17–21, 1969, Ridgecrest Baptist Assembly colloquium of the Home Mission Board of the Southern Baptist Convention, Mercer Main Library, Macon, Georgia, 54.

112. John Nichol, "Integrity of Witness," *Home Mission* 39, no. 1 (January 1968): 9–11.

113. Bill Sherman, "Yellow, Black, Pink, or Purple," *BS* 48, no. 2 (November 1969): 47.

114. William M. Watts, "Letters from Our Readers: Opportunity of Crisis," *HM* 39, no. 7 (July 1968): 3; Charles T. Heltman and Mrs. Walter C. Dean, "Letters from Our Readers: Reaction to King Ad," *HM* 39, no. 8 (August 1968): 2.

115. Jack L. Hamilton, "Letters from Our Readers: Reaction to King Ad," *HM* 39, no. 8 (August 1968): 2.

116. C. Norman Bennette Jr., "We Eulogized Martin Luther King," *HM* 39, no. 8 (August 1968): 5.

117. Leslie Whiteley, "Letters from Our Readers: Reactions on King," *HM* 39, no. 10 (October 1968): 2–3.

118. Mrs. J. T. Hammett, Jane Gill Tombes, Mrs. Sam McGinnis, and Norman D. Stephenson, "Letters from Our Readers: Reactions on King," *HM* 39, no. 10 (October 1968): 2–3.

119. Ottis Denny, "Letters from Our Readers: Instant Sociology," *HM* 39, no. 5 (May 1968): 2; Felix V. Greer and Mrs. Chester P. Jones, "Letters from Our Readers: Reaction to Race," *HM* 39, no. 3 (March 1968): 2; Mrs. William Lee Jones, "Letters from Our Readers: The Race Issue," *HM* 39, no. 4 (April 1968): 2.

120. "A Statement Concerning the Crisis in Our Nation," SBC, 1968, 67–69.

121. Ibid.; Walker Knight, "Editorials: After Houston, What?" *HM* 39, no. 7 (July 1968): 4.

122. "SBC Leaders Map Action on Race Stand," *HM* 39, no. 7 (July 1968): 28–29.

123. Arthur B. Rutledge, "The Executive's Words: Implementing the Statement," *HM* 39, no. 8 (August 1968): 7; Rutledge and Tanner, *Mission to America*, 145; Powell, *Persistence of Racism in America*; Barnett, "New Theological Frontier," 264–76.

124. Walker L. Knight, "Please, Don't Vote," *HM* 40, no. 8 (August 1969): 4.

125. Sam W. Williams quoted in Dallas M. Lee, "Justice is Something You Do," *HM* 40, no. 12 (December 1969): 17; Edge, "Where Are We," 17–20.

126. M. Thomas Starkes, "A Search for Revolutionary Power," *HM* 40, no. 1 (January 1969): 22–28; Ken McNeil, "Heaven for Whites, Hell for Negroes," *BS* 48, no. 6 (March 1969): 18, 20; B. Bryant, "Where Are We in Civil Rights," 21–23; Bill Junker, "Chat," *BS* 47, no. 8 (May 1968): 4–5.

127. Margaret Ann Niceley, "A little Can Be A Lot," *Window* 40, no. 5 (January 1969): 1.

Conclusion

1. Carter, *Living Faith*, 120; Powell, *Persistence of Racism in America.*

2. Weatherspoon, "Report of the Committee on Race Relation," 47–48, 340–43; Eighmy, *Churches in Cultural Captivity.*

3. Rosenberg, *Southern Baptists*, 114; C. Eric Lincoln, *Race, Religion, and the Continuing American Dilemma* (1984; repr., New York: Hill and Wang, 1999).

4. Queen, *Center of Gravity.*

5. Eighmy, *Churches in Cultural Captivity*; Queen, *Center of Gravity*; Kosmin and Lachman, *One Nation Under God*, 51–55; Hill, *Southern Churches in Crisis*; Samuel S. Hill Jr., *One Name but Several Faces: Varieties in Popular Christian Denominations in Southern History*, Jack N. and Addie D. Averitt Lecture Series at Georgia Southern University (Athens: University of Georgia Press, 1996).

6. Eighmy, *Churches in Cultural Captivity*; Manis, *Southern Civil Religions*; Newman, "Getting Right with God"; Queen, *Center of Gravity*; Marsh, *God's Long Summer.*

7. Harrell, *White Sects and Black Men*; Morgan, *New Crusades*; Oran P. Smith, *The Rise of Baptist Republicanism* (New York: New York University Press, 1997).

8. Hankins, *Uneasy in Babylon*, 243; "Resolution No. 1: On Racial Reconciliation on the 150th Anniversary of the Southern Baptist Convention," SBC, 1995, 80–81.

9. Hankins, *Uneasy in Babylon*, 240–71.

10. G. W. Simmons to Porter Routh, April 3, 1958, Box 82, Folder 2, ECR, SBHLA; A. J. Pugh to Porter Routh, December 23, 1958, Box 82, Folder 1, ECR, SBHLA.

11. Robert F. Martin, "Critique of Southern Society and Vision of a New Order: The Fellowship of Southern Churchmen, 1934–1957," *Church History* 52, no. 1 (1983): 66–80; Charles Donald Donahue, "The Yearning for a Prophetic Southern Culture: A History of the Fellowship of Southern Churchmen" (PhD diss., Union Theological Seminary, 1995).

SELECTED BIBLIOGRAPHY

Southern Baptist Publications

All-Indian Baptist (Albuquerque, NM), 1946–1957.

Ambassador Life (Birmingham, AL/Memphis, TN), 1947–1969.

The Baptist Student (Nashville, TN), 1945–1969.

The Christian Index (Atlanta, GA), 1953–1966.

The Commission (Richmond, VA), 1945–1969.

Royal Service (Birmingham, AL), 1945–1969.

Southern Baptist Brotherhood Quarterly (Memphis, TN), 1945–1969.

Southern Baptist Home Missions/Home Missions (Atlanta, GA), 1945–1969.

The Window of YWA/The Window (Birmingham, AL), 1947–1969.

Other Baptist Materials

In 1996 the Southern Baptist Convention restructured several of its agencies. The Home Mission Board became the North American Mission Board, and the Foreign Mission Board became the International Mission Board.

Foreign (International) Mission Board Archives, Richmond, VA.

Executive Correspondence 1954–1979, Baker James Cauthen Papers

Harris Mobley Papers

Homer R. Littleton Papers

Joanna C. Maiden Papers

Minutes of the Ghana Baptist Conference

Minutes of the Ghana Mission Minutes and Reports

Minutes of the Foreign Mission Board, 1945–1969
Minutes of the Nigerian Baptist Convention
Minutes of the Nigerian Baptist Mission

Home Mission Board (North American), Atlanta, GA
Minutes of the Home Mission Board

Southern Baptist Historical Library and Archives, Nashville, TN
Clifton J. Allen Collection
Executive Committee Records
Baptist History File
Una Roberts Lawrence Collection

Archives and Special Collections, Roberts Library, Southwestern Baptist Theological Seminary, Fort Worth, TX
T. B. Maston Papers

Contemporary Publications

Barnett, Das Kelly. "The New Theological Frontier for Southern Baptists." *Review and Expositor* 38 (July 1941): 264–76.

Barnette, Henlee. "Negro Students in Southern Baptist Seminaries." *Review and Expositor* 53 (April 1956): 207–11.

Bennett, John C. *Christianity and Communism.* New York: Association Press, 1948.

Edwards, Vetress Bonn. *Go South with Christ.* New York: Exposition Press, 1959.

Ezell, Humphrey K. *The Christian Problem of Racial Segregation.* Newark: Greenwich Book Publishers, 1959.

Goerner, H. Cornell. *America Must Be Christian.* Atlanta, GA: Home Mission Board, 1947.

Hill, Samuel S., Jr. "The Southern Baptists: Need for Reformulation, Redirection." *Christian Century* 80, no. 2 (January 9, 1963): 39–42.

Holmes, Thomas J. *Ashes for Breakfast.* Valley Forge, PA: Judson Press, 1969.

Kilpatrick, James J. *The Southern Case for School Segregation.* New York: Crowell-Collier Press, 1962.

Maston, T. B. *The Bible and Race.* Nashville: Broadman Press, 1959.

———. *Biblical Ethics: A Guide to the Ethical Message of Scriptures from Genesis through Revelation.* 1967. Reprint, Macon, GA: Mercer University Press, 1982.

———. *"Of One": A Study of Christian Principles and Race Relations.* Atlanta, GA: Home Mission Board, 1946.

— — —. *Segregation and Desegregation: A Christian Approach*. New York: Macmillan, 1959.

Myrdal, Gunnar. *An American Dilemma*. New York: Harper and Brothers, 1944.

Neff, Lawrence. *Jesus: Master Segregationist* (pamphlet). Atlanta, GA: Banner Press, 1964. Special Collection Department, Pitts Theological Library, Emory University, Atlanta, Georgia.

Niebuhr, H. Richard. *Christ and Culture*. New York: Harper Torchbook Edition, 1975.

Niebuhr, Reinhold. *The Irony of American History*. New York: Charles Scribner's Sons, 1952.

Talmadge, Herman. *You and Segregation*. Birmingham: Vulcan Press, 1955.

Tillich, Paul. *What Is Religion?* Translated by James Luther Adams. New York: Harper and Row, 1969.

Trillin, Calvin. *An Education in Georgia: The Integration of Charlayne Hunter and Hamilton Holmes*. New York: Viking Press, 1963.

Workman, William D. *The Case for the South*. New York: Devin-Adair, 1960.

Secondary Sources

Allitt, Patrick. *Catholic Intellectuals and Conservative Politics in America, 1950–1985*. Ithaca, NY: Cornell University Press, 1993.

Alvis, Joel L., Jr. *Religion and Race: Southern Presbyterians, 1946–1983*. Tuscaloosa: University of Alabama Press, 1994.

Ammerman, Nancy Tatom, ed. *Southern Baptists Observed: Multiple Perspectives on a Changing Denomination*. Knoxville: University of Tennessee Press, 1993.

Anderson, Terry H. *The Movement and the Sixties: Protest in America from Greensboro to Wounded Knee*. New York: Oxford University Press, 1995.

Anderson-Briker, Kristin. "Making a Movement: The Meaning of Community in the Congress of Racial Equality." PhD diss., Syracuse University, 1997.

Bailey, Kenneth K. *Southern White Protestantism in the Twentieth Century*. Gloucester, MA: P. Smith Publishers, 1964.

Bartley, Numan V. *The Rise of Massive Resistance: Race and Politics in the South during the 1950s*. Baton Rouge: Louisiana State University Press, 1969.

Bell, Derrick. *And We Are Not Saved: The Elusive Quest for Racial Justice*. New York: Basic Books, 1987.

Black, Earl, and Merle Black. *Politics and Society in the South*. Cambridge, MA: Harvard University Press, 1987.

Boles, John B., and Evelyn Thomas Nolen, eds. *Interpreting Southern History: Historiographical Essays in Honor of Sanford W. Higginbotham*. Baton Rouge: Louisiana State University Press, 1987.

Bordewich, Fergus M. *Killing the White Man's Indian: Reinventing Native Americans at the End of the Twentieth Century.* New York: Anchor Books, 1996.

Bowden, Henry Warner. *American Indians and Christian Missions: Studies in Cultural Conflict.* Chicago: University of Chicago Press, 1981.

Branch, Taylor. *Parting the Waters: America in the King Years, 1954–63.* New York: Simon and Schuster, 1988.

Brown, Sara Hart. "Congressional Anti-Communism and the Segregationist South: From New Orleans to Atlanta, 1954–1958." *Georgia Historical Quarterly* 80, no. 4 (Winter 1996): 785–816.

Campbell, William D. *The Stem of Jessie: The Costs of Community at a 1960s Southern School.* Macon, GA: Mercer University Press, 1995.

Carson, Clayborne. *In Struggle: SNCC and the Black Awakening of the 1960s.* Cambridge, MA: Harvard University Press, 1981.

Carter, Dan T. *Politics of Rage: George Wallace, the Origins of the New Conservatism, and the Transformation of American Politics.* New York: Simon and Schuster, 1994.

Carter, Jimmy. *Living Faith.* New York: Times Books, 1996.

Carter, Lawrence Edward, Sr., ed. *Walking Integrity: Benjamin Elijah Mays, Mentor to Martin Luther King, Jr.* Macon, GA: Mercer University Press, 1998.

Cauthen, Baker James, et al. *Advance: A History of Southern Baptist Foreign Missions.* Nashville, TN: Broadman Press, 1970.

Chappell, David. "The Divided Mind of Southern Segregationists." *Georgia Historical Quarterly* 82, no. 1 (Spring 1998): 45–72.

———. *Inside Agitators: White Southerners and the Civil Rights Movement.* Baltimore: Johns Hopkins University Press, 1994.

Cleveland, Len G. "Georgia Baptists and the 1954 Supreme Court Desegregation Decision." *Georgia Historical Quarterly* 59, Supplemental Issue (1975): 107–17.

Collins, Donald E. *When the Church Bell Rang Racist: The Methodist Church and the Civil Rights Movement in Alabama.* Macon, GA: Mercer University Press, 1998.

Commager, Henry Steele. *The American Mind: An Interpretation of American Thought and Character since the 1880s.* New Haven, CT: Yale University Press, 1950.

Conkin, Paul. *When All the Gods Trembled: Darwinism, Scopes, and American Intellectuals.* Lanham, MD: Rowman & Littlefield, 1998.

De León, Arnoldo. *Mexican Americans in Texas: A Brief History.* 2nd ed. Wheeling, IL: Harlan Davidson, 1999.

DeMott, Benjamin. *The Trouble with Friendship: Why Americans Can't Think Straight about Race.* New Haven, CT: Yale University Press, 1995.

Donahue, Charles Donald. "The Yearning for a Prophetic Southern Culture: A History of the Fellowship of Southern Churchmen." PhD diss., Union Theological Seminary, 1995.

Dyer, Richard. *White*. London: Routledge, 1997.

Eighmy, John Lee. *Churches in Cultural Captivity: A History of the Social Attitudes of the Southern Baptists*. Introduction and Epilogue by Samuel S. Hill Jr. Knoxville: University of Tennessee Press, 1972.

Ellwood, Robert S. *The Fifties Spiritual Marketplace: American Religion in a Decade of Conflict*. New Brunswick, NJ: Rutgers University Press, 1997.

Eskridge, Larry. "'One Way': Billy Graham, the Jesus Generation, and the Idea of an Evangelical Youth Culture." *Church History* 67, no. 1 (March 1998): 83–106.

Findley, James F., Jr. *Church People in the Struggle: The National Council of Churches and the Black Freedom Movement, 1950–1970*. New York: Oxford University Press, 1993.

Flynt, Wayne. *Alabama Baptists: Southern Baptists in the Heart of Dixie*. Tuscaloosa: University of Alabama Press, 1998.

Fredrickson, George M. *The Comparative Imagination: On the History of Racism, Nationalism, and Social Movements*. Berkeley: University of California Press, 1997.

Fromkin, David. *In the Time of the Americans: FDR, Truman, Eisenhower, Marshall, MacArthur, the Generation that Changed America's Role in the World*. New York: Alfred A. Knopf, 1995.

Gann, Lewis H. *Central Africa: The Former British States*. Englewood Cliffs, NJ: Prentice Hall, 1971.

García, Ignacio M. *Chicanismo: The Forging of a Militant Ethos among Mexican Americans*. Tuscon: University of Arizona Press, 1998.

Garrow, David J. *Bearing the Cross: Martin Luther King, Jr., and the Southern Christian Leadership Conference*. New York: Vintage Books, 1988.

Gates, Henry Louis, Jr. *Colored People: A Memoir*. New York: Alfred K. Knopf, 1994.

Giddings, Paula. *When and Where I Enter: The Impact of Black Women on Race and Sex in America*. New York: Quill William Morrow, 1984.

Greene, Melissa Fay. *The Temple Bombing*. Reading, MA: Addison Wesley, 1996.

Gutiérrez, José Angel. *The Making of a Chicano Militant: Lessons from Cristal*. Madison, WI: University of Wisconsin Press, 1998.

Hale, Grace Elizabeth. *Making Whiteness: The Culture of Segregation in the South, 1890–1940*. New York: Pantheon, 1998.

Hankins, Barry. "Southern Baptists and the Northern Evangelicals: Cultural Factors and the Nature of Religious Alliances." *Religion and American Culture: A Journal of Interpretation* 7, no. 2 (Summer 1997): 271–98.

———. *Uneasy in Babylon: Southern Baptist Conservatives and American Culture.* Tuscaloosa, AL: University of Alabama Press, 2002.

Harrell, David Edwin. *White Sects and Black Men.* Nashville, TN: Vanderbilt University Press, 1971.

Hill, Samuel S., Jr. *One Name but Several Faces: Varieties in Popular Christian Denominations in Southern History.* Jack N. and Addie D. Averitt Lecture Series at Georgia Southern University. Athens: University of Georgia Press, 1996.

———. *Southern Churches in Crisis.* New York: Holt, Rinehart, and Winston, 1967.

Hoover, Dwight W. *The Red and the Black.* Chicago: Rand McNally College Publishing, 1976.

Hullum, Evert. *We Spell Missions America.* Atlanta, GA: Home Mission Board of the Southern Baptist Convention, 1983.

Hunt, Alma. *History of Woman's Missionary Union.* Nashville, TN: Convention Press, 1964.

Hunter-Gault, Charlayne. *In My Place.* New York: Farrar, Strouse, Giroux, 1992.

Isichei, Elizabeth. *A History of Christianity in Africa: From Antiquity to the Present.* Grand Rapids, MI: William B. Eerdmans, 1995.

Iverson, Peter. *"We Are Still Here": American Indians in the Twentieth Century.* Wheeling, IL: Harlan Davidson, 1998.

Johnson, Troy R. "Roots of Contemporary Native American Activism." *American Indian Culture and Research Journal* 20, no. 2 (1996): 127–54.

Kelsey, George D. *Social Ethics among Southern Baptists, 1917–1969.* Metuchen, NJ: Scarecrow Press, 1993.

Kendall, W. Fred. *A History of the Tennessee Baptist Convention.* Brentwood, TN: Executive Board of the Tennessee Baptist Convention, 1974.

King, Noel Q. *Christian and Muslim in Africa.* New York: Harper and Row, 1971.

Kluger, Richard. *Simple Justice: The History of* Brown v. Board of Education *and Black America's Struggle for Equality.* New York: Random House, 1977.

Kosmin, Barry A., and Seymour P. Lachman. *One Nation Under God: Religion in Contemporary American Society.* New York: Harmony Books, 1993.

LaFeber, Walter. *America, Russia, and the Cold War, 1945–1992.* 7th ed. New York: McGraw Hill, 1993.

Lasch-Quinn, Elisabeth. *Black Neighbors: Race and the Limits of Reform in the American Settlement House Movement, 1890–1945.* Chapel Hill: University of North Carolina Press, 1993.

Lears, T. J. Jackson. "The Concept of Cultural Hegemony: Problems and Possibilities." *American Historical Review* 90, no. 3 (1985): 567–93.

Legum, Colin. *Pan Africanism: A Short Political Guide.* New York: Preager, 1962.

Leonard, Bill J. *God's Last and Only Hope: The Fragmentation of the Southern Baptist Convention*. Grand Rapids, MI: William B. Eerdmans, 1990.

— — —. "Southern Baptists and Southern Culture." *American Baptist Quarterly* 6, no. 2 (June 1985): 200–212.

Lincoln, C. Eric. *Race, Religion, and the Continuing American Dilemma*. Rev. ed. New York: Hill and Wang, 1999.

Manis, Andrew M. "'Dying from the Neck Up': Southern Baptist Resistance to the Civil Rights Movement." *Baptist History and Heritage* 34, no. 1 (Winter 1999): 33–48.

— — —. *Southern Civil Religions in Conflict: Black and White Baptists and Civil Rights, 1947–1957*. Athens: University of Georgia Press, 1987.

Marsh, Charles. *God's Long Summer: Stories of Faith and Civil Rights*. Princeton, NJ: Princeton University Press, 1997.

Martin, Robert F. "Critique of Southern Society and Vision of a New Order: The Fellowship of Southern Churchmen, 1934–1957." *Church History* 52, no. 1 (1983): 66–80.

Marty, Martin E. *Modern American Religion*. Vol. 3, *Under God, Indivisible, 1941–1960*. Chicago: University of Chicago Press, 1996.

Massie, Robert Kinloch. *Loosing the Bonds: The United States and South Africa in the Apartheid Years*. London: Doubleday, 1997.

Mathews, Donald G. "'We have left undone those things which we ought to have done': Southern Religious History in Retrospect and Prospect." *Church History* 67, no. 2 (June 1998): 305–25.

Mathews, Donald G., Samuel S. Hill Jr., Beth Barton Schweiger, and John B. Boles. "Forum: Southern Religion." *Religion and American Culture* 8, no. 2 (Summer 1998): 147–77.

May, Elaine Tyler. *Homeward Bound: American Families in the Cold War Era*. New York: Basic Books, 1988.

May, Henry F. "The Recovery of American Religious History." *American Historical Review* 70 (October 1964): 79–92.

McGreevy, John T. "Faith and Morals in the United States, 1865—Present." *Reviews in American History* 26, no. 1 (March 1998): 239–54.

McLaurin, Melton A. *Separate Pasts: Growing Up White in the Segregated South*. Athens, GA: University of Georgia Press, 1987.

Mertz, Paul E. "Mind Changing Time All Over Georgia": HOPE, Inc. and School Desegregation, 1958–1961." *Georgia Historical Quarterly* 77, no. 1 (Spring 1993): 41–61.

Moody, Dale. "The Shaping of the Southern Baptist Polity." *Baptist History and Heritage* 14, no. 3 (1979): 2–11.

Morgan, David T. *The New Crusades, the New Holy Land: Conflict in the Southern Baptist Convention, 1969–1991.* Tuscaloosa: University of Alabama Press, 1996.

Neill, Stephen. *A History of Christian Missions.* Rev. ed. New York: Penguin Books, 1986.

Newby, I. A. *Challenge to the Court: Social Scientists and the Defense of Segregation, 1954–1966.* Baton Rouge, LA: Louisiana State University Press, 1967.

— — —. *Jim Crow's Defense: Anti-Negro Thought in America 1900–1930.* Baton Rouge, LA: Louisiana State University Press, 1965.

Newman, Mark. "Getting Right with God: Southern Baptists and Race Relations, 1945–1980." PhD diss., University of Mississippi, 1993.

Nieman, Donald G. *Promises to Keep: African Americans and the Constitutional Order, 1776 to the Present.* New York: Oxford University Press, 1991.

Noll, Mark A. *The Scandal of the Evangelical Mind.* Grand Rapids, MI: William B. Eerdmans, 1994.

Norrell, Robert J. *Reaping the Whirlwind: The Civil Rights Movement in Tuskegee.* New York: Alfred A. Knopf, 1985.

Oliver, Roland. *The African Experience: Major Themes in African History from Earliest Times to the Present.* New York: Harper-Collins, 1991.

Pakenham, Thomas. *The Scramble for Africa: The White Man's Conquest of the Dark Continent from 1876 to 1912.* New York: Random House, 1991.

Parrinder, Geoffrey. *Religion in Africa.* New York: Preager, 1969.

Patterson, James T. *Grand Expectations: The United States 1945–1974.* New York: Oxford University Press, 1996.

Porter, Lee. "Southern Baptists and Race Relations." ThD diss., Southwestern Baptist Theological Seminary, 1965.

Powell, Thomas. *The Persistence of Racism in America.* Lanham, MD: University Press of America, 1992.

Queen, Edward L. *In the South the Baptists Are the Center of Gravity.* Preface by Martin E. Marty. Brooklyn, NY: Carlson Publishing, 1991.

Reed, Linda: *Simple Decency & Common Sense: The Southern Conference Movement, 1938–1963.* Bloomington, IN: Indiana University Press, 1991.

Robert, Dana L. *American Women in Missions: A Social History of Their Thought and Practice.* Macon, GA: Mercer University Press, 1996.

Rosenberg, Ellen M. *The Southern Baptists: A Subculture in Transition.* Knoxville: University of Tennessee Press, 1989.

Russell, Jean. *God's Lost Cause: A Study of the Church and the Racial Problem.* London: SCM Press, 1968.

Rutledge, Arthur B., and William G. Tanner. *Mission to America: A History of Southern Baptist Home Missions.* 2nd ed. Nashville, TN: Broadman Press, 1983.

Salmond, John A. "The Fellowship of Southern Churchmen and Interracial Change in the South." *North Carolina Historical Review* 69, no. 2 (April 1992): 179–99.

Scales, T. Laine. *All That Fits a Woman: Training Southern Baptist Women for Charity and Mission, 1907–1926.* Macon, GA: Mercer University Press, 2000.

Scrivin, Charles. *The Transformation of Culture: Christian Social Ethics after H. Richard Niebuhr.* Foreword by James Wm. McClendon, Jr. Scottsdale, PA: Herald Press, 1998.

Smith, Lillian. *Killers of the Dream.* Rev. ed. New York: W. W. Norton, 1961.

Smith, Oran P. *The Rise of Baptist Republicanism.* New York: New York University Press, 1997.

Smith, Page. *Rediscovering Christianity: A History of Modern Democracy and the Christian Ethic.* New York: St. Martin's, 1994.

Smith, Robert. *They Closed Their Schools: Prince Edward County, Virginia, 1951–1964.* Chapel Hill: University of North Carolina Press, 1965.

Spain, Rufus B. *At Ease in Zion: Social History of Southern Baptists, 1865–1900.* Nashville, TN: Vanderbilt University Press, 1967.

Spicer, Edward H. *Cycles of Conquest: The Impact of Spain, Mexico, and the United States on the Indians of the Southwest, 1533–1960.* Tucson, AZ: University of Arizona Press, 1962.

Staniland, Martin. *American Intellectuals and African Nationalists, 1955–1970.* New Haven, CT: Yale University Press, 1991.

Stanton, Mary. *From Selma to Sorrow: The Life and Death of Viola Liuzzo.* Athens, GA: University of Georgia Press, 1998.

Stricklin, David. *A Genealogy of Dissent: Southern Baptist Protest in the Twentieth Century.* Lexington, KY: University Press of Kentucky, 1999.

Taeuber, Karl E., and Alma F. Taeuber. *Negroes in Cities: Residential Segregation and Neighborhood Change.* New York: Atheneum, 1969.

Von Eschen, Penny M. *Race against Empire: Black American and Anticolonialism, 1937–1957.* Ithaca, NY: Cornell University Press, 1997.

Welch, Richard E., Jr. *Response to Revolution: The United States and the Cuban Revolution, 1959–1961.* Chapel Hill, NC: University of North Carolina Press, 1985.

White, O. Kendall, Jr., and Daryl White, eds. *Religion in the Contemporary South.* Southern Anthropological Society Proceedings 28. Athens, GA: University of Georgia Press, 1993.

Williams, Walter L. *Black Americans and the Evangelization of Africa, 1877–1900.* Madison, WI: University of Wisconsin Press, 1982.

Willis, Alan Scot. "A Baptist Dilemma: Christianity, Discrimination, and the Desegregation of Mercer University." *Georgia Historical Quarterly* 80, no. 3 (Fall 1996): 595–615.

— — —. "A White Man's Religion?: Missionaries, Africa, and the Race Question." *Proteus: A Journal of Ideas* 15, no. 1 (Spring 1998): 49–52.

Wilson, Charles Reagan, ed. *Religion in the South*. Chancellor's Symposium Series. Jackson: University Press of Mississippi, 1985.

Woodward, C. Vann. *The Strange Career of Jim Crow*. 3rd ed. New York: Oxford University Press, 1974.

Wuthnow, Robert W. *The Restructuring of American Religion: Society and Faith since World War II*. Princeton, NJ: Princeton University Press, 1988.

INDEX

126–31, 137–40, 143–44; religious persecution of, 127–28; stereotypes of, 125–26, 130; Termination policies and, 130–31; voting rights for, 127; World War II service by, 127
Inlow, Eva, 128
integration: acceptance of, 109; church, 33–35, 146–48, 166–69, 173–74, 179–82, 187, 189; educational, 140, 158–59, 169–73; intermarriage and, 20–23, 179, 181; theological arguments about, 11–12, 18–23
interracial marriage(s): biblical interpretations on, 20–23; integrated schools and, 21, 181; offspring of, 22–23; segregationists' fears of, 20, 160, 179. *See also* social equality
Islam: African spread of, 70, 74, 84; women's roles in, 78

Jackson, Hermione Dannelly, 85, 113, 158; double standard and, 155; international racism and, 43; migrant workers and, 141; segregation and, 102–3
Jenkins, Howard L., 68
Johnson, Charles D., 43
Johnson, Lyndon, 117, 175
Johnson-Reed Act, 51
Jojola, Andrea, 138–39
Jones, Jameson, 52
Journeyman Missionary Program, 183
Junker, Bill, 192

Keelin, Anne, 145
Kefauver, Estes, 52
Kennedy, John F., 87
Kerrigan, Lucille, 65
Khrushchev, Nikita, 63, 85
Killers of the Dream (Smith), 18
Kilpatrick, James J., 21

King, Edith Marie, 133
King, Martin Luther, Jr.: assassination of, 185–86; characterization of, 187–89; leadership of, 185
Kiser, Margaret Gooch, 158
kneel-ins, 166–68
Knight, Walker L., 64, 141; American Indian rights and, 143; free pulpits and, 26–27; integration and, 167, 168, 191–92
Ku Klux Klan, 25, 107, 154; segregation and, 21, 197; student protest against, 107–8

Language Missions Week, 135
Latinos: disease amongst, 140–41; education of, 140–41, 145; employment opportunities for, 140; evangelism of, 144–45; good will center, 134; housing conditions for, 141; melon strike and, 141–43; missionary statistics for, 121; poverty amongst, 136, 140; racism against, 131–36, 140–43
Law, Maxine, 84–85
Lawoyin, Samuel A., 76–77
Lawrence, J. B., 16, 44, 95, 122; belief in oneness of humanity, 57; communism and, 58; languages and, 123; social equality and, 150, 153; world leadership and, 94
Lee, Dallas M., 64, 140, 143
Leonard, Bill, 2–3; Baptist publications and, 6; southern identity and, 35
Lequire, Leila, 53
literature: Baptist racial, 5–8; women's views in, 8, 114; youth's views in, 8, 114
Littlejohn, Carrie U., 152
Lockard, W. David, 88
Lopez, Miguel A., 123

Macon, Leon, 7, 181, 188

by, 5–8, 114; themes of, 4; theology of, 3–4, 28–32, 112, 121, 149–50; women and youth, importance of, 8, 111–12, 114–15
Propst, Fred, 168–69
Pruden, Edward Hughes, 154

race as social construct, 121, 124–25
Race Relations Sunday, 178
racism in the U.S.: American Indian, 126–31, 137–40, 143–44; Baptist literature on, 5–8; as barrier, 57; Bible's relevance to, 11–12, 18–23, 53, 104; *Brown* decision's effect on, 104–6, 109; civil rights era and, 174–79; colonialism's tie to, 42–46; contemporary positions on, 198; definition of, 1; economic contribution to, 101–2, 142, 155; education's relation to, 4–5, 37–38, 55–56, 68–71, 73–74, 135, 137–40, 155–56; friendship building and, 55–56, 103–4, 132–36, 158; institutional, 5, 184–85, 196; international repercussions of, 51–52, 67, 80, 86–87, 91–92, 102, 136, 150, 165; Latino, 131–36, 140–43; missions' effect on, 17–18, 45–47, 81–82, 84–85; morality and, 4, 28–32; overcoming, 55–56, 103–4, 109–12, 132–33, 151–53, 158, 164–66; progressive themes on, 4–5; race inferiority and, 23; social equality and, 150, 153–55, 160; women and, 8, 54, 102, 114, 152–53; youth and, 8, 106–12, 152, 183–85, 193–94. *See also* segregation
racism, international: as barrier, 57; colonialism's tie to, 42–46, 200; communism's effect on, 57–60; domestic racism's tie to, 51–52, 67, 80, 86–87, 91–92, 102, 136, 150, 165

radicalism, 17–18
Ramsey, Brooks, 26
Rankin, M. Theron, 10, 50, 70; African nationalism and, 73–74; mission education and, 77
Redford, Courts, 63–64, 95; church integration and, 168; language missions and, 121; student unions at black colleges and, 152; world leadership and, 96
"Reflections" (Grace), 107
Reynolds, Edward, 170
Rhodesia: Africanization in, 88; apartheid policies of, 88–89; missions in, 87–89; political changes in, 89–91
Richardson, Lynn T., 169
Riddle, Jerry, 184
Roebuck, Doris, 128
Roebuck, Lee, 145
Rounds, J. B., 127, 139
Routh, E. C., 41–42, 53; materialism and, 99; Russian Baptists and, 60
Routh, Porter: integration and, 115, 169, 173; morality and, 32; spiritual needs and, 44
Royal Ambassadors program, 69, 70; black chapter of, 111; literature by, 6; missionary efforts, 134, 136–37
Royal Service, 22, 53, 63; ambivalence of, 112–13, 115–17; bias of, 177; *Brown* decision and, 105; demographics of, 6, 114; materialism and, 99, 101; Sunbeam Band program and, 106–7
Rummage, Ralph, 69
Russell, Mary Elizabeth, 105, 109, 161
Russell, William, 133
Russian Orthodox Church, 60
Rutledge, Arthur, 117, 178, 190–91

Sadler, George W., 44, 50, 56; African missions and, 73–74, 79
Saito, Itsuko, 54